Labor Standards in Intern Supply Chains

Labor Standards in International Supply Chains

Aligning Rights and Incentives

Daniel Berliner
Arizona State University, USA

Anne Regan Greenleaf
University of Washington, Seattle, USA

Milli Lake
Arizona State University, USA

Margaret Levi
Stanford University, USA

Jennifer Noveck
University of Washington, Seattle, USA

 Edward Elgar
PUBLISHING

Cheltenham, UK • Northampton, MA, USA

Published by
Edward Elgar Publishing Limited
The Lypiatts
15 Lansdown Road
Cheltenham
Glos GL50 2JA
UK

Edward Elgar Publishing, Inc.
William Pratt House
9 Dewey Court
Northampton
Massachusetts 01060
USA

Paperback edition 2016

A catalogue record for this book
is available from the British Library

Library of Congress Control Number: 2014959465

This book is available electronically in the **Elgar**online
Social and Political Science subject collection
DOI 10.4337/9781783470372

ISBN   978 1 78347 035 8 (cased)
ISBN   978 1 78347 037 2 (eBook)
ISBN   978 1 78347 036 5 (paperback)

Typeset by Columns Design XML Ltd, Reading
Printed and bound in Great Britain by TJ International Ltd, Padstow

Contents

Acknowledgments

This book had its origins in the involvement of Margaret Levi and, later, Anne Greenleaf and Milli Lake in the Advisory Committee on Trademarks and Licensing (ACTL) at the University of Washington (UW). The task of the committee is to ensure that products carrying the University of Washington logo are produced under conditions that satisfy the University's labor code of conduct. This proved a challenging job, given the complexities of contemporary supply chains and the variety of commitments and concerns represented on a committee composed of faculty, students, and staff from trademarks and licensing, athletics, the bookstore, and the president's office. It was here we gained our initial experience with clusters of interest and the difficulties of aligning the interests within and across clusters. We also gained considerable respect for and appreciation of the anti-sweatshop movement and the dedicated students who create and manage its campaigns. We came to understand the contributions of both the Worker Rights Consortium (WRC) and the Fair Labor Association (FLA) organizations the UW had joined to provide 'fire alarms' of labor violations and monitoring of code compliance. We learned about the internal workings of brands and their problems managing their suppliers, and we were impressed by the bravery of various organizations of workers and advocate groups who demand improved labor conditions in countries all over the world. We discovered the importance of universities in signaling appropriate ethics and values to students, alumnae, and wider publics, but we also discovered the difficulties of enacting and sustaining the university's value commitments in regard to supply chain workers.

Although ACTL members may not have been aware of how much they were teaching us and helping us, we are extremely grateful to Kathy Hoggan, Norman Arkans, Debra Glassman, Daniel Jacoby, Mary Kay Gugerty, Aseem Prakash, James Ritter, Louise Little, Scott David, Sagan Harlin, Shannon Kelly, Angelina Godoy, Rod Palmquist, Trevor Griffey, George Robertson, April Nishimura, Morgan Currier, Rachel Shervin, and all the other students, staff, and faculty who participated during the decade Margaret Levi served on the committee.

Many individuals and organizations supported the writing of this book. Our biggest debt is to the United States Studies Centre (USSC) at the University of Sydney, which provided major financial backing for the research and convenings that made it possible to write this manuscript. Sean Gallagher's commitment of USSC resources, intellectual and monetary, and Cindy Tang's financial management skills ensured the viability of our multi-continent collaboration. Additional funding was provided by: The Watson Institute, Brown University; Jere L. Bacharach Professorship, University of Washington; and the Harry Bridges Center for Labor Studies, University of Washington.

Our collaboration began in 2011 when Dena Ringold, Senior Economist, World Bank, solicited from us a background paper for the *2013 World Development Report: Jobs*. We are particularly grateful to Dena for guiding us in its preparation, including asking us the tough questions, and to the World Bank for covering our research costs. Christopher Adolph and Aaron Erlich were co-authors of the original piece. Their input and the reviewer comments of Amy Lunistra and Piotr A. Mazurkiewicz proved invaluable as we developed the background paper into a full-blown book.

The World Justice Project, most particularly Alejandro Ponce and Juan Botero, also proved invaluable partners. They graciously shared data with us and helped us in constructing the appropriate analysis for our purposes.

The Center for Advanced Study in the Behavioral Sciences at Stanford University, which Margaret Levi now directs, hosted us for a week of brainstorming and writing, without which this book could not have been completed. We particularly thank Iris Wilson, Sally Schroeder, Ravi Shivanna, Barbie Maycock, and Phil Main for being so welcoming and making the group so comfortable.

The Just Supply Chains project at the Watson Institute for International Studies (watson.brown.edu/research/projects/jsc) offered information and networks as well as the opportunity to present some of our material at conferences in 2012 and 2013. Richard Locke, Dean of Brown University's Watson Institute, and one of the founders of Just Supply Chains, was a source of inspiration and support to all of us from our first co-authored paper on labor rights in global supply chains. We cannot thank him enough.

Daniel Yoo provided invaluable research assistance. We are also grateful to a host of others who read papers or chapters and offered useful comments: Victor Menaldo, Joshua Cohen, Mark Anner, Tim Bartley, Andrew Schrank, Layna Mosley, David Weil, Gay Seidman,

April Linton, Renato Bignani, Roberto Pires, Mary Gallagher, Matt Amengual, Anand Rajaram, Michael Hiscox, and Jens Hainmueller.

For the Bangladesh chapter we owe thanks to Audrey Sacks of the World Bank, and Faisal Ahmed, Assistant Professor at Princeton University, Anne Greenleaf's previous co-authors, who provided the opportunity to gain in-depth knowledge and experience on the Bangladesh case, and specifically the labor situation, before the Rana Plaza tragedy. Anne also owes thanks to Mary Kay Gugerty and Stephen Kosack, Professors at the Daniel J. Evans School of Public Affairs at the University of Washington, who made it possible for Anne to travel to Bangladesh as part of a separate research project.

Several people provided critical guidance and deep contextual knowledge to the China chapter at the University of Washington including Susan Whiting, Kam Wing Chan, and Steve Harrell. In addition, Doris Duangboudda read multiple versions and provided important and constructive feedback.

Our fieldwork in Honduras depended on the advice and assistance of a number of generous individuals including Angelina Godoy and Quinn Kedley, as well as Mario and Dina Nathusius. We were incredibly lucky to find Carlos Roman who went above and beyond and truly became a partner in our research. Milli and Anne were inspired by the women at the Centro de Derechos de Mujeres as well as the inimitable Evangelina Argueta. The chapter on Honduras also would not have been possible without the input of Scott Nova, Jorge Perez Lopez, Linda Yanz, Auret van Heerden, Lance Compa and the many anonymous workers, union organizers, and NGOs who agreed to be interviewed for this project.

We also owe many personal thanks to our friends and families. Daniel Berliner would like to thank his brilliant co-authors, and the faculty and graduate students at the University of Washington who were always so welcoming and supportive. Anne Greenleaf thanks Stephen, Connie, and Abigail Greenleaf for their many years of support. She also thanks Edwin Schmitt, Patricia Tietgens, Michelle Zhang, Tian Feng Liu, Erik Hedborg, Allen Sanchez, Tina Xu, Yvonne Wang, and Kevin He for their friendship and assistance in Chengdu; and Dallas Schuster, Michele Statz, the D'Ambruosuo clan, and a wonderful group of fellow graduate students and faculty at the University of Washington. Without them, the time spent writing this book would have included far less laughter and happy memories. Milli Lake thanks her family, friends, and co-authors for their wisdom and inspiration. She also thanks her colleagues in Congo for many spirited debates about the realities of regulating labor rights in a very different global supply chain. Margaret Levi once again thanks her husband, Bob Kaplan, who was patient with Margaret, insightful about our claims, and generous with wine and hospitality to the five of us. Finally, Jennifer Noveck would like to thank her family and friends, who were encouraging and provided much needed comic relief: Tina Fenton, the Noveck-Snyder clan, the Ortiz family, the Reth-Macdiarmids, Matthew D. Miller, Joey Powers Kraves, and Christopher Kemp.

Abbreviations

ACFTU	All China Federation of Trade Unions
ACTL	Advisory Committee on Trademarks and Licensing
AFL-CIO	American Federation of Labor-Congress of Industrial Organizations
AIP	Apparel Industry Partnership (USA)
BJSD	Bangladesh Jatiyatabadi Sramik Dal
BKMEA	Bangladesh Knitwear Manufacturers and Exporters Association
BNP	Bangladesh Nationalist Party
CAFTA	Central American Free Trade Agreement
CCP	Chinese Communist Party
CDS	Coastal Development Strategy (China)
CES	Cadre evaluation system (China)
CFA	Committee on Freedom of Association (ILO)
CGT	Central General de Trabajadores (Honduras)
CLB	China Labour Bulletin
CLS	Core Labour Standards (ILO)
CLW	China Labor Watch
CSR	Corporate social responsibility
CWA	Communication Workers of America
ECHR	European Convention on Human Rights
ECOSOC	Economic and Social Council (UN)
ECSR	European Committee of Social Rights
ECtHR	European Court of Human Rights
EICC	Electronic Industry Citizenship Coalition
EPZs	Export processing zones
ESC	European Social Charter
FDI	Foreign direct investment
FLA	Fair Labor Association (USA)
FLSA	Fair Labor Standards Act (USA)
FTAs	Free trade agreements
HRW	Human Rights Watch
IACHR	Inter-American Commission on Human Rights
IACtHR	Inter-American Court of Human Rights

ICCPR	International Covenant on Civil and Political Rights
ICESCR	International Covenant on Economic, Social and Cultural Rights
ICFTU	International Confederation of Free Trade Unions
IFC	International Finance Corporation
IFPRI	International Food Policy Research Institute
ILC	International Labour Conference
ILO	International Labour Organization
ILRF	International Labor Rights Forum
ILWU	International Longshore and Warehouse Union (USA)
ITUC	International Trade Union Confederation
MFA	Multi-Fibre Agreement
NAFTA	North American Free Trade Agreement
NLRA	National Labor Relations Act (USA)
NLRB	National Labor Relations Board (USA)
NPC	National People's Congress (China)
OECD	Organisation for Economic Co-operation and Development
OSHA	Occupational Safety and Health Administration (USA)
RMG	Ready-made garment
SACOM	Students and Scholars Against Corporate Misbehaviour (Hong Kong)
SCI	Sustainable Compliance Initiative
SER	Social and environmental responsibility
SEZs	Special economic zones
UFCW	United Food and Commercial Workers (USA)
UNGC	United Nations Global Compact
UNHRC	United Nations Human Rights Council
UNITE	Union of Needle Trades, Industrial and Textile Employees (USA)
USAS	United Students Against Sweatshops
WGI	World Governance Indicators
WJP	World Justice Project
WRC	Worker Rights Consortium
WTO	World Trade Organization

Abbreviations

1. Introduction

> Subcontractors could pay the workers whatever rates they wanted, often extremely low. The owners supposedly never knew the rates paid to the workers, nor did they know exactly how many workers were employed at their factory at any given point. Such a system led to exploitation ... The fire ... which claimed the lives of 146 young immigrant workers, is one of the worst disasters since the beginning of the Industrial Revolution ... This incident ... highlights the inhumane working conditions to which ... workers can be subjected.
>
> (Cornell University, 2014)

This is not a description of one of the many factory fires in Bangladesh. Nor does it allude to contemporary immigrants. It refers to the Triangle Shirtwaist Company in New York City in 1911. Locked into the sweatshop, workers, disproportionately young and female, threw themselves out of windows to escape the flames – and fell to their deaths. Earlier union efforts to change the awful conditions in sweatshops, including at Triangle, had little effect. Public shock and outrage were the catalyst for the passage of legislation regulating health and safety. The factory was a disaster waiting to happen, but it took highly publicized and horrifying deaths to precipitate change.

Workers throughout the world continue to toil in unsafe conditions for low wages, long hours, and few, if any, benefits. They suffer preventable diseases from overwork and exposure to chemicals and toxins. Some are effectively enslaved, and others, like too many of the Triangle Shirtwaist Factory girls, are subject to sexual harassment. Immigrant workers are particularly vulnerable to exploitation. Government protections, especially where states are corrupt or have little enforcement capacity, are not always effective for citizens and more or less non-existent for immigrants. Where unions are weak or illegal, the collective voice of labor is curtailed. Even in countries where the laws presumably protect the right to organize, employers still threaten to fire workers who join union efforts, and in many places, even today, union organizers are assassinated.

Under what conditions should we expect labor rights in global supply chains to improve? This book asks what has been done and what can be done. Although we find that any change is difficult both to achieve and sustain, some progress is possible. Change comes, we argue, when the interests of key actors are aligned to improve labor standards. The achievement of alignment is not a given but requires political and economic processes, and often the explicit use of economic and political power, to compel stakeholders to form commonalties of interest.

Our aim is to specify the conditions that align the interests of employers, governments, and consumers with those of the workers. We do this with a particular focus on apparel, footwear, and consumer electronics brands, whose history we trace generally and through case studies of four countries that illustrate a variety of strategies and processes: the United States, Honduras, Bangladesh, and China. We find that the contemporary form of the global supply chain is the source of problematic working conditions we identify; improved labor standards require transformation in the motivations and practices of owners and managers of supply chain businesses and the governments that house them. Progress is most likely to come about as a result of the establishment of international norms, monitoring, media attention to labor violations, and anti-sweatshop activist campaigns and boycotts. Unfortunately, the precipitant to changes in policy and practice is, far too often, a horrible event such as the Triangle Shirtwaist Factory fire or the collapse of Rana Plaza in Bangladesh. Loss of innocent lives creates a public uproar, as well as opportunities for leverage by the international organizations, NGOs, labor unions, reformist government actors, sympathetic brand management, and others attempting to raise labor standards.

Global supply chains involve myriad actors with divergent interests and complicated relationships. We attempt to organize this complexity by focusing on four clusters of actors, their incentives and beliefs, and the changing configurations of alignment and misalignment among them that can lead to better, or in some cases, worse labor rights. The four clusters of actors we identify are supply chain workers and their allies, governments, businesses, and consumers.

We argue that actors can capitalize on opportunities for leverage along three dimensions. First, opportunities increase when there is a higher degree of alignment of interests within an actor's cluster. Second, opportunities increase when there are conflicts of interests within the cluster that is the target of opposition or change. Third, opportunities for leverage increase when there are greater cross-cluster alignments and coalitions. These configurations of interests within and across the four clusters of actors are malleable and reflect stakeholder incentive structures, their beliefs about the rewards and punishments that they face, and their beliefs about norms of appropriate behavior.

By developing this analytic framework, we hope to illuminate both opportunities for and challenges to improving labor rights globally. Our findings reveal that neither international institutions nor private regulatory schemes are sufficient to ensure sustained supplier compliance. We find that major openings for change generally occur in response to a combination of worker and consumer pressure directed at transforming the beliefs of firm management about the norms of appropriate behavior. Such pressure is likely to be most effective when highly publicized labor violations and disasters make the issues salient to important publics and actors. Probably the most important and sustainable mechanism for improved labor standards is government regulation backed up by effective enforcement.

Opportunities for leverage lead to improvements only if alliances and coordination are possible within and across clusters, but this is not always the case. Brands may be motivated to act but be stymied by their suppliers, who have strong economic investments in poor labor conditions. Workers and their allies may undermine each other because of inability to overcome collective action problems or as a consequence of strategic differences. Consumers, both individual and institutional, may not be persuaded to make purchasing decisions the campaigns demand. Distinctive viewpoints and interests within legislatures and among government agencies and branches can yield inaction or repression, rather than improved labor standards.

Government may be the key player for ensuring sustained labor rights, but the capacity and motivations of government actors vary considerably. In Bangladesh and Honduras, the governments are ineffective due to weak state capacity, corruption, and intense political competition that favors business interests over workers. While China has relatively stronger state capacity, local governments collude with supplier firms to boost investment and revenue while the central government continues to actively repress and prohibit independent unionization and collective bargaining. Both negatively affect Chinese workers' rights. Finally, although the United States previously had a fairly strong regulatory environment with effective enforcement for labor, since the 1980s there has been an unraveling of American unions, the breakdown of labor enforcement capacity, and serious backsliding in labor rights for many of America's workers. Without the incentives necessary to encourage government actors to actively commit to upholding labor standards, victories on factory floors are likely to be sporadic, issue specific, and tenuous.

This book develops our argument by using a multi-method approach, relying on evidence from both cross-national quantitative empirical analysis and in-depth qualitative case studies. Chapter 2 introduces the global context for labor standards and discusses the incentives and motivations that multinational brands face in developing more efficient, productive, and ultimately profitable, supply chains. After reviewing the costs and risk calculations of firms generally, we then examine the efforts of four multinational brands, Levi Strauss & Co., Nike, Apple, and Alta Gracia, to uphold and improve labor rights at their supplier factories abroad.

Chapter 3 builds our analytic framework, which focuses on four key clusters of actors, defined by their relationship to the process of production, and identifies when and where opportunities may be leveraged to improve labor standards. We then build a framework for thinking about how interest alignment within and across the clusters of actors can result in opportunities for leverage to improve working conditions for workers in global supply chains. Chapter 3 also describes the mechanisms of influence that can alter the incentives and, therefore, the alignments within and between clusters of actors. We outline common patterns in the processes that lead to positive changes in working conditions in global supply chains.

In Chapter 4, we discuss the role of international organizations and global governance initiatives in contributing to the development of an international framework for workers' rights and global labor standards. We identify three mechanisms through which international institutions have contributed to improving labor standards: formal monitoring and enforcement; the diffusion and internalization of global norms pertaining to labor rights; and capability building provided to firms and governments by international organizations, NGOs, foreign governments, or corporations. We suggest that where international initiatives have had the greatest success is in establishing global norms to which advocates of labor rights appeal.

Chapter 5 presents quantitative statistics using new data from the World Justice Project to evaluate some of the potential mechanisms for improving both labor standards on paper and their enforcement in practice. The chapter finds that the level of economic development, democracy, and left-leaning governments are associated with better labor standards, all else equal. We also test other variables that have been identified in the literature as being important for upholding labor rights including state capacity, foreign direct investment, arm's-length contracting, ratification of ILO conventions, UN Global Compact membership, and Fair Labor Association inspections.

Chapters 6 through 9 explore four in-depth country cases. We begin with a discussion of labor standards in the United States. The US case illustrates how domestic labor rights that were hard won in the early twentieth century have been eroded by declining union power, hostile business interests, and weak incorporation of labor interests into either of the two dominant political parties. Simultaneously, however, American consumers and NGOs have pushed hard for improvements for workers elsewhere in global supply chains.

Chapter 7 examines efforts in Honduras to compel Nike and Russell to improve labor standards. Using original qualitative data in the form of interviews and fieldwork, we document the response in 2012 when Honduran workers faced sudden unemployment without compensation due to the closure of their factories. Campaigns against Nike and Russell by Honduran workers, the Worker Rights Consortium, and universities altered the incentives of both corporations. Consequently, some workers were able to negotiate settlements, either through compensation or re-employment. Unfortunately, this important victory has not set in motion any broader improvement in labor rights, primarily because the Honduran government remains corrupt and weak.

Labor rights, or lack thereof, in Bangladesh are examined in Chapter 8. The starting point is the equilibrium between apparel brands and their suppliers, the Bangladeshi government, Bangladeshi workers and their allies, as well as apparel consumers that existed before and after the Rana Plaza tragedy. Rana serves as an important example of how a horrible tragedy can become an important moment of opportunity for leverage for workers and their allies. However, we interpret the resulting changes with caution. Without a long-term and credible commitment by consumers and retailers to punishing brands and suppliers who violate workers' rights, sustained improvements are unlikely, especially given the current domestic political equilibrium in Bangladesh.

Our qualitative cases conclude with that of China in Chapter 9. The examples of two mega-suppliers, Yue Yuen and Foxconn, demonstrate the conflict of interest that exists between brands and suppliers, collusion between supplier factories and local governments against workers, and the nature of labor resistance in contemporary China. As with the Bangladesh and Honduras cases, transnational campaigns and media attention did, temporarily, change the calculations of both supplier factories at a specific moment in time. The central government's continued prohibition of independent unionization and its emphasis on local economic development and revenue generation create immense barriers to sustainable improvements in labor standards in China.

The Triangle Shirtwaist tragedy precipitated the alliances and coalitions that advanced major improvements to labor rights in the United States in the early twentieth century. While the problems of many global supply chain workers in 2014 when this book was written are remarkably similar to those of the US sweatshop workers in 1911, the modern brand era is much more complicated and international. It is to those complexities, and the challenges and opportunities they create for improving labor standards, that we now turn.

2. The world brands create

Brands transformed the manufacturing process and created the contemporary global supply chain with its complex of suppliers and subcontractors. No longer is production likely to be the provenance of the company whose name the product bears. The brand designs the product, institutes quality controls, locates inputs globally, gives over manufacture to suppliers and subcontractors (often overseas), and then sells what is produced through its own stores and through other retailers. It is Ricardo's comparative advantage to its extreme, with a constant search for the best return at the lowest cost on almost every conceivable margin. The result is a vast, widely extended and decentralized international network of suppliers, producers, and retailers combined with centralized brand control over design, quality, and marketing. This is notably the case in apparel, footwear, and electronics, the industries on which this book focuses.

Brands are motivated by the drive for profit and growth, the same motivation that has long inspired business to seek 'the conquest of new markets and ... the more thorough exploitation of the old ones' (Marx and Engels [1848] 1952, p. 5). In the absence of external pressure, few brands had incentives to protect labor rights and multiple reasons to ignore violations. The incentives almost entirely lay in lowering labor and transaction costs while simultaneously producing fast fashion and new and 'hot' consumer goods. Aligning the interests of brands with those of the employees in their supply chains generally demands effective action by a subset of workers and their allies, political officials, and consumers. The transformation of the brand's cost calculus is most likely to come about as a consequence of some combination of government pressure, unionization, boycotts, and campaigns that tarnish brand reputations.

LOCATIONAL DECISIONS OF BRANDS

One important and ongoing concern for brands is where they locate production and find inputs. Cost savings tend to drive these decisions. Changes in relative prices (e.g., new technology that makes transport of

7

goods cheap) induce restructuring of companies, with some functions being shed to other firms. The economic theory of transaction costs, particularly Oliver Williamson's line of inquiry (1975, 1985), focuses on precisely the issues long absorbing corporate leaders' attention: how to efficiently reorganize companies in order to reduce labor costs, increase productivity, and maximize return on investment. The emphasis is on designing the optimal structure for the company in response to changes in the price of key inputs; the location, quality, and quantity of demand; and the costs of transport and communication.

Labor costs are of equal consideration. Productivity, the total wage package (including benefits), and worker militancy or quiescence all figure into the firm's cost equation. Breaking or avoiding unions is consistent with management concerns about both optimal structure and cost savings. Unions tend to raise the cost of wages and benefits and reduce management flexibility, creating an added incentive to find a more malleable and lower-cost workforce. This was part of the reason firms relocated from the industrial North of the United States to the 'sunshine belt' of the South and Southwest or to countries in other parts of the world. Beverly Silver (2003) addresses this set of issues in terms of various 'fixes' firms deploy. Sometimes a 'technological fix' reduces the wage package by sufficiently raising productivity or decreasing the number of workers. For ports, a fixed asset, containerization, was the employer's long-term cost-cutting solution. In other instances, the fix is 'spatial' with the firm moving production elsewhere; the automobile industry is exemplary here.

Brands consider the transaction costs of vertical versus horizontal integration, as the Williamson model suggests, but they are also on the constant lookout for ways to lower the costs of labor, as Silver suggests. In addition, according to Hagel and Brown (2005), there are firms such as Hong Kong-based Li & Fung that are keen to optimize on innovation than efficiency, and they attempt to increase value through connectivity and coordination, leveraged capability building, and dynamic specialization (Locke, 2013).

Some firms can provide certain outputs more efficiently or at higher quality than others. By contracting out, a firm at a comparative disadvantage creates rents that are shared by both the contracting firms. In general, firms contract out for services that are not core to the firm. Apparel, footwear, and electronics brands generally define their core competency as research, design, marketing, sales, and, in some instances, the creation of financial services for consumers (Gereffi, 1994); manufacturing is no longer core. Nor for some brands is the management of the supply chain itself; increasingly more of this work is outsourced to companies specializing in logistics.

What is offshored, and where, depends on numerous factors. Call centers require speakers in the language of the customer, thus, it is not surprising that India is a popular location for English-speaking firms. High-technology products require multiple inputs available quickly. Here, the advantage goes to China. On the other hand, the production of apparel requires little in the way of skills or education, and for this kind of work, Bangladesh and Honduras are good sites.

TYPOLOGIES OF SUPPLY CHAINS

An earlier, more sociological, literature referred to supply chains as commodity chains: 'a network of labor and production processes whose end result is a finished commodity' (Hopkins and Wallerstein, 1986, p. 159). By one account, in the 1980s and 1990s, two types of international economic networks existed: producer-driven and buyer-driven commodity chains (Gereffi, 1994). Producer-driven commodity chains characterized capital-intensive industries, including automotive, aerospace, computers, semiconductors, and some machinery. Profits derived from scale and technological advances. Ownership of manufacturing stayed with the multinational firm.

If Gereffi's distinction was once useful, it no longer is. Today almost all supply chains are buyer driven, or in the language of economists and logistic engineers, demand driven. Demand-driven chains result from the search for higher-value products and lower-cost production worldwide. Local firms in developing countries become suppliers to larger corporations often based in a very different place on the map. Among the lead coordinating firms in these chains are brands such as Wal-Mart, Target, Nordstrom, Amazon, Best Buy, Nike, Reebok, H&M, Ralph Lauren, Tommy Hilfiger, Li & Fung, Apple, IBM, and Dell. The transaction costs of contemporary production have elicited more horizontal integration than vertical. The brand sheds ownership of all but its core functions.

While attempting to elicit brand loyalty from consumers, the brand's loyalty to its suppliers is highly conditional. The business benefit of demand-driven supply chains is their flexibility in reducing transaction costs. 'Such flexibility is often achieved through spatially dense contracting networks, permitting the manufacturer to select factories according to specific production requirements' (Applebaum and Gereffi, 1994, p. 44). Brands can respond quickly to changes in demand or increases in costs imposed by labor demands or government regulations by moving to another supplier, sometimes in another country. The mobility of the corporations heightens both their independence from particular suppliers and their power relative to those they contract with.

Or, at least, it did. As technology advances, multinational brands increasingly seek 'a much smaller number of larger, more capable, and strategically located suppliers. Supply chain production hubs are concentrating in big emerging economies, both because of their abundant supply of workers and local manufacturers and also because of their expanding domestic markets' (Gereffi, 2013). The rise of such so-called 'supply chain cities' and hubs is a fairly recent development in the fast-moving world of brands, and they reflect the specialization and division of labor that characterizes the requirements of low-value versus high-value supply chains. The capital city of Dhaka in Bangladesh exemplifies a concentrated locus of garment production in sweatshop conditions that recall the fire-prone and environmentally hazardous tenement-based sweatshops of early nineteenth-century America. The rise of the massive Chinese supplier complexes represents the newest iteration of sweatshops; the factories are large, shiny, and structurally sound, if not always totally safe from fire, dust, and other interior pollutants.

Differences in capital and technology requirements affect not only where suppliers are likely to be concentrated but also the power relationship between suppliers and buyers. Of the three industries of interest here, garment production has the lowest level of capital and technology requirements. Aside from sewing machines, manufacturing requires no specialized machinery. Locational concentration may occur, as in Bangladesh or Central America, but brands tend to have little dependence on any particular supplier.

Footwear manufacture, on the other hand, requires specialized machinery that has become more sophisticated over time. Effluent treatment processes for tanning entail aerators, decanters, compact stations, and monitoring stations for chemicals. Specialized machines for leather, rubber, and metal have developed in shoe production to stretch bootlegs, crimp rubber and metal moldings, burn or smooth edges, and attach eyelets, rivets, and heels. Waste management and pollution prevention involve technology. The high levels of design and quality control demanded by brand footwear, especially athletic footwear, presents risks to suppliers who have purchased expensive machinery that cannot be repurposed for other manufacturing processes, but it also creates dependence by buyers on those suppliers who can afford the investment in machines and quality control.

Electronics has the highest level of technology and quality requirements; components must meet exacting standards and be available on short notice. Consequently, the suppliers have become large firms within a geographically proximate network of subcontractors. They are at the core of the 'supply chain cities', which tend to be concentrated in a few countries such as China, India, and Brazil, countries with the capacity to provide infrastructure and other corporate requirements. One effect is a subtle shift in the power relationships between brands and their suppliers. Apple, for example, is now as dependent on Foxconn, Pegatron, and other mega-suppliers as the mega-suppliers are on Apple.

LABOR PRACTICES

Throughout the twenty-first century, brands have come under fire for violations of labor standards within their supply chains. Brands often turn a blind eye and sometimes condone child labor, sexual harassment, forced servitude, and wages well below the country's minimum; they do not enforce freedom of association or occupational health and safety. In the following chapters we explore a variety of strategies to align the incentives of firms and governments with those of the workers: inter-national institutions, brand auditing of its own supply chain, government regulation, labor organization, consumer pressure, and transnational advocacy campaigns.

Here we focus on several brands based in the United States. European and Asian corporations are equally important, but it is largely American firms that initiated the new global supply chains. Moreover, the US population remains the largest consumer market for brand output. The story is not simply one of economic interests, however. The narrative makes clear that each of these companies had a different set of beliefs about the best way to succeed in a competitive environment and that these beliefs were affected by the values of their leadership. Levi Strauss, Nike, Apple and Knights Apparel began with very different corporate cultures (Kreps, 1990; Miller, 1992), that is, principles that organizational leadership upholds even when it seems costly to do so. These initial corporate cultures have subsequently evolved in distinctive ways that shape how each brand organizes and locates production, and the labor standards they uphold.

Levi Strauss

Levi Strauss is not in the human rights business, but to the degree that human rights affects our business, we care about it. (Peter A. Jacobi, former President and COO of Levi Strauss & Co., quoted in Landler, 1998)

Levi Strauss & Co. was a family business founded in San Francisco, California in 1853 to sell wholesale dry goods. For 68 years, since the appearance of its first pair of jeans in 1873 with denim sourced from New Hampshire's Amoskeag Manufacturing Company (Levi Strauss & Co., 2014a), the entire supply chain was located within the United States. In order to become a multinational firm with global reach and expand production into Europe and Asia, in 1965 Levi Strauss & Co. created Levi Strauss International and Levi Strauss Far East.

Throughout the late 1990s and well into the 2000s, Levi Strauss & Co. struggled financially. Some speculated it was because the company 'clung to century-old tradition of manufacturing, at least in part, in the United States' while its competitors had been primarily producing in Mexico or Asia for some time (Kaufman, 1999). But the profitability decline was as much an issue of failure to innovate as of decline in relative efficiency. The company had not been as dynamic as its competitors; it was essentially making the same products it had for the past 100 years (Pollack, 1989; Prior, 2014).

In 1985 the family bought back the company, which remains privately held to this day (Levi Strauss & Co., 2014b). The leadership of Levi Strauss began to recognize that the firm had not fully reaped the cost savings from reorganizing around its core competencies (design and marketing) and relocating its manufacturing to the developing world. By the late 1990s the company began slowly closing down its American and Canadian plants. CEO Peter Haas said that ending its North American manufacturing enabled Levi Strauss to become a '"marketing company" that would focus mostly on shaping and maintaining its brand image. It would make money from licensing its name' (Kaufman, 1999). In 2003 the last American factory, based in San Antonio, Texas, closed (Cosgrove-Mather, 2003).

In 1991 Levi Strauss & Co. instituted its first corporate responsibility standards, which it referred to as 'terms of engagement'. According to the company's heritage timeline, it was the 'first multinational apparel company to establish labor rights, health, safety and environment standards for vendors' factories where clothes are produced' (Levi Strauss & Co., 2014a). Levi Strauss already had a history of principled commitments to worker equity: when it opened its first plant in the American South in 1960, it insisted that the factory be racially integrated, four years before federal law mandated desegregation in 1964 (ibid.).

Creation of the terms of engagement was partially a response to activist demands and partially a consequence of renewed family control of the business. In the late 1980s and early 1990s labor rights activists and academics exposed several factories in the developing world that were using prison labor and child labor. Some were in the Levi Strauss supply chain. Soon after drawing up the terms, the company conducted audits of more than 40 countries and found facilities in China and Burma that used prison labor (Areddy, 2010).

Schoenberger (2000) argues that the Levi Strauss decision to implement corporate social responsibility standards is attributable to the Haas family values and the belief that 'ethical orientation is ultimately good for business'. Although it is unclear how much being a private company influenced Levi Strauss & Co.'s dealings with its supplier factories abroad, the case of Alta Gracia and Knights Apparel CEO Joe Bozich (see below) lends support to the argument that some corporate responsibility decisions are easier when a company is privately held.

Subsequently, Levi Strauss took progressive first steps towards ensuring a more ethical supply chain. The company was one of the original participants in the Fair Labor Association (FLA) in 1997 and is a partner of the International Labour Organization (ILO) Better Work program, begun in 2009.

The corporate culture of Levi Strauss, with its ethical business orientation, was in stark contrast to many of Levi Strauss & Co.'s competitors. The company's active involvement in inhibiting child labor is a case in point: 'to a considerable extent, norms and practices of corporate responsibility in relation to child labor may be characterized in terms of a more or less tacit acceptance "that's just the way things were done over there"' (Nielsen, 2005, p. 565).

When developing sourcing standards for suppliers, Levi Strauss & Co. management tried to 'select partners whose practices are compatible with our aspirational and ethical values' and who would not tarnish its brand image (quoted in Compa and Hinchliffe-Darricarrere, 1995, p. 675). Both positive concerns over upholding company principles and negative fears of losing profit went into the management calculus. In 1992, the company's terms focused on privately regulating and monitoring wages and benefits, working hours, child labor, prison labor, discrimination and disciplinary practice at supplier factories. The original terms did not include the right to collective bargaining and independent unionization (ibid., p. 677).

Labor rights activists were able to leverage the company's commitment to ethical principles, particularly where there was evidence of egregious abuses, such as prison or child labor. Although China was attractive to many multinationals for its cheap and abundant workforce, activists were also able to build on the international outcry in reaction to the Tiananmen Square massacre in 1989 and pressure Levi Strauss & Co. to leave the country (Areddy, 2010).

In the United States, politicians were also taking note of popular and international concern about human rights abuses abroad. In August 1992, the Child Labor Deterrence Act (the Harkin Bill) was proposed in the US Congress, which would have banned the importation of products that used child labor into the United States (Nielsen, 2005, p. 568).[1] Finally in 1993, Levi Strauss announced that it would gradually leave China due to the country's 'pervasive violation of human rights' (Areddy, 2010). Although the company drastically reduced the scale of production in China, it never fully withdrew from the country. Moreover, no other firms facing similar allegations during the same time period withdrew from China (Landler, 1998).

Levi Strauss & Co. fully returned to China in 2008 and, as of January 2014, had shifted the vast majority of its production to Asia (Levi Strauss & Co., 2014c). The company now has 432 contractor factories in Asia, with more than half in China and India alone. However, in response to a segment of consumers clamoring for American-made products, Levi Strauss & Co. reports 51 contractor factories in North America as of January 2014; the ten located in the United States are all in California.

In 2013, Levi Strauss & Co. also revised its terms to include freedom of association and the right to collective bargaining. According to its *Sustainability Guidebook* section on General Labor Practices and Freedom of Association (Levi Strauss & Co., 2013), the company has a zero tolerance policy for factories that restrict, discourage or infringe upon workers' rights to unionize. While the terms recognize that legal regulations on unionization vary greatly from country to country, they are vague when it comes to their application to governments that actively restrict freedom of association and collective bargaining, most notably China.

The history of Levi Strauss's manufacturing location changes and CSR efforts over time illustrates why the firm was responsive to the exposure of egregious labor violations in supplier factories. It worried about declining profits as a consequence of a tarnished brand reputation, but its response was also affected by a corporate culture derived from family values in support of good labor standards. Over time, however, the need to remain competitive and reduce labor costs pushed manufacturing back to Asia and to countries with explicit repression of independent unionization efforts.

Nike, Inc.

Unlike Levi Strauss & Co., Nike's production was not based in the United States at its founding. The business started in the 1950s when Phil

Knight, co-founder of Nike, contacted Japanese shoemaker Onitsuka Co. (now Asics) and persuaded the firm to manufacture running shoes for distribution in the United States even though there were American shoe manufacturers at the time (Nike, Inc., 2014). In 1970 there were 1100 footwear factories in the United States, but by 1985 there were only 300 (Hollie, 1985a). By the end of 1985, Nike was importing 90 percent of its shoes (Hollie, 1985b); by 2011, 99 percent of all shoes sold in the United States were imported (Whoriskey, 2011). Even New Balance, which is considered the last major athletic shoe brand that manufactures in the United States, reports that only one of out every four pairs of shoes it sells in America is made in America.

Nike continually seeks to lower transaction costs while retaining quality by locating new supplier factories, primarily within Asia, that better meet its needs. Nike broke relations with Onitsuka in 1972 and started buying from production sites in South Korea and Taiwan (Nike, Inc., 2014), where wholesale costs were significantly lower (Tharp, 1981). South Korea actively encouraged investment by foreign multi-nationals, giving tariff exemptions to exporters, providing subsidized credit and export credits, and reducing income taxes on export earnings (Rodrik, 1995, pp. 61–2). However, after the South Korean President Park Chung Hee was assassinated in 1979, the economic and political environment for business changed. Throughout the 1980s pro-democracy protests were often coupled with labor protests, resulting in wage increases. As early as 1981, buyers started 'to bypass South Korea in favor of other producing countries with cheaper wage rates and more stable political conditions' (Tharp, 1981).

Increased development in both Korea and Taiwan further raised the cost of labor and business (Locke et al., 2007a). Knight's renewed search for cheaper production motivated his first visit to China in 1980 (Forney, 2004); by the mid-1980s the majority of Nike's production facilities were in China. Nike did not take any equity positions in its contractors (Harrison and Scorse, 2010, p. 250). Rather, it sourced heavily from foreign-owned exporting firms whose owners came from other parts of Asia, including Korea, Taiwan, and Japan. Indeed, in many cases Nike contracted with the same Taiwanese and Korean owners as previously; the owners of supplier firms left their own countries for the cheaper labor and laxer regulatory environment of China.

Nike, like Levi Strauss, began to feel pressure from anti-sweatshop activists in the late 1980s and by the early 1990s became the primary target of activist campaigns. Despite the fact that Nike had over 900 supplier factories around the world with more than 600 000 workers, many of these campaigns focused on labor violations in Indonesia

(O'Rourke, 2003, p. 7). This was probably because American Federation of Labor-Congress of Industrial Organizations (AFL-CIO) representative Jeff Ballinger so persuasively documented poor working conditions and non-compliance with labor laws within the country (Harrison and Scorse, 2010, p. 249). Similar data collection and documentation did not exist in China or any other supplier countries in this period.

In 1992 Nike responded by establishing a code of conduct for both labor and environmental standards (O'Rourke, 2003, p. 7). Nike's code was closely modeled on Levi Strauss & Co.'s terms of engagement issued earlier the same year (Doorey, 2011, p. 592), but it reflected an evolving, rather than the initial, corporate culture:

> For decades, Nike asserted that it had no responsibility for working conditions in its suppliers' factories. John Woodman, a senior Nike employee, expressed this sentiment in 1991, when he told a reporter that it was 'not within our scope to investigate' conditions of work in contractor factories. (Ibid.)

In a major shift of policy, Phil Knight told the National Press Club in 1998 that the 'Nike product has become synonymous with slave wages, forced overtime, and arbitrary abuse', and said that 'the American consumer does not want to buy products made in abusive conditions' (Cushman, 1998). In the same speech, Knight agreed to allow outsiders from labor and human rights groups to join Nike's auditors for factory inspections in Asia and said that the company would also raise the minimum age for hiring new workers to 18 and 16, depending on local laws. To address continuing criticism, Nike created the Safety Health Attitude, People and Environment (SHAPE) internal monitoring system, signed on to the United Nations Global Compact (UNGC), and created a corporate responsibility and compliance division.

Despite these efforts, the Worker Rights Consortium (WRC) and United Students Against Sweatshops (USAS), American-based organizations that will be more fully described in Chapter 6, continued to pressure Nike to go further and disclose its full supplier factory list to the public. They campaigned with universities to withdraw Nike's logo licensing if the company did not comply: 'Nike decided that the cost of forgoing the university market was too high, and in October 1999, it reluctantly agreed to disclose its suppliers to its university customers that demanded factory list disclosure' (Doorey, 2011, p. 590). In 2005, Nike became the first company to disclose a complete list of factories to the public.

The Nike corporate culture was evolving. Nike had previously led the movement against factory disclosure. Brands under fire in the United States claimed, and some continue to claim, that 'factory identity is valuable proprietary information' and disclosure would 'hinder their ability to remain competitive in the global marketplace' (ibid., p. 588).

Since 1992, Nike has put in an immense amount of effort and funding into addressing labor violations in its supplier factories abroad. Problems remain and violations are persistent even though Nike has been auditing some factories for many years. In thorough evaluations of the effectiveness of Nike's monitoring and compliance programs, Locke et al. (2007a) find that private monitoring alone was not successful in producing sustained outcomes.

Nike is the world's largest publicly listed apparel and footwear company, which enhances Nike's bargaining power vis-à-vis its footwear suppliers (Forbes, 2014). The company has pushed footwear suppliers hard on costs and has greatly reduced supplier profit margins. Even Yue Yuen, the biggest footwear manufacturer in the world and a supplier on whom Nike depends, was only able to pass on a third of its rising costs to Nike (Chan et al., 2013, p. 102). However, Nike's size does not always provide leverage with suppliers. Given the different demands and timelines of the fashion industry, Nike and other apparel and footwear firms:

> sometimes enter into short-term contracts with these companies or place very limited orders with them (or both). The result is diminished influence on these suppliers, and in particular, diminished ability to regularly monitor the production processes and working conditions at the supplier factories. (Locke et al., 2007a, p. 8)

For reasons perhaps having more to do with garnering consumer support than transaction costs of production, Nike recently started using American suppliers again even though American firms face serious problems with sourcing various components of shoes (outsoles, eyelets, and shoelaces) and in finding technicians available to fix shoe machinery and equipment. The majority of component suppliers and machinery experts have moved to Asia to be closer to producers (Aeppel, 2008). As of July 2014, Nike has 719 supplier factories, employing 990 325 workers worldwide. Seventy supplier factories (9 percent of the total) are in the United States, but the factories are small and only employ 12 495 workers (Nike, Inc., 2014). In contrast, 192 factories are in China (26 percent), employing 240 578 workers, 24 percent of all workers supplying Nike.[2]

Nike exemplifies a company that learned how bad publicity and a tarnished brand reputation would reduce profits. Activist revelation of abuses, campaign actions, and media attention effectively compelled Nike to pay greater attention to the conditions of workers in its supply chain.

Its corporate culture has consequently evolved although activist skepticism and surveillance remain high.

Apple

> Apple is facing its 'Nike moment' ... Unless we hold Apple's feet to the fire, they're going to get away with profiting off the same sweatshop conditions and driving a global race to the bottom while fooling the public and making it look like they're getting better, just like Nike did. The Nike and Apple experiences, although in two different industries, are one and the same. (Teresa Cheng, international campaign coordinator for USAS, quoted in Jones, 2012)

In August 2012, Apple surpassed Microsoft to become the largest American company ever, based on a stock-market value of US$623.52 billion (Browning et al., 2012). By 2014, Apple was ranked as the 15th biggest company in the world by Forbes and considered the most valuable brand, with the highest market value and the fifth in profit.

Apple's success has been attributed to many factors, including its innovative design and product line, the ability to know what customers want (even before they do), and a 'rock star' design and marketing effort. However, 'the magnitude of Apple's commercial success is paralleled by, and based upon, the scale of production in its supply chain factories, the most important of them located in Asia' (Chan et al., 2013, p. 1). As Apple has achieved global dominance as the world's most valuable brand, its primary supplier, Foxconn, has also become the world's largest electronic manufacturer and contractor.[3]

Apple's manufacturing was not always based in Asia, however. Steve Jobs and Steve Wozniak inaugurated the company in 1976 in Cupertino, California. Initially the focus was on the design and production of personal computers, with a great deal of its production based in the United States. Thousands of American employees built Apple computers in Texas, Colorado, and California throughout the 1980s and early 1990s (Prince and Plank, 2012). In 1980, the firm opened a 150 000ft^2 plant in Carrollton, Texas. Later in 1983, Apple opened an automated plant in Fremont, California after shutting down a pilot factory in Cupertino. In 1991, it opened a 360 000ft^2 plant in Fountain, Colorado, and in 1992 a plant in Elk Grove, California that was later expanded.

In order to capture profits from savings in labor costs, as well as the efficiency and quality benefits of working with mega-suppliers in Asia specialized in producing consumer electronics, Apple began to leave the United States. By 2004, the Elk Grove facility became the last of Apple's American manufacturing lines to be shut down. Apple had been manufacturing circuit boards in Singapore as early as 1981, but by 2004 the majority of its production subcontractors were in China (ibid.). As of 2013, more than 90 percent of Apple's products were assembled in China (Guglielmo, 2013). The decision to move to Asia was largely guided by Timothy Cook, Apple's Chief Operation Officer, and now the CEO of Apple, as of August 2011 (Duhigg and Bradsher, 2012).

Moving production to Asia has not been without problems. By 2006, Apple faced scrutiny due to the behavior of one its major suppliers in China, Foxconn. Shanghai journalist, Wang You, and his editor, Weng Bao, reported that employees in Foxconn's Shenzhen factory were working more than the legal daily amount (12 hours per day) and were only paid about 1000 yuan (US$125) per month. Foxconn sued Wang and Weng for tarnishing its reputation (Xinhua, 2006). At the time, the lawsuit was for 30 million yuan (US$3.77 million), which was the largest compensation claim of its kind in China. Reporters Without Borders, and other activist groups directly petitioned Steve Jobs to unfreeze the journalists' assets and drop the lawsuit (Lee, 2006).

The lawsuit was eventually dropped, but the media attention and pressure on Apple was minor in comparison to later events. Between January and May 2010, 13 young migrant workers attempted or committed suicide at two different Foxconn facilities in Southern China. By the end of 2010, there had been 18 suicide attempts, resulting in 14 deaths and four critical injuries. While Dell, IBM, HP, Samsung, Nokia, and many other multinational brands contract with Foxconn to manufacture their products, the bulk of international outrage, media attention, and labor activist campaigns targeted Apple. Due to the highly secretive nature of Foxconn, it was and continues to be difficult to get information on the day-to-day working conditions. Therefore, many relied upon accounts from Nicholas Kristof, actor Mike Daisey, and Hong Kong-based Students and Scholars Against Corporate Misbehaviour (SACOM) who all reported that workers suffered serious workplace abuses (Glass, 2012).

For example, SACOM's May 2011 report noted that workers were subjected to humiliation and threats from supervisors, not allowed to take a single break in ten-hour shifts, not allowed breaks to drink water and were housed in prison-cell like dormitories. Workers who complained were ignored, humiliated, put on blacklists, and fired. China Labor Watch (CLW) (China Labor Watch, 2014c, p. 4) reported that before 2010 workers in Apple's supplier factories were logging over 300 working hours per month, with more than 120 hours of overtime. Although some of Daisey's account, as portrayed in *The Agony and Ecstasy of Steve Jobs*, turned out to be exaggerated or even fabricated, Apple's reputation was damaged. Furthermore, SACOM, China Labour Bulletin (CLB), and CLW's reports corroborated other media reports of poor working conditions and labor law violations at the facilities.

In early 2012, Apple responded to mounting criticism and pressure by becoming a participating company in the Fair Labor Association (Fair Labor Association, 2012a). The company subsequently worked collaboratively with the FLA to conduct audits of Foxconn facilities (Fair Labor Association, 2012a; Lucas et al., 2013). Apple has taken other positive steps in response to the Foxconn suicides and continuing accusations of labor rights abuses in its supplier factories. It now conducts independent audits of Foxconn facilities, and it has significantly grown the Supplier Employee Education and Development (SEED) program and the program requiring worker rights training of factory supervisors and workers in its supply chain (Apple, 2013, 2014). More than 3.8 million managers and workers have participated since the inception of the training program in 2007, with 1.5 million participating in 2013 alone (Apple, 2014, p. 7).

Facing criticism both in terms of shipping American jobs overseas and poor working conditions in Chinese supplier factories, in December 2012 Apple announced that it would begin manufacturing a computer, the MacBook Pro, in the United States in the next year (Gross, 2012). The high cost of manufacturing in the United States, as well as the fact that the majority of the components of the computer would still be produced by subcontractors outside of the United States, has led many to speculate that this was a 'token gesture' or a 'PR move' by the company (Goldman, 2012b; Cheng, 2013).

Since Tim Cook became the CEO of Apple in 2011, the Apple corporate culture appears to have improved its commitment to raising labor standards. Under his watch, the Supplier Responsibility Program (SRP) seems to have grown significantly stronger. Apple University, in partnership with the SRP, established an Academic Advisory Committee to help the SRP benefit from independent research on the sources and correctives of endemic labor problems (Apple, 2013, p. 24).[4]

Without question, Apple seeks to enhance its reputation with the various initiatives to improve labor standards on the one hand, and its US commitments on the other. Yet, this perspective underplays the visible change in corporate culture vis-à-vis labor rights under Cook. The driving commitment of his predecessor, Steve Jobs, was to high-quality, beautiful, and innovative products; Jobs revealed no serious concern about labor standards. Cook, in speech and action, reveals far more commitment to an ethical supply chain (see, e.g., Cook, 2013).

Apple remains a target for campaigns to improve labor standards, in part because of its visibility and in part because the campaigns have evoked responsiveness from the company. Simultaneously, the change in Apple leadership has also produced some transformation in its corporate culture, leading to serious efforts to improve labor rights and standards within its supply chain. Profit, of course, is always a bottom line, and it remains to be seen what Apple's trade-offs will be in the future.

Knights Apparel

One brand took an alternative path once it had established a serious market share. In 2010, Knights Apparel, the largest supplier of collegiate licensed apparel in the United States (Nike is second), opened a factory in the Dominican Republic to produce collegiate clothing under the new brand name Alta Gracia. It is the first garment factory to pay its workers a living wage, certified by an independent auditor. Calculated by considering the basket of goods and services a family needs, the living wage amounts to more than 300 percent of the legally mandated minimum wage in the Dominican Republic. Workers have the right to unionize and engage in collective bargaining. They have health and other benefits, and they work in safe, healthy, and environmentally sustainable conditions. The WRC certifies that Alta Gracia continues to provide the living wage and meet other high labor standards, and the firm provides the WRC auditor with an office in the factory, encourages her to meet with workers off premises, and offers access to its books.

Alta Gracia is the brainchild of Joe Bozich, the CEO of Knights Apparel. Personal tragedy influenced his decision to create a factory that ensures its workers and their children a path out of poverty through a good job. But he also believes good jobs are a good business model. Knights expected to subsidize Alta Gracia for three years, but it is breaking even after 18 months. Bozich has plans to open a second factory. The company does take a smaller return on Alta Gracia products in order to ensure that it can sell the garments at the same price point as its closest competitor and that retailers get their standard margin. There is no advertising for Alta Gracia other than the hangtags and posters that let consumers know what the living wage has meant for the workers, the website,[5] and considerable word of mouth and campaigning by supporters, including several student groups.

By setting its standards in collaboration with representatives of the WRC, USAS and other vocal critics of violations of universities' codes of conduct in supply chains, Bozich was able to build and manage a factory that they support while winning their patience in his efforts to improve the conditions in contracted factories. Moreover, they have assisted him in marketing by purchasing their own t-shirts for their student members from Alta Gracia and encouraging other university student groups and campus labor unions to do the same.

As a consequence of rising wages, the increased spending power of the workers means they can now buy their children equipment and clothes needed for school, move to better housing, and get loans. Small transport and food service businesses have sprung up to meet the needs of workers who can now afford taxis and purchased lunches.

With Bozich and Knights Apparel, a corporate culture committed to ethical principles and innovative strategic planning produced a high-quality product, profitable to the business owners and advantageous to the workers.

GLOBAL SUPPLY CHAIN DYNAMICS

The cases above offer examples of brands making commitments to improve labor standards in their supply chains. This book is motivated by the desire to understand why, when, and how brands are likely to make such commitments and whether or not they will be successful and sustainable. In order to do this, we must develop a broader analytic framework that takes into account the complex web of actors and relationships involved in the governance of modern global supply chains. We begin this challenging task in the next chapter.

However, at least in the four cases presented here, activist campaigns that tarnish the brand's reputation among its consumers – or the potential threat of such campaigns – appear to be the trigger. Even those companies, such as Levi Strauss, with a history of corporate social responsibility did not always react to labor rights abuses in their supply chains until effectively compelled to admit to them. Knights Apparel, taking stock of the political environment, acted pre-emptively. It makes a difference to have a corporate culture that values good labor standards, but it matters only when those values can be conjoined with profitable business practices.

Establishing a commitment to better labor standards and changing the corporate culture (if it needs to be changed) to include such a commit-ment is a first step. But it is only a first step. The big issue remaining is how best to ensure that corporate codes of conduct are, in fact, implemented throughout the supply chain.

Gereffi et al.'s (2005) influential work concentrates on asymmetrical power relationships in vertically integrated manufacturing networks where global brands retain control over high-value-added functions but offshore labor-intensive production processes. When suppliers wish to 'upgrade' (i.e., move up the value chain), they are more likely to be responsive to corporate demands, be it for product quality, speed, or higher labor standards. The assumption of much of this work is that when global brands can dictate the terms of business to their suppliers, they must have the power to dictate that their suppliers follow whatever codes of conduct brands decide to impose. Therefore, auditing and monitoring allows brands to identify and punish the non-compliant. A strategic supplier, fearing loss of orders, will, consequently, raise standards.

In this context, a number of global brands have introduced corporate codes of conduct that include various labor rights provisions. These codes vary widely in content (Esbenshade, 2004; Locke et al., 2007b, 2009). Some employ vague language and abstract principles that are difficult to implement or enforce, others include detailed provisions for labor rights, and yet others are geared at simply protecting brands from legal accountability for subcontracted employees. In his work on Mexico and Guatemala, for instance, Rodríguez-Garavito (2005) found that many codes emphasized working conditions and hours but lacked attention to freedom of association rights (see also Barrientos and Smith, 2007).

Even when codes include strong labor protection provisions, lack of internal enforcement or independent auditing limits their usefulness in creating meaningful improvements for workers. Brands with strongly worded codes of conduct but weak enforcement have often been accused of 'greenwashing'. Certainly it is rare for brands to pull out of factories with documented violations, especially if there is strong demand for turnaround on a particular product; generally the brand's excuse is that it is capability building in an attempt to bring the factories up to standard (Locke, 2013).

Brands, however well intentioned, have additional problems in enforcing their codes within the supply chain. First, they have limited information about their own supply chains. Although codes of conduct are usually intended to apply to all suppliers, the reality is that brands do not always know where their products are made. Second, suppliers do not always have adequate incentives to adhere to the code. When a brand's principal supplier subcontracts orders to other factories, subsidiary firms are often non-compliant, either because of ignorance of the code or because it is costly to do so (and easy to evade detection). Indeed, the brands are often sending mixed signals to suppliers by asking them to compete on price and simultaneously raise labor standards.

The extent to which a global brand has sufficient power over its suppliers to enforce compliance is very contextual. Locke (ibid.) documents how large suppliers in Asia, for example Foxconn, have specialized skills and knowledge and have carved out niche markets for themselves. As detailed in Chapter 9, such suppliers have significantly increased their bargaining power in relationship to global brands based in the developed world. A single brand may have to develop multiple tools and strategies in order to address labor violations in different industries and supply chains.

The mobility of small companies who produce at the bottom of the supply chain is another persistent problem, particularly in the garment industry. According to O'Rourke (2001), 'the problem is not with individual factories or evil managers. The problem is a global production system that ... encourages highly mobile, fly-by-night, secretive, and completely unaccountable garment factories'. When challenged by workers forming unions or pressured by MNCs trying to induce compliance with private regulatory schemes, smaller factories that rely on low-skilled workers and unsophisticated technology can and will simply shut their doors without paying severance to workers and relocate.

Countries with low state capacity have difficulty enforcing national law against delinquent factory owners, particularly when the owners are foreign nationals. Enforcement may not be in the interest of the regime if they believe enforcement will discourage future investments. Although the problems with fly-by-night ownership are well known to activists and corporations alike, scholarly research on these actors is thin.

While the brand–supplier relationship is critical, domestic governments are also important in upholding labor standards. As we will see in the country chapters that follow, the Honduran and Bangladeshi governments are challenging to brands because they are riddled with corruption and lack much of the basic infrastructure and the capacity to monitor or enforce labor laws. China is challenging in a different way. Chinese local governments actually have some capacity to enforce laws and arbitrate on behalf of workers. However, local officials often find it in their interest to collude with supplier factories. The rewards of collusion with mega-suppliers are even greater as they bring more jobs and tax revenue to local areas than small and medium-sized enterprises. Layering and interacting private regulatory schemes with public institutions, as suggested by Locke (2013), is more difficult to implement under these conditions, although not impossible.

In the chapters that follow we explore the various strategies employed to ensure that brands develop and effectively implement a corporate code of conduct. Our investigation of international institutions suggests and the country cases further reveal that more than a code is necessary to ensure supplier compliance. Aligning the interests of brands, suppliers, and supply chain workers requires, first, the combination of worker ally and consumer pressure that attempts to transform the beliefs of firm management about the appropriate norms of behavior. We have seen that process at work in the cases above. However, the second, and probably most important and more sustainable mechanism, is government regulation backed up by effective enforcement.

NOTES

1. The Harkin Bill was re-proposed in 1993, 1995, 1997, and 1999.
2. Our other case studies include Bangladesh, home to only three Nike supplier factories, employing 15 366 workers; and Honduras with nine supplier factories and 18 701 workers (Nike, Inc., 2014).
3. While this case study focuses primarily on the brand perspective of Apple itself, we also focus in Chapter 9 on the supplier and government perspective, with an analysis of Foxconn.
4. As full disclosure, Margaret Levi is a member of that committee.
5. http://altagraciaapparel.com/.

3. Aligning interests across global supply chains: an analytic framework

Under what conditions should we expect labor rights in global supply chains to improve? How do we make analytic sense of the complex universe of actors and interests involved in global supply chains, as well as their governance and the multitude of relationships and modes of influence among them? What forms of social pressure do we expect to lead to changes in behavior, and under what circumstances? We attempt to organize this complex landscape with an analytic framework focusing on four clusters of actors, their incentives and beliefs, and the changing patterns of interest alignment and misalignment among them. While this framework retains substantial complexity, our aim is to identify the particular changes and relationships that we expect to be most significant in leading to better labor rights.

We focus on four key clusters of actors, defined by their relationship to the process of production: supply chain workers and their allies, governments, businesses, and end consumers. Each of these clusters in turn comprises myriad types of actors in different geographic locales and structural positions in the supply chain. We emphasize the different configurations of interests within and across these clusters, which vary in their degrees of alignment or conflict.

Our primary concern is the extent to which opportunities for leverage to improve labor standards are present in a given configuration of interests. Opportunities for leverage are just that: opportunities. Some actor or coalition of actors, within or outside of existing organizations, may or may not take advantage of such opportunities to press for changes to the existing governance of labor rights. Some opportunities pass with no such change. In other cases, positive improvements take place, but are likely to be short-lived unless firmly institutionalized. In this sense, positive changes to labor rights in global supply chains are likely to be isolated, limited, and fleeting, even when they do take place.

How do such opportunities for leverage arise? We argue that opportunities for leverage for a given actor are increasing along three dimensions. First, opportunities are greater when there is greater alignment of interests within an actor's cluster. Second, they are greater when there is greater conflict of interests within the cluster that is the target of opposition or change. Third, opportunities for leverage are greater when there exist greater cross-cluster alignments and coalitions with actors in other clusters.

Finally, we argue that the configurations of interests within and across the four clusters of actors are not constant and unchanging but instead reflect stakeholder incentive structures, their beliefs about the rewards and punishments that they face, and their beliefs about norms of appropriate behavior. In the global supply chains we focus on in this book, beliefs about rewards and punishments are most likely to change when new, often disturbing information is revealed about practices and conditions that workers face. Sometimes this revelation is due to high-profile incidents, such as the Triangle Shirtwaist Factory fire in the United States, and sometimes due to political action, such as when activist groups successfully bring labor violations to the attention of global media.

The stages of this process are represented, in abstract form, below:

1. New information (resulting from high-profile incidents and/or political action).
2. Modifications of incentives/beliefs about rewards and punishments and/or the modification of beliefs about norms of appropriate behavior.
3. Changes in configurations of interests within and across clusters of actors.
4. New opportunities for leverage, which may or may not be utilized.
5. Improved labor rights, which may be more or less isolated, limited, or short term.

We should be clear, however, that alignments of interest among stakeholders do not always serve to advance or protect workers. Sometimes the opposite is the case; businesses, consumers, and even governments may be aligned in opposition to workers.

The main goal of this chapter is to define and detail the clusters of relevant actors that interact in this framework. First, however, we briefly introduce the clusters and our concepts of interest alignment within and across them, and the mechanisms of influence that can alter those alignments.

CLUSTERS, INTERESTS, AND ALIGNMENTS

We define the clusters of actors by their relationship to the production process, revealing four clusters with certain kinds of interests attached to each:

- supply chain workers and their advocates and allies;
- governments, broken down into relevant legislative, judicial, and administrative/executive agencies;
- businesses, including brands, suppliers, wholesalers, and retailers;
- consumers, primarily individual consumers but also institutional purchasers.

Businesses organize factors of production, including labor, in order to make or sell goods for profit. Workers supply labor for compensation and seek the best return and conditions they can get, and their allies/ advocates try to promote these goals on the workers' behalf. End consumers purchase goods for use with an eye to both price and quality. Government actors regulate the system as a means to achieve desired ends for the country (e.g., jobs, economic development) and benefits for themselves (e.g., remaining in office, side payments).

We focus on clusters of actors, rather than individual actors, for two reasons. First, the universe of actors relevant to the governance of labor rights in global supply chains is so large and complex that we must impose some simplifying assumptions in order to make any framework for analysis tractable. Second, the clusters capture defining preferences and thus the boundaries of the group. That being said, the strategies, payoffs, and values of actors within clusters can diverge, creating conflict within clusters, alliances across clusters, and opportunities for leverage.

For example, while both brands and suppliers seek profit, their time horizons and their competitive and regulative environments vary and can promote discord. While both local and national government officials may seek economic growth, the first focuses on a particular region of the country and the second on the country as a whole, and they may face very different logics of political promotion and survival. Workers and their allies can differ significantly over goals and strategies, particularly when some seek protection of domestic workers and unions that are counterproductive to improving the well-being of workers in the global supply chain. Some consumers hold strong social values while most care about little beyond cost and quality.

Further, while the core interests of each cluster are clearly different from each other, and often in direct opposition, we highlight potential alignments of interest across clusters, and the coalitions that can sometimes result, as crucial in creating and exploiting opportunities for leverage. Cross-cluster alignment of interests between the worker and government clusters can arise when political parties depend upon or compete for labor votes. The worker and consumer clusters align when ethical consumers or institutional purchasers have normative beliefs that lead them to seek out 'fair trade' products. When negative media attention, activist pressure or the risk of scandals gives brands incentives to take actions to improve labor rights and working conditions, the result is an alignment of interests between workers and their allies and brands. But it is an alignment that also requires intra-cluster conflict between brands and the suppliers who resist the changes brands demand.

In addition to examples that make change in workers' interests possible, it is also important to emphasize the fact that cross-cluster alignments and coalitions can operate to stymie and roll back the rights of workers. This is the case when brands or suppliers share interests or cooperate with government in opposition to labor standards. Indeed, we expect such aligned interests between business and government clusters to be far more common empirically than aligned interests between either of those clusters and workers.

Combining the varying degrees of alignment and conflict of interests within and across clusters reveals the configurations that are most likely to create opportunities for leverage to advance labor standards. Generally, but not always, this requires workers and their allies to impose economic or political costs on other actors. Strikes, slowdowns, and boycotts (which require further coordination with some critical subset of consumers) are examples of how workers can impose costs on business. Electoral clout and demonstrations are means for imposing political costs on at least some members of the government cluster. A coordinated worker cluster, or even a powerful subset of the worker cluster, is only likely to succeed, however, when they can take advantage of either a division within the business cluster, generally between the brands and their suppliers, or a strong and effective state apparatus whose interests they are able to align with their own.

Such configurations create new avenues of collective action and points of leverage, but too often they are no more than isolated moments of alignment within broader contexts of structural imbalance among the different clusters of actors. The more likely scenario is that the divisions within the worker and government clusters permit business to get its way.

Table 3.1 summarizes how different configurations of alignment might shape the interactions of two different clusters of actors. This table is presented without reference to the specific clusters under consideration, in order to present a prototypical case. In practice, the specific identities of the clusters in the relationship may shape the interactions in more nuanced ways.

Table 3.1   Examples of different configurations of interests within and across clusters

	Cluster B: Low Alignment Within Cluster	Cluster B: High Alignment Within Cluster
Cluster A: Low Alignment Within Cluster	Little chance of cross-cluster alignment	Opportunity for actors in B to act collectively and/or forge coalitions with some actors in A: *Advances interests of B*
Cluster A: High Alignment Within Cluster	Opportunity for actors in A to act collectively and/or forge coalitions with some actors in B: *Advances interests of A*	Either opportunities to substantially advance shared interests, or source of substantial conflict, depending on whether interests are shared or not across A and B

It is important to note, however, that the opportunities for leverage created by these configurations remain only opportunities. In many cases, actors fail to successfully take advantage of them or are blocked by actors with opposing interests. Even when opportunities for leverage are successfully used, changes are often limited or are short-lived. In order to sustain improvements over longer periods of time, we emphasize the necessity of institutionalization through formal rules with monitoring and enforcement provisions.

We have now introduced, if not yet fully explored, the clusters of actors in our framework and the potential configurations of alignment and conflict of interest among them. We now briefly turn to the preceding stage of our process of change: sources of modification in the beliefs and incentives of key actors.

INCENTIVES AND BELIEFS

We argue that disturbing and salient information about what is happening in supply chains can trigger modifications in beliefs and incentives that in turn lead to changes in alignments of interest and points of leverage among actors. To understand this process better we will use a specific example: the Triangle Shirtwaist Factory fire of 1911 in New York City.[1] Of the 146 workers who died, most were girls in their teens and twenties. In the aftermath of the horrific images of young immigrant women jumping to their deaths and the subsequent revelations of the unsafe conditions the management created, the actors in our clusters experienced a variety of new pressures – material, informational, and psychological – that transformed incentives and beliefs.

For the business cluster, the bad publicity, the trial and ultimate conviction (in a civil but not criminal suit) of the factory owners, and the introduction of new regulations established punishments for labor standard violations. At the least, those in the business cluster came to believe the behavioral incentives had changed. Some business actors, probably a minority given the persistence of sweatshops for many years after, were embarrassed and alarmed by the shocking effects of standard business practice and changed their beliefs about how it was normatively appropriate to run a factory.

Workers and their allies also experienced incentive and belief changes. The International Ladies' Garment Workers' Union (ILGWU) had struck against sweatshop conditions in 1910 and, with its allies, pushed for protective legislation but with limited success. Public outrage produced an environment where actions on behalf of workers, even including unionization, became more acceptable. In terms of incentives, individuals now saw the possibility of career ladders in the labor movement. In terms of belief modification, activists came to believe that they now lived in a world where they might actually have some influence if they made use of the opportunity. As an example, Frances Perkins, a social worker who witnessed the fire from the street below and went on to become the US Secretary of Labor under Franklin Delano Roosevelt from 1933–45, helped found and chair the Committee on Public Safety. She worked closely with the ILGWU to lobby for worker safety legislation in New York State.

The change in the incentives government officials experienced was largely an effect of their calculus about the rewards and punishments voters would deliver at the ballot box. They also worried about bad publicity that would affect their capacities and popularity. Moreover, like the workers and their allies, some legislators already wanted reform but first had to believe it was possible. When even the bosses of Tammany Hall (New York City's infamous political machine) supported the proposed bills, Robert F. Wagner, then the Majority Leader of the New York State Senate and later the US Senator who crafted the National Labor Relations Act, knew passage was very likely indeed. The end result was a series of progressive labor laws and the establishment of the beginning of an inspectorate for occupational health and safety.

Consumers as citizens possibly experienced a short-term change in their incentives to express outrage, and there was some demonstrable belief change about the positive contributions of unions and government action on workers' behalf. Public outrage, even if short term, played an important role in changing the calculus and beliefs of actors in the other clusters.

The Triangle Shirtwaist fire triggered an alignment of interests both within and across clusters. In this case, although not in all that we will discuss, key actors took advantage of the opportunity produced by this alignment of interests to lobby for, pass, and enforce legislation that significantly improved labor standards for workers in the years that followed.

THE CLUSTERS

The example of the Triangle Shirtwaist Factory fire illustrates the broad range of actors involved in creating improvements for labor standards. It further exemplifies the respective interests of those actors and the ways in which beliefs about the rewards and punishments they face shape their actions. Moving beyond the US case, in the following we review in general terms the actors that comprise each cluster within contemporary global supply chains. We pay particular attention to the various conflicts and alignments of interests that may exist.

Supply Chain Workers and their Allies

Those with the deepest interest in protecting labor rights are supply chain workers themselves. Although economic security, fear of reprisals, and ignorance about their rights may inhibit action, workers nonetheless have the clearest stake in improving the legal and administrative regime regulating employment practices. Their allies, found among NGOs, religious organizations, community-based organizations, and trans-national activists, sometimes offer the voice and lobbying capacity that unorganized workers lack.

Workers in supply chain factories are often working far from home and have come to factories in search of jobs that they have been unable to find at home. A consequence of this is that they are often willing to work long hours under stressful conditions so that they can send much-needed money back to their families (Rivoli, 2005; Locke, 2013). Many prefer to work overtime to supplement their base salaries but want to be paid for the overtime work they do at the agreed-upon rates (without being cheated). They may be willing to repeat the same task for many hours, day in and out, under stressful working conditions and for low wages, but they prefer environments that do not jeopardize their personal safety and health, live in clean, not overly crowded dorms, and eat nutritious and well-cooked food. They expect to be treated fairly and with respect. If not, they may leave their employer as soon as they can and/or engage in individual or even collective resistance.

Unions

A prime way for workers to advance their interests vis-à-vis employers is by organizing and engaging in collective bargaining. Labor unions were a major organizational means workers used to win and protect rights in most of the now developed countries. However, unions are declining within most of the Organisation for Economic Co-operation and Development (OECD) countries; in many developing countries, the percentage of workers represented by unions is as low as 1–2 percent of total employment (Hayter and Stoevska, 2011). Nonetheless, where they exist, they often play an essential role in campaigns for labor rights (Anner, 2011). They can pursue collective bargaining with employers to seek better wages or working conditions, and they can threaten strikes, job actions, and whistle-blowing to allies to promote their interests. Where direct bargaining with employers fails, unions may also assist workers in taking cases to domestic courts or filing grievances with labor ministries or other agencies. Unions can also lobby the state or otherwise advocate for favorable policy changes, such as laws protecting a minimum wage, restricting the number of hours that can be worked per week, or outlawing pregnancy tests as conditions of employment. The potential for unions to achieve significant gains for workers depends a great deal on the political context in which they operate.

Non-governmental organizations (NGOs)

NGOs can improve labor standards for workers in global supply chains by offering credible information of what is happening in the factories and firms of supply chains, providing training and education to workers, and by coordinating global and domestic campaigns. They often play a vital role in alerting key stakeholders in other clusters to workplace violations.

Subcontracting within supply chains poses a challenge to acquiring adequate information among stakeholders. In the locations in which labor rights violations occur, local NGOs (including religious organizations and community-based organizations), together with unions and workers, are uniquely positioned to gather information through at least two different kinds of monitoring roles: they can provide 'fire alarms', alerting others to violations, and they can act as formal monitors. Some

NGOs play both roles, while others (such as the Fair Labor Association and the Worker Rights Consortium) specialize in one or the other.

Training and educating workers in global supply chains is another service they may provide. Factory workers in particular (alongside agricultural workers) typically have extremely low levels of education and little knowledge about their rights (Rodríguez-Garavito and De Sousa Santos, 2005). NGOs offer information not otherwise easily accessible; some also attempt to raise consciousness and provide advocacy tools. In Honduras, for example, as well as elsewhere, NGOs play powerful roles in educating workers about basic rights enshrined in domestic law, training them how to count hours of overtime worked, and assisting them in organizing and building unions.

International organizations
Various international organizations act as allies of workers in their monitoring, advocacy, and enforcement and labor rights. These include regional and international human rights courts and commissions such as the Inter-American Commission for Human Rights (IACHR) or the European Court of Human Rights (ECtHR). They also include various UN bodies and committees. The most important international organization acting explicitly on behalf of workers is the International Labour Organization (ILO). Established as part of the League of Nations in 1919, the ILO was the first specialized agency of the United Nations. It is the primary international organization responsible for creating and overseeing international labor law, and it engages in various monitoring, capacity-building and advocacy activities (discussed at length in Chapter 4). The ILO frequently partners with governments and brands in efforts to raise the global floor for workers around the world and promote best practices.

Alignment and conflict in the worker cluster
Supply chain workers are interested in having jobs and sufficient pay to support themselves and potentially their families, in better wages, and in fair treatment and working conditions. Unions and NGOs have interests in promoting those same goals for workers, as well as their own interests in organizational growth and survival.

There are, however, numerous potential sources of conflict among these actors. Globally, workers in different countries find themselves competing for scarce jobs in any given industry. Within countries, workers in different industries may find themselves with competing interests over policy, for example between export-oriented and import-competing industries (Hiscox, 2001, 2002), or between skilled and unskilled workers (Rudra, 2008). Even within single firms, political differences can yield disagreements over the value of unions. Workers may also place different priorities on different goals, for example between rights to association and collective bargaining on the one hand, and wages and available overtime hours on the other. When workers face threats of retribution or even violence, they may value personal safety and job security over all other potential interests.

Some of these sources of conflict are material in nature, whereas others have their origins in beliefs over the state of the world that workers find themselves in, including what actions are likely to have positive or negative consequences. Unions seeking to work together in a single country may face differences in beliefs over what the most effective strategy is likely to be.

Workers' allies, including unions, NGOs, and transnational campaigns, also face many potential sources of conflict. Their organizational goals in resources and survival, and in preserving their reputation and integrity, may come into conflict with the interests of workers that they seek to promote. They may also have markedly different beliefs over the best strategies to employ, and how best to work with relevant actors in other clusters – most notably brands and suppliers themselves.

The many potential sources of divergent interests and beliefs may reduce the ability of workers and their allies to act collectively and effectively. Levels of alignment or divergence will vary from case to case, within and across countries and at different points in time.

Governments

Governments, like workers, are comprised of a diverse collection of actors with competing interests and beliefs. When governments are aligned against labor, this can serve as a strong impediment to improved working conditions. However, more often than not, in apparel- and electronics-producing countries government actors have interests that are misaligned or seriously lack capacity. Many of the case studies presented in this book illustrate divergent interests among different actors in the government cluster.

Different types of regimes also affect outcomes. Democracies potentially allow for more equitable representation of diverse groups including workers and their allies. For this reason, they typically experience fewer collective bargaining violations than autocracies (Bueno de Mesquita et al., 2003; Neumayer and de Soysa, 2006; Caraway, 2010; Mosley and Uno, 2007; Mares and Carnes, 2009).

Politicians and parties

Pro-labor political parties have often been crucial for enhancing labor rights, but analysis of their role is complicated by the cross-national variety of electoral arrangements and experiences. Leftist political parties, typically aligned with and supported by workers' organizations, consistently spend more on social welfare than their conservative counterparts (Hibbs, 1977; Korpi, 1978; Korpi et al., 1998; Huber and Stephens, 2001; Bueno de Mesquita et al., 2003), and labor parties generally have a commitment to institutionalizing improved labor standards (see, e.g., Murillo, 2001; Murillo and Schrank, 2005). Government partisanship can therefore be an intervening variable in the relationship between global economic integration and labor rights.

Judiciary

Many countries have adopted remarkably similar labor laws on the books but the enforcement and interpretation of those laws diverges dramatically. Many apparel- and electronics-producing countries house highly corrupt judicial systems or lack independent judiciaries altogether. Where judges or other domestic institutions can get away with corrupt practices and where foreign and domestic firms are willing to use bribes and payoffs, workers stand little chance of resolving grievances through formal institutional channels. In addition, domestic courts may also lack independence or be beholden to the will of the executive office. Where the executive is either anti-labor or strongly aligned with business, a lack of judicial independence may pose considerable challenges for labor activists and the lawyers representing them.

Labor ministries

Labor ministries can be an important institution for effective workplace regulation but like courts, they vary in their commitments and for many of the same reasons. Where the interests of relatively autonomous and effective labor ministries are aligned with those of workers, those ministries may be able to raise labor standards even in regimes that are broadly hostile to labor in the aggregate (Amengual, 2010, 2014; Schrank, 2011). Labor ministries may also be brought into alignment with workers through capability-building programs such as the ILO-sponsored Better Work program discussed in Chapter 4.

Alignment and conflict in the government cluster

Governments are charged with upholding the rule of law, and most countries have substantial protections for workers' rights on the books.

Yet government agencies, officials, and legislators, even within the same government, often diverge in interests and goals.

Political parties can represent very different groups in society and have divergent beliefs about the state of the world, and about the most appropriate and effective ways of pursuing the national interest. Central and local governments often have distinct sets of incentives that may lead them to act in contradictory ways. Furthermore, when governmental actors value private gain over the duties of public office or economic growth, even at the price of lower labor standards, the consequence is high susceptibility to business influence and capture. This is probably the most common state of affairs both historically and in the contemporary world.

Businesses

Brands, retailers, suppliers, and logistic companies form a coherent business cluster given their relationship to the production process (in that they organize labor and production in order to make and sell goods for profit). However, they play different roles in global value chains and thus often develop distinctive and often competitive interests. Suppliers source and manufacture components, brands design and market products, retailers (who are sometimes the brands themselves) sell final products, and logistic companies coordinate sourcing, delivery, and other features of the supply chain.

Suppliers

Suppliers have an interest in receiving a steady and reliable stream of orders that generate a high marginal return. They want to make the fullest possible use of their productive capacity for as much of the year as possible (in order to amortize their fixed costs). To reduce transaction costs and risk, many attempt to develop long-term, stable relationships with global buyers. To do this, they need to deliver (quickly and reliably) high-quality products at acceptable prices. They may also need to ensure that their production practices do not create any reputation risks for their global customers. Suppliers also have a strong interest in containing or even reducing their production costs, of which labor costs are among the most important. Consequently, they have incentives to restrain wage increases, limit overtime pay and benefits, and underinvest in various services (canteens, dormitories, health clinics, recreation halls).

Moreover, in order to respond to the growing demands by buyers (both existing and potential new customers) for lower prices, smaller batches, and shorter lead times, suppliers structure their production processes in ways that permit them to ramp up production quickly but without incurring additional fixed costs. This can mean imposing excessive overtime hours on their workers and relying on migrant and/or contract workers that they can quickly hire and fire, depending upon their production schedules. Thus, even when these suppliers embrace corporate responsibility programs and engage in various private initiatives aimed at improving working conditions within their factories, the pressures they face often drive them to engage in labor and production practices that undermine these efforts.

Brands
We discussed brands at length in Chapter 2. Their interests lie in profitability, efficiency, and innovation. They also prefer to avoid controversies or scandals that tarnish brand reputation. Largely in response to labor rights campaigns and unwanted media attention, many have developed corporate codes of conduct, corporate social responsibility programs, and monitoring of subcontractors to ensure compliance within the supply chain and build capability of firms. In this category we include those brand retailers, such as Wal-Mart and Target, who are also the major buyers of what suppliers sell.

Logistic companies
Logistic companies are increasingly taking over the jobs of coordinating sourcing and delivery. Their growth represents yet a further evolution in firms shedding tasks that are outside the core competency of the firm. The interest of logistic companies lies in keeping transport and transaction costs as low as possible, given that these are the margins on which their profits depend. It is often these decisions that influence what countries become popular as sites of raw materials and manufactured goods and which have become too expensive.

Alignment and conflict in the business cluster
Businesses share a basic interest in organizing factors of production in order to make profit, yet this does not mean that they have shared interests on other dimensions. Moreover, as we observed in Chapter 2, variations in corporate cultures can produce divergent beliefs among and between brands and suppliers about appropriate business norms and practices.

Subcontractors and brands are particularly prone to misalignment of interests. The contracting corporations have a valuable asset in the brand name, with a reputation to protect among investors and consumers. They also have deep pockets. Many subcontractors, on the other hand, operate on slim margins, usually produce for several brands, and often have few incentives to uphold the labor standards contractually required by the brands. Some take what money they can but fold or move or reinvent themselves, as circumstances require. Given that businesses exist to make financial profits, calculation about punishment and rewards associated with labor violations, low-cost production, and public image will be entirely different depending on the position of the business within the supply chain, and the beliefs of managers and executives about the consequences of upholding basic standards.

End Consumers

End consumers purchase goods with an eye to both price and quality. Despite a growing concern for labor standards among certain consumers, and the emergence of a small but committed 'ethical purchasing' movement, consumers are still predominantly motivated by cost. However, in certain instances, their interests can be captured or brought into line with the interests of workers and their allies. When this happens, it changes the incentives and beliefs of brands, providing a potential source of leverage to raise labor standards.

Ethical consumers

Ethical consumers constitute a tiny proportion of all end consumers, but they sometimes exert considerable influence on sourcing and marketing strategies (see, e.g., Levi and Linton, 2003; Esbenshade, 2004; Shamir, 2010; Linton, 2012; Hainmueller et al., 2014). Ethical consumption generally works through boycotts or through campaigns that use positive signifiers, such as Fair Trade certification or the promise of a living wage, to promote ethically sourced products.

Institutional purchasers

Recently, ethical consumption campaigns organized by NGOs and student groups have targeted institutional purchasers such as churches, universities, and government contractors (Seidman, 2007; Levi et al., 2011). While the threat of losing a few institutional contracts may not severely damage company revenue in the short term, as shown in Chapter 7, the threat of losing multiple institutional purchasers may be a cause for concern. Campaigns that threaten the long-term reputation of brands among end consumers, as well as those that attract enough attention for importing states to threaten sanctions or even market closures, are likely to be the most effective in influencing corporate and factory policy (Seidman, 2007; Greyser, 2009).

Alignment and conflict in the consumer cluster
Despite examples of workers and their allies successfully aligning the interests of a subset of consumers with those of supply chain workers, this is not the norm. Most end consumers, rather than having an interest in improving labor standards, are still motivated by low costs and flashy products. Indeed, the distinctions among consumers, even activist consumers, are becoming increasingly salient. Among individual consumers, different tastes and values give rise to niche markets that may help particular workers in global supply chains but not all workers. 'Buy American' campaigns conflict with an emphasis on ethically sourced products from workers in the global South. Institutional purchasers make choices that individual consumers might not have made.

CONCLUSION

In order to better understand the complex interactions across numerous different types of actors in global supply chains, we have proposed in this chapter an analytic framework centered around four clusters of actors and the alignments and conflicts of interest among them. We focus on supply chain workers and their allies, businesses, governments, and end consumers. Each of these groups share a set of common interests defined by their relationship to the process of production. However, alignments of interest will often form across these clusters, just as conflicts will often form within them. We argue that opportunities for leverage by actors promoting better labor standards will be greater when they are facilitated by greater alignment of interest within their own cluster, greater alignment or coalitions with actors in other clusters, and greater conflicts within the clusters of their targets of influence. These configurations of interest conflict and alignment, in turn, are not constant. Instead, they can change when new information alters the incentives and beliefs of actors in global supply chains.

This framework helps us to understand the events that have taken place in examples like the Levi-Strauss, Nike, Apple, and Alta Gracia cases in the previous chapter, or the numerous cases presented in the chapters to come. Our framework highlights when and why opportunities for leverage are likely to arise. However, it also highlights just how rare such opportunities will be, how high the barriers will be to taking advantage of them, and how limited and short-lived they will be in most cases.

NOTE

1. See http://www.ilr.cornell.edu/trianglefire/index.html.

4. The international framework for labor standards

Among the earliest efforts designed to raise labor standards are those that emerged from international organizations. As members of the worker and ally cluster, international organizations use their power to try to align government and business interests with those of global supply chain workers. Unfortunately, evidence suggests that these initiatives generally fail to provide the large and sustained improvements they appear to promise. Where they have had some success is in establishing the norms to which all advocates of better labor rights appeal.

This chapter reviews the existing international framework governing labor rights. We identify three mechanisms through which international institutions and global governance initiatives have shaped, or sought to shape, the behavior of governments and business vis-à-vis workers. First is the formal monitoring and enforcement associated with violating internationally recognized labor standards. These include the International Labour Organization (ILO)'s formal complaints and enforcement procedures through which it disciplines and monitors compliance from its member states. Second is the diffusion and internalization of global norms pertaining to labor rights that may shape the behaviors of brands, governments, and employers. Third is the capability building provided to firms and governments by international organizations, NGOs, foreign governments, or corporations in order to improve labor rights and promote best practices at the bottom of global supply chains.

Before we evaluate the three mechanisms, we first discuss the evolution of the international framework governing workers' rights. We particularly focus on the ILO. Although it is not the only important international stakeholder, it has its own internal enforcement mechanisms, it has been at the forefront of creating and promoting new norms governing the protection of workers' rights, and it brings together governments, employers, and workers to promote policies and programs to support labor protections.

THE ORIGINS OF THE INTERNATIONAL
FRAMEWORK GOVERNING LABOR RIGHTS

The incorporation of labor rights into international institutions was a highly contested process (Kang, 2012, p. 19). Trade union rights first emerged during the early period of European industrialization, when workers began to demand representation and protection of their interests in industrial and political contexts. At the same time that workers were making gains in the form of new domestic protections, workers and elites in Europe sought to promote these new laws at a global level. In the early days of the movement, workers' rights were often limited to members within exclusive trade guilds. Protections were not afforded widely to employees and they rarely included any demands for the right to organize or bargain collectively. At the turn of the nineteenth century, a more expansive conception of labor rights emerged, and the movement began to gain support from churches, academics, and the clergy.

Throughout the late 1800s, the labor movement made further gains, either as new domestic laws protecting collective bargaining began to emerge, or existing laws criminalizing the practice were overturned. In the same period, the movement to abolish slavery gained global momentum. Efforts to achieve basic international recognition of workers' rights culminated in 1891 when Pope Leo XIII issued the *Rerum Novarum* articulating that states had an obligation to uphold workers' rights (Kang, 2012). Over the decades that followed, workers found additional strength through new transnational organizations, such as international trade secretariats. The international trade secretariats facilitated communication between different countries' trade unions and provided logistical support to domestic workers' organizations. In 1864 the First International, a federation of workers' groups, was created, followed by the Second International in 1889. These institutions paved the way for the first International Congress on Labor Legislation, held in 1897, and the follow-up intergovernmental conference of the International Association for Labor Legislation in 1905 (ibid.). These organizations began drafting early international labor conventions, particularly regarding health and safety measures, in the early 1900s, banning night work for women and banning the use of white phosphorus in the manufacturing of matches.

The first international trade union congress took place in Berlin in 1913. A subsequent conference in Leeds, which included the International Federation of Trade Unions and a number of representatives from various national union federations, formulated a list of demands that later became a blueprint for the ILO. The creation of the ILO was also heavily contested. It was finally established as the product of a protracted compromise between legislators, investors, socialists, and trade unionists (Cohen and Barr, 1944; Rodgers et al., 2009). Kang argues that protecting labor rights at the international level was seen as both an ethical good, relating to human rights and dignity, and an international consensus recognizing a relationship between industrial peace and international peace (Kang, 2012, p. 24).

The ILO's 1944 *Declaration of Philadelphia* included the provisions that:

> The [International Labour] Conference reaffirms the fundamental principles on which the organization is based and, in particular, that – (a) labour is not a commodity; (b) freedom of expression and of association are essential to sustained progress; (c) poverty anywhere constitutes a danger to prosperity everywhere; (d) the war against want requires to be carried on with unrelenting vigor within each nation, and by continuous and concerted international effort in which the representatives of workers and employers, enjoying equal status with those of governments, join with them in free discussion and democratic decision with a view to the promotion of the common welfare.

In its current form, the ILO comprises three main bodies: the International Labour Conference (ILC), the Governing Body, and the Office. The Office is the secretariat of the organization and the Governing Body is the executive. The Governing Body meets three times a year, in March, June, and November and is responsible for all decisions on ILO policy, the agenda of the International Labour Conference, the ILO's budget for submission to the International Conference, and the election of the Director-General. The International Labour Conference establishes the policies, practices, and priorities of the ILO, establishes and adopts international labor standards, and provides a global forum for the discussion of key labor-related questions. The conference meets once a year in Geneva, and brings together government, worker and employer delegates of ILO member states. Each member state is represented at the conference by two government delegates, an employer delegate and a worker delegate. Government representatives are predominantly cabinet ministers responsible for labor affairs in their own countries (International Labour Organization, 2014a). Each delegate has equal rights regardless of status and each can vote as they wish. International organizations can attend the conference as observers.

The Governing Body and the Office are aided by tripartite committees covering major industries. They are also supported by committees of experts on such matters as vocational training, management development, occupational safety and health, industrial relations, workers' education, and special problems of women and young workers.

After the formal creation of the ILO and following World War II, the creation of the United Nations spawned a new international human rights regime. The UN Human Rights Council (UNHRC) was established, alongside the UN Economic and Social Council (ECOSOC). Over the course of the subsequent decades, trade union rights became incorporated into the new international human rights framework and the right to freedom of association and collective bargaining were enshrined in international law, along with many other economic and social rights relevant to the plight of workers.

Yet with the advent of the Cold War, what limited gains the labor movement had made in the preceding decades began to be rolled back. Western states began to exhibit a growing hostility towards labor move-ments, which were often considered to be associated with the socialist policies of the Soviet Bloc. Right-wing and center-right political parties in Europe and the Americas began targeting labor movements domestic-ally and abroad. The global geopolitical context of the Cold War meant that domestic labor politics were often mapped onto East–West conflicts, often largely to the detriment of workers' rights.

GLOBAL MECHANISMS FOR MONITORING AND ENFORCEMENT

The ILO

The ILO is the primary international body responsible for creating, monitoring, and enforcing international labor law. Much like other UN human rights mechanisms, the ILO examines the application of labor standards in its member states and identifies areas of weakness and non-compliance. While countries can choose whether or not to ratify ILO standards and conventions, the ILO continues to monitor labor practices in all countries.

The ILO has a total of 158 conventions on a range of labor issues. Each convention is open for ratification by ILO member states. The conventions are supported by a supervisory system that comprises two mechanisms: (1) the regular system of supervision (which involves the examination of periodic reports submitted by member states on the measures they have taken to implement the provisions of ratified conven-tions) and (2) its special complaints procedures. It should be noted that despite the ILO's positive resolution of a number of cases through its complaints procedure (some of which are discussed below), complaints sometimes take years to resolve, if they are resolved at all.

The regular system for supervising the application of ILO standards is based on the examination of reports sent by ILO member states to the Director-General. Article 22 of the ILO Constitution requires member states to submit reports yearly to the Director-General. Once reports are submitted, they are examined by two ILO bodies (the Committee of Experts on the Application of Conventions and Recommendations and the Tripartite Committee on the Application of Standards, a standing committee of the ILC). These bodies assess the application of ILO standards in law and practice in each member state. Their analysis may also take into account observations submitted by employer and worker representatives (International Labour Organization, 2014b).

In addition to the regular system of supervision, the complaints procedures can work in three ways. First, unions and workers may file a representation against any member state, which, in its view, 'has failed to secure in any respect the effective observance within its jurisdiction of any convention to which it is a party' (International Labour Organization, 2014c). A tripartite committee is then set up to examine the representation and the government's response, and to issue a report and recommendation. If the Governing Body of the ILO deems the government's response to the recommendations unsatisfactory, it may publish the representation and the response.

Second, one member state may file a complaint against another member state for failure to comply with a ratified convention. When a member state is accused of committing or refusing to address persistent and serious violations, the Governing Body can set up a Commission of Inquiry, consisting of three independent members, to investigate the complaint and make recommendations. To date, only 11 Commissions have been established. When a country fails to fulfill its recommendations, the Governing Body can take action under Article 33 of the ILO Constitution and 'may recommend to the Conference such action as it may deem wise and expedient to secure compliance therewith' (International Labour Organization, 2014d).

Third, in 1951 the ILO set up the Committee on Freedom of Association (CFA) composed of an independent chairperson and nine members (three government, three employer, and three worker representatives). The CFA examines complaints about freedom of association violations, whether or not the country concerned had ratified the relevant conventions. Both employers' and workers' organizations can initiate complaints. If the CFA finds a violation has occurred, it issues a report and recommendations through the Governing Body. Since 1951, the CFA has examined over 2300 cases (International Labour Organization, 2014e). More than 60 countries on five continents have acted on its recommendations and improved freedom of association conditions in certain instances over the past 25 years.

Other International Agreements

Other international organizations and treaties also protect labor rights. These include various regional courts as well as the European Social Charter, the International Covenant on Economic, Social and Cultural Rights (ICESCR), and the International Covenant on Civil and Political Rights (ICCPR). The regional and international systems have varying degrees of influence, but the European system has arguably provided the most concrete labor rights protections anywhere.

The European Convention on Human Rights (ECHR), which created and governs the European Court of Human Rights (ECtHR), provides for freedom from slavery and forced labor (Article 4), freedom of assembly and association (Article 11), and freedom from discrimination (Article 14). Due to the fact that the European Court decisions are binding for all EU member states, decisions from the EU have the potential for wide-reaching implications across Europe (Ewing and Hendy, 2010). In the case of *Demir and Baykara* v. *Turkey* (European Court of Human Rights, 2008), the court ruled in favor of an inherent right to collective bargaining and the right to strike, protected under Article 11 of the ECHR. The Court found unanimously that Turkey had unjustly interfered with the right to collective bargaining by annulling a collective agreement between Tum Bel Sen trade union and local authority Gaziantep Municipal Council. The decision protecting the right to strike set a precedent for collective bargaining rights across Europe, ensuring that European courts must revert to this standard should similar cases come before them in the future (Ewing and Hendy, 2010).

The European Social Charter (ESC) similarly prohibits forced labor, prohibits the employment of children under the age of 15, protects the right to earn one's living in an occupation freely entered upon, protects an 'economic and social policy designed to ensure full employment', upholds fair working conditions as regards pay and working hours, upholds the freedom to form trade unions and employers' organizations, protects the rights to collective bargaining, conciliation and voluntary arbitration, guarantees protection in the case of dismissal, protects the right to strike, and upholds access to work for persons with disabilities. The ESC is not a court, and its enforcement mechanism is more akin to that of the ILO. Member states must submit periodic reports on their measures of implementation to the European Committee of Social Rights (ECSR). The ECSR investigates complaints and makes recommendations based on its findings. The ECSR has relied heavily on the ILO Core Labor Standards (CLS) in its decisions, which are binding on member states.

The ILO's CLS are also protected under Articles 6–9 of the ICESCR, which enumerates the rights to just and favorable conditions of work, the right to form and join trade unions, the right to strike, and the right to social security and social insurance. The UN's Economic and Social Council is entrusted with monitoring implementation of the ICESCR, and receives periodic reports from state parties. The Council makes recommendations that follow a similar process to those of the ECSR. Recommendations are based on reports submitted by member states. They are designed to encourage, promote, and support respect for labor rights by governments.

Finally, various labor standards are enshrined in the Inter-American system and the African system.[1] The Inter-American Court of Human Rights (IACtHR) has upheld the rights to freedom of association and non-discrimination among others. In *Escher et al.* v. *Brazil* (2009), the Inter-American Court found that Brazil violated the right to freedom of association by monitoring the phone lines of union organizers. The Court cited the state's obligation 'not to interfere in the exercise of the right to hold meetings or form associations', and its obligation to adopt measures to ensure the effective exercise of this right (Inter-American Court of Human Rights, 2009). The Court ruled that restrictions to freedom of association constitute 'serious obstacles to the possibility of individuals defending their rights, presenting their claims, and seeking change or a solution to the problems that affect them'. The state of Brazil was ordered to pay compensation to the victims of the case. While its rulings are non-binding, the Inter-American Commission on Human Rights (IACHR) has also frequently issued communications on working conditions in *maquilas* and farms in Guatemala, Honduras, El Salvador, and Mexico, pertaining to failure to pay the minimum wage, use of child labor, forced overtime, unsanitary and unsafe conditions, and dismissals of, and violence against, labor leaders. Activists use these communications to lobby domestic governments for greater protections, and a number of the Commission's cases have eventually been taken to the Inter-American Court.

There are a number of instances in which the ILO and other international bodies have successfully encouraged member states to comply with international labor obligations through binding and non-binding decisions, communications, and recommendations. However, given that there are few consequences for non-compliance in reality, the ability for international bodies to effect change through direct monitoring and enforcement remains inherently limited. The ILO and others simply do not have the resources or the teeth to ensure compliance in each member state.

INFORMAL MECHANISMS OF INFLUENCE: THE DIFFUSION AND INTERNALIZATION OF NEW NORMS

Norms are rules of appropriate behavior, with enforcement through social pressure, internalization, and other non-legal and non-formal means. Improvements in labor standards are likely to follow when employers or governments adopt new frames of understanding about what constitutes acceptable treatment of workers, or when they perceive a threat of exclusion from a valued community if they fail to apply its norms.

Many political scientists note that global norms of appropriate behavior can powerfully drive the actions of states and firms (Jepperson et al., 1996; Finnemore and Sikkink, 1998; Ruggie, 2007; Kollman, 2008). The abolition of slavery is one prominent example in which changing norms regarding forced labor have significantly restructured the ways in which actors in global supply chains understand the choices they face regarding the treatment of their workforce. Options such as forced or slave labor, which in previous eras were subject to standard cost–benefit calculations, have, in many sectors, become almost entirely removed from consideration. For the vast majority of businesses, such shifts go beyond employers simply shying away from potential normative disapproval of their actions. It is fair to say that the moral objections to slavery have, for most, been truly internalized. While this is just one particularly high-profile historical example – and even here slavery persists in much of the world – it demonstrates the necessity to take normative change seriously; the internalization of evolving norms concerning slavery demonstrates the potential for normative change to be replicated in other areas in the future.[2]

Of the international labor regime, Hassel (2008) argues that the development of four CLS by the ILO has allowed for a 'point of convergence', defining a core of acceptable behavioral norms relating to labor rights and business strategies. Hassel describes the ways in which the ILO's mainstreaming of an international labor regime in the form of the four CLS has meant that those standards have come to shape national laws, corporate codes of conduct, and government initiatives more effectively.

The decision to promote the four CLS over its conventions and treaties was implicitly motivated by the promise of normative change. Key decision-makers within the ILO expressed concern that although the ILO's 158 conventions were widely ratified, they were proving ineffective at raising the global floor. Practitioners considered that a focus on just four standards would provide opportunities for more strategic, systematic, and targeted outreach and advocacy.

The four CLS, drawn from eight of the ILO's 158 treaties, vary considerably in their content. The first two prohibit forced and child labor, the third seeks to overcome systematic discrimination and ensures that a country makes the most efficient use of its workforce, and the fourth promotes and protects processes that help workers protect their other rights. While specific rights and standards pertaining to occupational hazards, working conditions, hours, overtime and health and safety concerns are not included in the four standards, the fourth CLS – freedom of association and collective bargaining – is essential for ensuring fair working conditions. The standards are as follows:

1. Elimination of forced and compulsory labor (defined in Conventions 29 and 105).
2. Abolition of child labor (defined in Conventions 138 and 182).
3. Elimination of discrimination in respect of employment and occupation (defined in Conventions 100 and 111).
4. Freedom of association and collective bargaining (defined in Conventions 87 and 98).

When analyzing the emergence of new norms in the area of labor rights, it becomes apparent that attitudes towards the first CLS (forced labor) differs greatly from the discourse around the last (freedom of association and collective bargaining). Whereas forced and compulsory labor, child labor, and other forms of bodily harm have been almost universally decried, the right to collective bargaining remains deeply divisive.

As an example, the vast majority of national governments have ratified ILO Conventions 29 and 105 (on which the first CLS is based). Conventions 29 and 105 prohibit the use of forced and compulsory labor, which include slavery, abduction, misuse of public and prison works, forced recruitment, debt bondage, bondage of domestic workers, and human trafficking (Ruwanpura and Rai, 2004). Forced and compulsory labor is considered a baseline right recognized by most (although not all) businesses and governments.

Similarly, the vast majority of states have outlawed at least the worst forms of child labor. ILO Conventions 138 and 182 (the basis of the second CLS) establish guidelines for setting a minimum age to work. Children under age 18 may not do hazardous work, although this age limit is lowered to 16 when under strict supervision. Age 15 is established as a basic overall minimum, while ages 13–15 are suggested only for light work that does not affect educational training, including agricultural work. The ILO conventions require the elimination of the 'worst forms of child labor':

1. All forms of slavery or practices similar to slavery.
2. The use, procuring or offering of a child for prostitution, for the production of pornography or for pornographic performances.
3. The use, procuring or offering a child for illicit activities, in particular for the production and trafficking of drugs.
4. Work that by its nature or the circumstances in which it is carried out, is likely to harm the health, safety or morals of children.

The ILO's Recommendation 190 more specifically defines 'hazardous work' to be the exposure of children to physical, psychological or sexual abuse, work underground or underwater, work at dangerous heights or confined spaces, work with dangerous machinery, work in unhealthy environments, unnecessarily long work hours, or work that confines the child to the premises of the employer (International Labour Organization, 1999). Even states that have not legally prohibited all forms of child labor have laws prohibiting children from doing certain types of dangerous and hazardous work. For example, the Indian Ministry of Labour excludes children from a list of hazardous jobs and industries, such as loom industries, mines, foundries and slaughterhouses (Government of India, 2014). Child labor in the household or in subsistence agriculture has proved a thorny area for policy-makers because it has been difficult to establish and enforce limits in these settings. Additionally, in some contexts this type of work is deeply institutionalized and families depend on the unpaid work their children provide for subsistence.

The rights to freedom of association and collective bargaining (protected in Conventions 87 and 98) have long been critiqued by governments and even, in some cases, workers. These conventions ensure that workers have the freedom to form unions and can participate in civil and political life without retaliation or repression. State parties to Conventions 87 and 98 (which have 153 and 164 state parties respectively) permit workers and employers to freely create and participate in organizations to promote and protect their interests. They further agreed to establish mechanisms to ensure the right to organize and to encourage formal negotiations between employers' and workers' organizations. As we show in the US chapter, violations within this category of rights have rarely attracted widespread condemnation and, in many cases, unions have come under direct attack. Although collective bargaining rights are protected by law in most domestic contexts, and are recognized in the codes of conducts of many major brands, it is difficult to argue that there is any kind of global norm recognizing their importance.

Socio-political context has similarly determined how the elimination of employment and occupational discrimination (upheld in Conventions 100 and 111) has been received. The ILO considers this standard central to achieving greater socioeconomic equality and to promoting development through the more efficient allocation of resources. Discrimination includes 'any distinction, exclusion or preference' made 'on the basis of race, color, sex, religion, political opinion, national extraction or social origin, which has the effect of nullifying or impairing equality of opportunity or treatment in employment or occupation' (International Labour Organization, 1958). Freedom from discrimination in the workplace remains contentious either formally (in contexts where women are prohibited by law from certain types of work) or informally (where employment announcements may forbid applicants from certain religious or ethnic groups).

At specific moments in history, such as after the US civil rights movement or the end of apartheid in South Africa, freedom from workplace discrimination can be said to have reached a point of normative convergence. In both of these contexts, the failure to employ a qualified individual on the basis of their race would be perceived by the general public and the vast majority of employers as unconscionable. In the United States and most of Western Europe it would now be similarly incomprehensible to discriminate on the basis of gender or sexuality. However, while strong norms regarding racial, ethnic or gender discrimination exist in some domestic contexts, discrimination on these bases remains widespread in many countries around the world.

It is notable that workplace health and safety, abuse over working hours, forced pregnancy tests, and other occupational hazards are not incorporated in the ILO's four CLS. Although such practices may result in dire consequences for workers, they have not attracted the same degree of universal condemnation as, for example, forced labor, even within the bureaucracy of the ILO. As we discuss in the chapters on the United States and Bangladesh, there are moments in which international attention has been focused on monitoring and regulation of basic health and safety in the workplace such as following the Triangle Shirtwaist Factory Fire in the United States or the Rana Plaza factory disaster in Bangladesh. In the aftermath of tragedy, health and safety has emerged as part of a global conversation about labor regulations among some stakeholder groups. However, such conversations have rarely been sustained in the absence of other material incentives. It is notable that protections from excessive working hours remain divisive even among workers themselves.

When assessing the potential for global norms to shape local labor practices, we consider two broad arguments promoted by scholars and practitioners. On the one hand, norm enthusiasts (Finnemore and Sikkink, 1998; Risse-Kappen et al., 1999; Hassel, 2008) believe that the inclusion of increased protections for workers on the books, and normative convergence around certain core standards, serve to 'socialize' actors towards new frames of understanding, fundamentally altering the options available to corporations, governments, and consumers in the workplace. In this sense, the prohibition and condemnation of certain practices (such as slavery or child labor) serves, over time, to raise the global floor by institutionalizing and internalizing new norms of acceptable and unacceptable behavior.

Hassel (2008) suggests that its focus on the four CLS has increased the ILO's reach and influence over member states and corporations. The fact that the ILO's four CLS form the basis of so many corporate codes of conduct lends some support to Hassel's argument. The standards have also influenced the texts of many free trade agreements (FTAs). The Office of the United States Trade Representatives' Office of Labor Affairs negotiates labor provisions in bilateral FTAs signed by the United States. Labor provisions differ in detail across the various FTAs, but they generally include commitments to respect fundamental labor rights, to effectively enforce labor laws, to provide domestic procedural guarantees, and to promote public awareness of labor laws and establish consultation and dispute settlement mechanisms. The four CLS have also been incorporated into some processes of the World Bank and the International Monetary Fund (Anner and Caraway, 2010).

On the other hand, norm skeptics assume that the adoption of new labor protections in national laws and company codes of conduct are simply 'cheap talk' designed to distract attention away from continued poor practice (Hathaway, 2002; Aaronson and Zimmerman, 2007; Lafer, 2011). Indeed, the extent to which new protections on the books have translated into better practices remains unclear. Even when ratified by states, ILO conventions are not systematically implemented and we may expect the exact opposite. In her work on international human rights treaties, Simmons (2009) has observed a phenomenon of 'false positives': states that commit to treaties even though they have no intention of upholding the principles involved. Such false positives often arise when states with poor rights performance seek 'social camouflage' in order to avoid or blunt criticism from the international community. The result is that ratification of international human rights treaties correlates only weakly, if at all, with states' actual human rights practices.

Mosley (2010) offers some initial evidence that a similar phenomenon may be at work for several ILO conventions, in that ratifying and non-ratifying states do not differ significantly in their labor practices. Disparities between law and practice in exporting countries, as well as among private voluntary initiatives (discussed in Chapter 2) suggest that unless the interests of key stakeholders can be aligned, it is unlikely that the diffusion of new norms into laws and codes of conduct – no matter how pervasive – will go very far in providing genuine protections to workers. Where true, what looks like normative convergence on paper may in fact mask the continued prevalence of poor standards.

Capability Building

Among the most prevalent forms of international technical assistance programs are capability-building initiatives, often spearheaded by the ILO. These initiatives are designed to promote best practices, provide material assistance to governments and brands operating in weak state environments and encourage an iterative process of learning and innovation. Capability-building programs are in direct response to the short-comings of internal auditing and monitoring (Rabellotti et al., 2008) or to the failure to implement or comply with national or international labor law. Technical assistance may involve collaborations among global brands, their auditors, and suppliers to improve production processes, or they may consist of public–private partnerships in which government labor inspectors monitor and provide feedback to local suppliers. The premise is that suppliers lack the technical expertise and resources to address the 'root causes' of compliance failures. Global brands engage with suppliers to prevent violations by providing technical expertise that will increase firm efficiency and thereby increase profits, which hypo-thetically would translate into better working conditions and higher wages for workers. Some capability-building programs empower shop floor workers either by giving them the power to stop the line of production to address quality problems or by offering further training.

Ongoing capability programs include Nike's Generation 3, the Fair Labor Association's 3.0, and Social Accountability International's SAI 800 certification. Perhaps the largest and most interesting capability-building experiment is the Better Work program, a joint effort of the ILO and International Finance Corporation (IFC). The original Better Work initiative was a partnership with the Cambodian government. Since its initiation in 2007, the model has been replicated in Haiti, Jordan, Lesotho, Indonesia, Vietnam, and Nicaragua. There are plans to extend it to Morocco and Bangladesh in the near future. The program has three components:

- Compliance Assessment Activities in factories: auditors evaluate if the factories are adhering to ILO's four CLS and national labor laws.
- Continuous Improvement: Better Work staff facilitate dialogue between the managers and workers to address their report's findings and submit regular progress reports.
- Stakeholder Engagement: buy-in for the program and activities occurs at all levels, including government, employers, unions and workers, and international buyers.

Better Work reports that, as a direct result of its efforts since 2007, over 90 percent of garment factories in Cambodia now pay their workers their correct wages, including overtime, and allow for maternity and annual leave (International Labour Organization, 2014f).

To ensure long-term sustainability, Better Work requires international garment buyers such as GAP, Levi Strauss, and Adidas, to pay for factory audits and related activities. Although large public and private donors (including Levi Strauss) contributed funds to commence the initiative, Better Work's goal is to make each program financially sustainable in five to seven years (ibid.). Early assessments of Better Work reveal that repeat ILO visits with detailed feedback to factory managers on how to correct deficiencies in the production process have been the most effective at remedying workplace violations and guaranteeing compliance with domestic and international labor law (Polaski, 2006).

The United Nations Global Compact

The United Nations Global Compact (UNGC) takes an alternative approach to ensuring best practices through capability building. Launched in July 2000, after being announced by Kofi Annan at the 1999 World Economic Forum meeting, the Compact incorporates nine principles on human rights, labor standards, and the environment, with the addition of a tenth anti-corruption principle in 2004 (United Nations Global Compact, 2014). The four labor principles mirror the ILO's four CLS. As of 2014, the Compact had over 8000 businesses among its 12 000 participating stakeholders in nearly 150 countries around the world.

The UN Global Compact explicitly rejects compliance-oriented monitoring and enforcement (Berliner and Prakash, 2012, 2014). Instead it offers 'a framework of reference and dialogue to stimulate best practices and to bring about convergence in corporate practices around universally shared values' (Kell and Ruggie, 1999, p. 5). Ruggie (2002, pp. 31–2) explains:

> Its core is a learning forum. Companies submit case studies of what they have done to translate their commitment to the GC principles into concrete corporate practices. This occasions a dialogue among GC participants from all sectors: the UN, business, labour and civil society organisations. The aim of this dialogue is to reach broader, consensus-based definitions of what constitutes good practices than any of the parties could achieve alone ... The hope and expectation is that good practices will help to drive out bad ones through the power of dialogue, transparency, advocacy and competition.

In line with these goals, the Global Compact imposes only two requirements on new members: a 'Letter of Commitment' to support the ten principles and an annual submission of a 'Communications on Progress' report. In terms of substance, the reports must include a statement of continued support, a description of actions taken on at least two issue areas (changed in 2009 to require that all four issue areas must be addressed within five years of membership), and any measurement of outcomes. The deadlines for filing these self-reports is lax and verification of their content virtually non-existent. Officially, the Compact relies on the public or activists to highlight poor performance or disingenuous reporting through a Global Compact complaint system, but the website does not make complaints publicly available.

Not surprisingly, critics find the complaint system ineffective and lacking in transparency, and the impact on actual firm behavior to be limited (Sethi and Schepers, 2014). Berliner and Prakash (2015) conduct an analysis of roughly 3000 US-based firms over the period 2000 to 2010. They find that Compact membership leads to better performance in more superficial dimensions of corporate social responsibility (CSR), such as having an official corporate human rights policy or recycling program, but worse performance in more costly dimensions, such as having labor rights concerns in their supply chains or substantial pollution levels.

The large literature on technical assistance programs paints a mixed picture. It is evident that neither global brands nor their suppliers are adequately motivated to make the kinds of fundamental changes necessary to significantly improve working conditions in the absence of clear incentives to do so. Capability-building programs and international or third-party monitoring and compliance efforts may help improve working conditions in isolated factories, but such initiatives seem unlikely to have the reach or capacity to result in long-term change. It is only in combination with effective state regulation, or aligning the interests of key stakeholders, that we may expect to see meaningful shifts in policy and practice.

CONCLUSIONS

The ILO has markedly shaped the international context within which businesses, workers, and governments interact with each other over labor standards. ILO treaties, especially those that make up the four CLS, have come to define the basic standard against which other laws, codes, and practices are evaluated. Today, the CLS are incorporated into many nations' laws, many brands' internal codes of conduct, and the rules of many other international and transnational institutions, such as trade agreements and the United Nations Global Compact. In this way, as Hassel (2008) has argued, the CLS have effectively become a point of normative convergence that have diffused across many different types of actors.

This sort of norm diffusion is one mechanism through which the international framework for labor standards has successfully shaped the behavior of governments and businesses, although to an often very limited extent. The other mechanisms examined in this chapter, however, show even less promise. Formal monitoring and enforcement by the ILO has too little authority and reach to shape the behavior of governments or brands. Capability-building efforts, based on evidence to date, seem unlikely to bring about long-term changes in behavior, largely because of their own lack of stringent monitoring and enforcement.

While these mechanisms of international influence are crucial in defining the institutional and normative context within which the key actors in global supply chains operate, we believe we need to look beyond them to the specific relationships between each set of actors in different parts of the supply chain, and the beliefs and incentives that shape their interests. The case studies of the United States, Honduras, Bangladesh, and China employ this approach.

NOTES

1. Asia does not yet have a regional human rights system or human rights court.

2. It should be noted that forms of slavery and forced labor persist around the world, even in the United States. Sometimes this takes the form of debt bondage (see, for example, Burkhalter, 2012 concerning the case of tomato plantations in Florida). Other times it involves the confiscation of worker passports or the trafficking of persons. See, for example, Greenhouse (2014) concerning the case of workers in the electronics industry in Malaysia.

5. Labor standards around the world: a quantitative examination

Alignments of interest and opportunities for leverage are likely to change across space and time in ways that quantitative data cannot capture. There are thus limits to what country-level quantitative measures can tell us, especially measures that exist for only one point in time. Nonetheless, the results presented in this chapter highlight some underlying factors that hinder or facilitate improvements of labor standards. They provide the backdrop against which the actors in our four clusters operate. We find important evidence on the roles of state institutions, political parties, international treaties, and business interests in shaping the incentives and beliefs of actors. These findings help us think about how different alignments of interests across global supply chains might open up new opportunities for leverage.

To summarize our conclusions, our most consistent finding is that a country's level of development shapes its labor standards. Although obvious, the crucial importance of structural economic factors in accounting for variation in labor standards around the world is underlined by the robustness and strength of this result. Beyond economic development, our analysis highlights how an examination of a full sample of countries produces different conclusions than a sample comprised only of developing countries particularly important in global supply chains.[1] We also find that distinct sets of factors may be associated with the protection of freedom of association and collective bargaining rights on the one hand, and patterns of enforcement by state authorities on the other.

Across these differences, our analysis suggests which features of government can matter. Democracy and the power of left-wing political parties are sometimes associated with improvements in labor standards. Although state capacity is a powerful explanatory factor across all countries, when examining supply-chain-intensive countries alone state capacity offers little explanatory power beyond what is already explained by differences in economic development. That is, given that wealthier countries tend to have greater state capacity, differences in state capacity are not associated with differences in labor standards once we have taken development into account. We find some evidence supporting hypotheses regarding differences between foreign direct investment (FDI) and arm's-length contracting (Mosley and Uno, 2007; Mosley, 2010) and regarding the diffusion of labor standards via global supply chains (Greenhill et al., 2009). Countries that have ratified more ILO conventions tend to have better labor rights but not better labor enforcement.

Finally, we find intriguing results regarding different private initiatives designed to institutionalize global norms of corporate social responsibility (CSR), although these findings must be treated with extreme caution given the nature of the available data. Among supply-chain-intensive countries, those with more UN Global Compact (UNGC) member firms tend to have worse labor standards, whereas those with more Fair Labor Association (FLA) inspections tend to have better labor standards. This could reflect the spread of CSR norms institutionalized in initiatives with weak enforcement and monitoring provisions (Global Compact) versus stronger provisions (FLA), but could also be a manifestation of complex selection processes by which firms decide to join these initiatives.[2] Clearly, evaluation of the causal impact of either of these initiatives would require more nuanced data than the cross-section of country-level statistics used in this analysis.

This chapter first reviews approaches taken by other scholars to measuring labor standards, then introduces our new measure based on data from the World Justice Project. It then introduces our approach to modeling labor standards around the world and the variables included in our models, before presenting and discussing the results.

MEASURING LABOR STANDARDS

Scholars vary in their approaches to measuring labor standards across countries and, in some cases, over time. Mosley and Uno (2007) compiled a measure of collective labor rights violations covering the period 1986 to 2002 for 90 developing countries, based on reports from the US State Department, the ILO, and the International Confederation of Free Trade Unions (ICFTU). Although this measure has broad temporal coverage and fine-grained level of detail, it also has some shortcomings. The measure captures only the number of different types of labor rights violations, rather than their intensity or specific patterns of enforcement. It is also not yet available for points in time more recent than 2002. The Cingranelli Richards Human Rights Data Project has also coded a measure, based on US State Department and Amnesty International reports, of labor rights across all countries for a longer period of time, reaching almost to the present. However, this measure only takes values of 0, 1 or 2, and as such is less informative than the Mosley and Uno measure. Both of these measures are also subject to well-known biases in human rights reporting by the US State Department and other organizations (Ron et al., 2005; Clark and Sikkink, 2013; Hill et al., 2013; Fariss, 2014). Other measures, such as the Heymann and Earle (2010) legal rights database or the Organisation for Economic Co-operation and Development (OECD) indicators of employment protection, only cover a limited period of time or set of countries. The ILO publishes data on workplace injuries and fatalities, but these are very incomplete and inconsistent from country to country.

Instead of relying on one of these existing measures, we turn to a new source of data from the World Justice Project (WJP). The WJP has developed a Rule of Law Index, 'a quantitative assessment tool designed to offer a comprehensive picture of the extent to which countries adhere to the rule of law in practice' (World Justice Project, 2012). In 2012, this index included 48 individual indicators, grouped into nine categories: Limited Government Powers, Absence of Corruption, Order and Security, Fundamental Rights, Open Government, Regulatory Enforcement, Civil Justice, Criminal Justice, and Informal Justice. These indicators, in turn, are constructed from over 400 individual variables drawn from surveys of over 97 000 people and over 2500 experts around the world. While one of the WJP's 48 indicators is 'Fundamental labor rights' in the Fundamental Rights category, we construct a broader measure. This is because numerous individual variables in other categories of the WJP data also reflect relevant dimensions of labor standards. We combine 26 individual variables from the Absence of Corruption, Fundamental Rights, Regulatory Enforcement, and Civil Justice categories to create our own measure of labor standards.

Our approach offers several advantages over existing measures of labor standards, as well as some drawbacks. Our measure is directly based on surveys of in-country individuals and experts, avoiding potentially biased perceptions of out-of-country experts or foreign policy documents as in the US State Department reports. Our measure reflects the actual enforcement of labor standards, not simply *de jure* standards or the frequency or breadth of their violation. Finally, our measure covers both developed and developing countries for the contemporary period, rather than being limited to specific types of countries or a historical period.

However, our measure has thus far only been collected for one recent point in time (2011–12), and so does not allow us to evaluate temporal changes. This necessarily limits us to correlational claims; the concepts included in our models are all so deeply interrelated that we are unlikely to be able to assess the direction of causality based on statistical associations alone. In addition, while the countries included in the data come from around the world and from both developed and developing countries, the WJP excludes Honduras, one of our cases in this book. Finally, surveys of in-country individuals and experts introduce potential biases, including those derived from a lack of information about working conditions on the 'factory floor'. While most country scores appear sensible based on prior knowledge, others are somewhat puzzling, such as the relatively high score for the United Arab Emirates. Despite these shortcomings, we believe that this new approach to measuring labor standards across the world can offer valuable insights.

To construct our measure of labor standards, we create an index based on the average values of country-level responses to 26 questions from the WJP expert and general questionnaires (see Appendix Box 5A.1 for the full list of questions, at the end of this chapter). The first two questions are from general population surveys, while the rest are from qualified respondent questionnaires. These questions reflect two different dimensions of labor standards: labor rights and labor enforcement. The first eight questions are those we consider to reflect labor rights more than labor enforcement, as they primarily concern the ability of workers to form unions, bargain collectively, and strike. The remaining 18 questions are those we consider to reflect labor enforcement, as they primarily concern the potential enforcement of rules through monitoring and sanctions.[3]

Figures 5.1 and 5.2 plot the two sub-measures against each other for the countries included in the WJP data, and an averaged total measure against countries' level of development. The countries that are the focus of case studies in this book, Bangladesh, China, and the United States (Honduras does not appear in the 2012 WJP data), are circled. Figure 5.1 plots the average country scores for the WJP labor rights measure against the average country scores for the WJP labor enforcement measure, highlighting both the similarities and differences. Some countries score high values on both measures, especially developed democracies in Northern Europe, for example, Sweden, Norway, and Belgium. Some score low values on both measures, for example, Pakistan, Bangladesh, and Ethiopia. Others, for example, Singapore and the United Arab Emirates, score well on the enforcement measure but poorly on the rights measure. Finally, some, for example, Nepal, Burkina Faso, and Venezuela, score poorly on the enforcement measure relative to their scores on the rights measure.

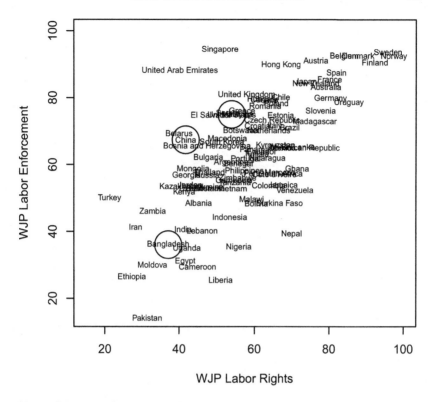

*Figure 5.1   Visualization of labor rights and labor enforcement measures
derived from 2012 World Justice Project data. Bangladesh,
China, and the United States are circled*

Figure 5.2 plots the aggregated *WJP Labor Standards* measure (scaled
to run from zero to 100), combining both the labor rights and labor
enforcement measures, against the log of countries' GDP per capita. A
very strong relationship is apparent, as for the most part more developed
countries have far better labor standards than less developed countries. A
few countries are markedly off the diagonal, such as Madagascar and
Uruguay with better labor standards than expected, and Pakistan,
Turkey, South Korea, and the United States (among others) with poorer
labor standards than expected based solely on the level of economic
development.

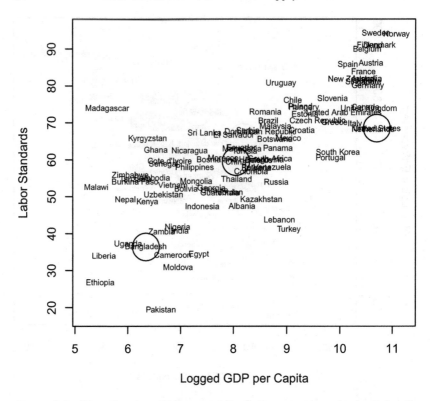

Figure 5.2 *Visualization of labor standards measure (aggregating labor rights and labor enforcement) derived from 2012 World Justice Project data, plotted against logged GDP per capita. Bangladesh, China, and the United States are circled*

MODELING LABOR STANDARDS

In order to assess what factors are associated with stronger labor standards across countries, we construct a series of quantitative models using different samples of countries and different independent variables that may or may not be correlated with labor standards. The goal of these models is not to support explicitly causal claims about what makes labor standards better or worse, but rather to simply explore what factors may be associated with better labor standards across countries.

It is important to be wary of the limitations of these methods. For example, a finding that countries with a given characteristic we may call

'X' have better labor standards than countries without that characteristic does not necessarily mean that X leads to better labor standards. It is possible that this is the case, but equally possible that better labor standards lead to X in a reverse relationship, or that some other underlying factor makes countries likely to both have X and have better labor standards.

We evaluate the relationships in the data in two different samples of countries. The first includes all countries for which the WJP data and our independent variables are available, whether they are developed or developing countries, and whether or not they are embedded in global supply chains. A list of all the countries included in the WJP can be found in Box 5A.2 of the Appendix to this chapter. The second sample includes only developing countries that are major exporters of garments or electronics products, in order to more closely capture the sample of countries most relevant to the analysis of labor standards in contemporary global supply chains. The first condition, developing countries, is defined by excluding those countries that joined the OECD by the end of 1973 (no new members joined between New Zealand in 1973 and Mexico in 1994). The second condition is defined as any countries whose exports in either the garment or electronics industries were valued at more than US$1 billion in 2011. The resulting sample, which we refer to as the 'restricted' and 'supply-chain-intensive' sample, includes 32 countries.[4]

We also investigate three different dependent variables. The first is the full *WJP Labor Standards* measure, constructed by averaging the results of all 26 labor relevant sub-indicators together and scaling to run in principle from 1 to 100. In practice, this measure ranges from 19.5 (Pakistan) to 94.4 (Sweden). The two other measures capture the indicators reflecting only *Labor Rights* and *Labor Enforcement*, respectively. This allows us to separate factors that might be more strongly associated with freedom of association and collective bargaining rights, versus those that might be more strongly associated with the ways in which authorities respond to violations of labor standards.

Independent Variables

We measure *Democracy* using the Polity2 measure from the Polity project, an index of different autocratic and democratic features of regimes. This measure ranges from −10, reflecting a full autocracy, to 10, reflecting a full democracy. There are many reasons that more democratic countries may have better labor standards, including the empowerment of workers' interests through an electoral process, and the respect for rights such as freedom of association. On the other hand, democracies also empower competing interest groups, and may create greater incentives for governments to sideline workers' interests in favor of other economic goals.

We measure the level of economic development using the variable *Log GDP/Capita* of each country, based on data from the World Bank's World Development Indicators (World Bank, 2013). Many of the structural, economic, and demographic changes that shape labor standards will be reflected in countries' levels of development, such as increased structural bargaining power for workers as surplus labor decreases, and the prevalence of industries higher up the value chain.

We also include in some models measures of *State Capacity*, but are limited by the strong correlation that exists across countries between state capacity and the level of development. In practice, most wealthy countries have relatively high state capacity and most poor countries have relatively low state capacity. Across our full sample, a measure of state capacity based on data from the World Governance Indicators (WGI) is correlated with logged GDP per capita at 0.86. This extremely high correlation leaves little variation in one of the variables that is not already captured by the other, strongly limiting what we can learn from including both in a single model. We are careful to present models including the level of development and state capacity both separately and together.

While the WJP data include measures of many relevant facets of state capacity, including order and security, regulatory enforcement, and civil justice, using these to measure state capacity in our models of labor standards would be problematic. This is because our measure of labor standards was constructed using many of the same individual indicators that go into the WJP measures of other institutional features. For example, many of the questions about labor enforcement are also parts of the WJP 'Regulatory Enforcement' measure. Thus using a WJP-based measure of state capacity would include some of the exact same information in both our independent and dependent variables.

In order to include an independent measure of state capacity, we instead use 2011 data from the WGI, taking the sum of the 'Rule of Law' and the 'Government Effectiveness' measures. Each of the WGI indicators is based on an unobserved components model of multiple individual governance indicators, both survey based and expert based, and is scaled to run from roughly -2.5 to 2.5, centered on 0. Our combined measure ranges from -3.15 to 4.22. The Rule of Law component 'reflects perceptions of the extent to which agents have confidence in and abide by the rules of society, and in particular the quality of contract enforcement, property rights, the police, and the courts, as well as the likelihood of crime and violence'. The Government Effectiveness component 'reflects perceptions of the quality of public services, the quality of the civil service and the degree of its independence from political pressures, the quality of policy formulation and implementation, and the credibility of the government's commitment to such policies' (World Governance Indicators, 2014).

We also include variables to measure different types of global economic integration. *Log Exports/GDP* is the logged share of exports in the economy, to capture the importance of globalized production to each country. *Log FDI/GDP* is the logged share of foreign direct investment (FDI) in the economy, to capture the prevalence of directly foreign-owned production. Indeed, Mosley (Mosley and Uno, 2007; Mosley, 2010) argues that exports and FDI will have different and opposing effects on labor standards, with production via arm's-length contracting (reflected in exports) driving standards down and production via hierarchically organized multinational firms (reflected in FDI) driving standards up. Greenhill et al. (2009) on the other hand, argue that globalization will have differential effects on labor standards depending on *where* a country's exports are sold. They argue that exports to countries with high labor standards themselves will place upward pressure on a country's own standards, whereas exports to countries with low standards will place downward pressure, as stakeholders in the destination country place varying demands and pressures on producers. As a way of capturing this logic, in some models we replace the exports measure with two separate measures, of *Exports to High-income Countries* and *Exports to Low-income Countries*. Each of these is the logged share of exports to high- or low-income countries in a given country's economy.

We also include a series of additional independent variables meant to capture other factors that could potentially shape labor standards across countries, while being aware that not all types of influence that take place in this realm will show clear manifestations in cross-national correlations in country-level data. *Left Party* measures the proportion of the preceding ten years (up through 2011) that a left-wing political party held the country's executive office, based on data from the World Bank Database of Political Institutions (DPI). If left-wing political parties represent the interests of workers in ways that result in stronger labor standards, then we should see effects of this variable.

We include two measures to capture two different potential roles of ILO conventions. First, we measure *Log ILO Conventions*, the logged number of total ILO conventions a country has ratified, out of over 150 total possible conventions. This variable ranges from 2.2, reflecting the United Arab Emirates' nine ratifications, to 4.7, reflecting Spain's 106 ratifications. However, the ILO has more recently emphasized eight conventions as reflecting its Core Labor Standards (CLS), so we construct an additional variable in case it is these conventions in particular that may have an effect. However, since the majority of countries have ratified all eight CLS conventions, we instead examine the length of time countries have experienced since ratifications. The variable *Log CLS Years* measures the logged total number of CLS convention-years for each country. That is, if a country has ratified one convention for 20 years and another two for five years, its total number of convention-years would be 30. This measure ranges from a low of 3.6, reflecting the United States' 36 convention-years, to a high of 6, reflecting Norway's 412 convention-years.

We include a measure to capture the prevalence of *Labor NGOs*, to capture their potential role in mobilizing for better labor standards. This measure comes from the database of NGOs affiliated with the United Nations Economic and Social Council (ECOSOC), which includes listings of the substantive areas that each NGO works on. While only NGOs with a certain level of capacity and international orientation will affiliate with ECOSOC, we mitigate this bias by measuring the logged percentage of total ECOSOC-affiliated NGOs in each country that list labor as one of their areas of expertise. Nonetheless, we must interpret any results for this variable with caution, as more NGOs may focus on labor issues precisely in countries with poorer labor standards.

Finally, we include two measures to capture different types of initiatives associated with labor standards, although again we must bear in mind potential selection issues regarding why firms participate. The first refers to the United Nations Global Compact (discussed in Chapter 4). We measure the logged number of *UN Global Compact* members in a given country, proportional to the size of the economy. This variable can be considered to measure the penetration of global CSR norms among firms in each country, but with an emphasis on forms of norm adoption that impose few enforceable obligations. The second comes from the *Fair Labor Association*, which makes available a database of the over 1500 inspections it has conducted to date, reflecting random selections of roughly 5 percent of suppliers of affiliated companies each year. The number of these inspections per country, adjusted by the total size of each country's economy, provides a rough proxy for commitment to more enforceable norms than those in the UN Global Compact among a country's producers. We measure the logged number of FLA inspections in a given country, proportional to the size of the economy. However, it is important to note that the FLA has also been criticized by many for the weakness of the standards in its code of conduct, and for an unwillingness to criticize and sanction the firms on which it largely depends for resources (Compa, 2004; Esbenshade, 2004; Anner, 2012). While these are important criticisms, we consider the prevalence of FLA inspections in a country to at least represent a higher level of commitment to international labor norms and their enforcement than represented by the prevalence of memberships in the UN Global Compact.

RESULTS

We discuss the results of a series of linear regression models using combinations of three different dependent variables, two different samples of countries, and a series of different independent variables. In order to avoid problems of multicollinearity, many of the independent variables are included only one at a time as additions to a base model including variables of core importance. Table 5.1 summarizes the statistically significant results of each model. The full results are presented in Tables 5A.1 through 5A.6 in the Appendix to this chapter.

Table 5A.1 includes the results of models using the full *WJP Labor Standards* measure and a full sample of countries. Table 5A.2 includes results of models using the full *WJP Labor Standards* measure as the dependent variable, but a sample of only supply-chain-intensive developing countries. Tables 5A.3 and 5A.4 present models using the same two samples of observations, respectively, but with the *WJP Labor Rights* component measure as the dependent variable. Finally, Tables 5A.5 and 5A.6 present models using the same two samples, respectively, but both with the *WJP Labor Enforcement* measure as the dependent variable. The following discussion focuses on the different results across all of these models for each variable considered in order.

The effect of democracy is positive, but not statistically significant, in the models of the *WJP Labor Standards* measure. In Table 5A.1/Model 1, the coefficient for democracy is 0.3, reflecting a maximum potential difference of roughly six points (on the 0–100 labor standards scale) between a full autocracy and a full democracy. This difference, however, is not statistically significant, in any of the models using the full dependent variable, with either the large or small samples of countries. In Tables 5A.3 and 5A.4, however, using the *WJP Labor Rights* measure as the dependent variable, the effect of democracy is positive and statistically significant in the majority of the models. Looking ahead to the models in Tables 5A.5 and 5A.6, using *WJP Labor Enforcement* as the dependent variable, democracy is no longer significant. This shows that where democracy has an effect on labor standards, it is only on the protection of freedom of association and collective bargaining rights, and

Table 5.1   Summary of model results presented in full in Tables 5A.1–5A.6 of the Appendix to this chapter

Variable	Relationships with Labor Standards	Relationships with Labor Rights	Relationships with Labor Enforcement
Democracy	None	Positive in both samples	None
Log GDP/Capita	Positive in both samples	Positive in full sample only	Positive in both samples
Log Exports/GDP	None	None	Positive in full sample only
Log FDI/GDP	Positive in some models of restricted sample	None	Positive in some models of restricted sample
State Capacity	Positive in full sample; in restricted sample only when not controlling for GDP/capita	Positive in full sample only	Positive in full sample; in restricted sample only when not controlling for GDP/capita
Left Party	Positive in restricted sample only	None	Positive in full sample only
Log ILO Conventions	None	Positive in full sample only	None
Log CLS Years	None	Positive in full sample only	None
UN Global Compact	Negative in restricted sample only	None	Negative in restricted sample only
Labor NGOs	None	None	None
Fair Labor Association	Positive in restricted sample only	None	Positive in restricted sample only
Exports to High-income Countries	Positive in restricted sample only	Positive in full sample only	None
Exports to Low-income Countries	Negative in restricted sample only	Negative in both samples	None

Note: Full sample uses all countries available in WJP data. Restricted sample uses only developing countries with 2011 exports greater than US$1 billion in either garment or electronics sectors. Only statistically significant findings are discussed.

70

not on patterns of government enforcement. In Table 5A.3/Model 1, the coefficient for democracy is 0.65, relatively large considering the range of the variable from −10 to 10. This reflects a potential difference of roughly 13.7 points in labor rights (on a 0–100 scale) between a full democracy and full autocracy. In Table 5A.4/Model 1, using the restricted sample of 31 supply-chain-intensive countries only, the coefficient is a slightly larger 0.68.

The level of development, measured with *Log GDP/Capita*, shows very strong results across most of the models. Its coefficient is positive and statistically significant in all or nearly all of the models using *Labor Standards* or *Labor Enforcement* as the dependent variable. For the models using *Labor Rights* as the dependent variable, the coefficient is smaller in magnitude but remains positive and statistically significant in models using the full sample of countries. However, among the models using the restricted sample of supply-chain-intensive countries only, the coefficient is smaller in magnitude and much more uncertain, being insignificant in all but two of the models. These results show that the level of development is a very strong factor shaping labor standards, but that it is more strongly related with the enforcement dimension than the rights dimension. The effects are substantively quite large. The co-efficient in Table 5A.1/Model 1 is 7.06, for a variable whose observed range runs from 5.4 to 11.1. The results of this model would predict a difference of 11 points on the *Labor Standards* measure between two countries separated by one standard deviation on the *Log GDP/Capita* measure. In practice, the effects of development on labor standards may run through a myriad of individual mechanisms, but these results stand to highlight the importance of structural and economic factors.

The *Log Exports/GDP* variable captures the overall extent of countries' exposure to global trade, but its coefficient is not statistically significant in any of the models using either of the first two dependent variables. Interestingly, its coefficients are mostly positive in the models using *Labor Standards* as the dependent variable, and mostly negative in the models using *Labor Rights* as the dependent variable, but the results are too uncertain to reach conventional levels of statistical significance. However, in the models in Table 5A.5 – using *Labor Enforcement* as the dependent variable and a full sample of countries – the coefficients for exports *are* positive and statistically significant. This indicates that across all countries, those for which exports make a greater share of the economy have stronger patterns of state enforcement of labor standards, although this is no longer significant in the models in Table 5A.6 using supply-chain-intensive countries only.

The results for the *Log FDI/GDP* variable support some of the arguments of Mosley (Mosley, 2008, 2010) regarding differences between production via hierarchical multinational firms and production via arm's-length contracting. While the variable's coefficients are insignificant and mostly small in magnitude in the models using the full sample of countries, they are positive, substantively large, and in some cases statistically significant in the models using the restricted sample of supply-chain-intensive countries only. Particularly, in several of the models using the restricted sample and either *Labor Standards* or *Labor Enforcement* as the dependent variable, the results show that FDI is significantly associated with stronger outcomes. This offers some support for Mosley's argument that, at least among developing countries where substantial garment and electronics production is located, those where more production is directly foreign owned are likely to have better labor standards.

Evaluating the effects of the *State Capacity* variable requires particular care, as that variable is so highly correlated with GDP per capita. Thus, we evaluate the role of state capacity both in models omitting the *Log GDP/Capita* variable and in models including it – and thereby assessing only the effect of that portion of the variation in capacity that is not already accounted for by the level of development. In the models using the full sample of all countries – across all three dependent variables – the results clearly highlight an important role for state capacity. In these models, capacity has a positive and statistically significant coefficient whether or not the models also control for GDP per capita. The results are more mixed, however, in the samples of supply-chain-intensive countries only. In the models using *Labor Standards* as the dependent variable, capacity is only positive and statistically significant when omitting the *Log GDP/Capita* variable. When that variable is included, not only is state capacity no longer statistically significant, but its coefficient is almost exactly zero – indicating that among developing countries involved in the bulk of global garment and electronics production, there is *no* relationship between state capacity and labor standards that is not already accounted for by countries' level of economic development. Using *Labor Rights* as the dependent variable, state capacity is not statistically significant in any models using the restricted sample of observations, whereas using *Labor Enforcement* as the dependent variable, capacity is again significant only in models omitting GDP per capita. These results further highlight that state capacity offers little explanatory power beyond economic development for the strength of labor standards – both rights and enforcement dimensions – specifically among supply-chain-intensive countries.

The *Left Party* variable, measuring the proportion of the preceding ten years in which a left-wing party held the executive office, shows significant results in some models. While in all models the coefficient is positive, it is only statistically significant in the restricted sample for the *Labor Standards* dependent variable and in the full sample for the *Labor Enforcement* dependent variable. That is, these results offer some evidence that left-wing political parties govern in ways resulting in stronger labor standards, although the precise nature of these relationships remains unclear from the mixed results.

The two different measures capturing different dimensions of country ratifications of ILO conventions, *Log ILO Conventions* and *Log CLS Years*, show similar results. Both are positive and statistically significant only in the models using *Labor Rights* as the dependent variable and the full sample of countries. That is, the strength of country commitments to ILO conventions is associated with better labor rights (but not with better labor enforcement) across all countries, but not across a sample of supply-chain-intensive countries only.

The effect of the number of UN Global Compact member firms in each country is actually negative and statistically significant in some models, specifically those using a restricted sample and either *Labor Standards* or *Labor Enforcement* as the dependent variable. That is, the results of these models show that among supply-chain-intensive countries, labor standards are actually *worse* in countries with greater penetration of CSR norms in the form of Global Compact memberships. There are different possible interpretations of this finding. The first is that, in line with the findings of Berliner and Prakash (2015), Compact members actually take advantage of the weak-to-non-existent monitoring and enforcement provisions of the Compact and ultimately exhibit worse performance on CSR dimensions that would require costly changes. Under this interpretation, the spread of CSR norms institutionalized in initiatives without strong enforcement provisions may serve to actually weaken labor standards in global supply chains. However, a second possible interpretation is that the finding is driven by the selection process by which firms decide to join the UN Global Compact. Firms operating in countries with poor labor standards may face greater pressure – which may be external or internal, and material or normative – to join CSR initiatives. It may thus be that poor labor standards drive Global Compact membership, rather than the other way around. Finally, it is possible that the two possible interpretations represent two different data-generating processes that are both at work simultaneously.

The *Fair Labor Association* variable shows markedly different results to the *Global Compact* variable. Among models using the restricted sample of supply-chain-intensive countries, and with either *Labor Standards* or *Labor Enforcement* as the dependent variable, the prevalence of FLA inspections is significantly and positively associated with *better* labor outcomes. Similarly to the results of the *Global Compact* variable, these findings must be interpreted cautiously. One interpretation is that FLA prevalence reflects the spread of CSR norms institutionalized in an initiative with stronger monitoring and enforcement provisions than the Global Compact, and as such is better able to engender stronger labor standards. However, it is important to bear in mind the criticisms of the FLA's monitoring and enforcement procedures as well. The positive relationship may be driven not by FLA inspections themselves, but by changing norms among producers in a given country that lead them to be more willing to join initiatives with stronger monitoring and enforcement provisions. On the other hand, a selection process may drive this finding as well, such that only in countries with better labor standards already are firms willing to expose themselves to the greater international scrutiny that may come with FLA affiliation.

Finally, the results for the *Exports to High-income Countries* and *Exports to Low-income Countries* variables offer some indirect support to arguments made by Greenhill et al. (2009) about supply chain diffusion of labor standards. In the models using *Labor Standards* as the dependent variable, and using the restricted sample of supply-chain-intensive countries only, countries with greater exports to high-income destinations tend to have better labor standards, while countries with greater exports to low-income destinations tend to have worse labor standards. Since it is in high-income destinations where consumers, activists, regulators, and other stakeholders are likely to demand better labor standards, this finding is in line with the hypothesis of supply chain diffusion. However, the same finding does not emerge in the sample of all countries. For the *Labor Rights* dependent variable specifically, on the other hand, a similar finding *does* emerge in the sample of all countries. For the *Labor Enforcement* dependent variable, on the other hand, the relationships are not statistically significant. Thus, to the extent that these findings offer support to the supply chain diffusion hypothesis, they point to a greater role in changing freedom of association and collective bargaining rights in producing countries, and a lesser role in changing patterns of state enforcement.

CONCLUSION

This chapter used a new source of quantitative data in order to investigate the variation in labor standards across countries. While this analysis is not able to isolate specific strategies of influence or alignments of incentives that may or may not take place among the actors in our framework, it is able to offer preliminary evidence on the structural, political, and transnational factors that are likely to shape labor standards in broad ways.

First, we find that different factors shape labor rights and labor enforcement. For example, democracy, ILO ratifications, and exports to high-income countries all show evidence of being associated with stronger labor rights, but *not* with stronger labor enforcement. This supports our focus on the rewards and punishments that actors face, rather than just the rules that exist in international or domestic law, or private codes of conduct. The United States, Honduras, and Bangladesh case studies that follow illustrate that democracy, ILO ratifications and exports to high-income countries are not sufficient for upholding labor rights. The China case likewise demonstrates that ILO ratifications and exports to high-income countries may lead to improved labor rights in law, but weak enforcement in practice.

Second, we find different results when analyzing supply-chain-intensive countries separately from all countries. Factors associated with labor standards are likely to be substantially different in countries highly integrated into global supply chains from those that are not, and cross-national analyses of labor standards should be explicit about the scope conditions for their arguments. Bangladesh, China, and Honduras are all highly integrated into global supply chains as producer countries, and so our results from the restricted sample of cases may be more relevant to their experiences than to those of countries that are less integrated into global supply chains, such as Côte d'Ivoire or Kazakhstan.

Third, we find specific evidence supporting important roles for several key factors, such as economic development, regime type, and left political parties. Economic development emerges as one of the most powerful and robust factors shaping labor standards, highlighting the crucial role of the economic structures providing the backdrop against which the different dynamics in our framework can play out. As the China case study will illustrate, early stages of economic development often bring about improvements in labor rights violations as workers enter weakly regulated factories. However, all four cases show that development does not necessarily bring strong labor rights enforcement across industry, space or time. Nor does development guarantee that all forms of labor rights will improve on paper or in practice. Actors may align on certain rights, such as child labor, but never align on others, such as collective bargaining.

We find some evidence for the ability of political factors, including democracy and left political parties, to shape either labor rights or labor enforcement. This highlights the importance both of the preferences of actors in the government cluster, and of configurations of interests across clusters whereby workers and their allies are well represented in state institutions. For example, while Bangladesh is a democracy and China continues to be an autocracy, at this point in time both national governments fail to incorporate or adequately represent workers or their allies' interests in politics. Both continue to suffer from enforcement problems, albeit on very different scales.

We find only limited importance for state capacity, especially in supply-chain-intensive countries. Variation in state capacity offers little or no explanatory power beyond what we already learn from variation in economic development. Although this must be interpreted cautiously due to the high correlation between these two variables, one interpretation is that increases in state capacity in countries like Bangladesh or Honduras, if not accompanied by broader increases in economic development and political incorporation of workers' interests, are unlikely to substantially improve labor standards.

We also find some evidence consistent with previous arguments that have been made that different types of international economic integration have different effects on labor standards. Mosley and Uno (2007) and Mosley (2010) argue that integration via foreign direct investment, as opposed to arm's-length contracting, can have positive effects on labor standards. We find evidence in some models that countries with more FDI have better labor standards, but only among the restricted sample of supply-chain-intensive countries. Greenhill et al. (2009) argue that countries exporting to destinations with stronger labor standards see their own labor standards improve. In order to capture this intuition, we include variables measuring exports to high-income destinations (where labor standards will be stronger) and low-income destinations (where they will be weaker) separately. We find that exports to high-income destinations are associated with stronger labor standards and labor rights, while exports to low-income destinations are associated with worse labor standards and labor rights. However, we find no such relationships for labor enforcement. The continuing problems with enforcement detailed in the Bangladesh, China, and Honduras chapters, despite those countries' focus on exports to advanced industrialized countries, corroborate this finding.

These arguments, at their core, reflect the effective exercise of influence operating across clusters of actors in our framework, as well as across the globe, because the initial incentives for some businesses to ensure better labor standards comes from their exposure to stakeholders with pro-standards preferences. These stakeholders are often workers and their allies or consumers with socio-political preferences in favor of strong labor rights. Thus, our results offer some evidence, from a new source of data, supporting the important role of these forms of influence in aligning incentives in support of labor rights.

We find some evidence of a limited role that international norms can play. We find that countries that have ratified more ILO conventions tend to have better labor rights, but not better labor enforcement. Further, this relationship is only apparent among the full sample of countries. Last, we find some preliminary evidence that different types of transnational initiatives can have different effects depending on their institutional design. We find that, among supply-chain-intensive countries, those with more UN Global Compact members tend to have *worse* labor standards and labor enforcement, while those with more FLA inspections tend to have *better* labor standards and labor enforcement. One interpretation is that these findings stem from the more rigorous monitoring associated with the FLA. However, the data available leave open the possibility that these findings instead are an artifact of factors leading business to join these initiatives in the first place. And, as the Foxconn case illustrates in Chapter 9 focusing on China, intensive monitoring by the FLA at one place and time do not guarantee continued improvements in labor rights enforcement over time, space or industry.

While these results are able to offer some limited support for, or evidence against, propositions about the roles that specific actors might play in aligning incentives with labor rights in global supply chains, the nature of the data make it difficult for these to yield anything beyond suggestive conclusions. The strength of this type of quantitative analysis is in identifying empirical regularities that can help explain the observed variation in labor rights across countries. In a context where many improvements in labor rights take place in isolated contexts or specific moments in time, we are interested in dynamics that may not be represented by such aggregated statistics. Thus we see this analysis as a complement to the specific case studies that follow, as these can focus more directly on the specific actors and interests involved.

NOTES

1. We refer to these as 'supply-chain-intensive' countries, defined as developing countries whose exports in *either* the garment or electronics industries were valued at more than US$1 billion in 2011.

2. That is, the findings may reflect not membership in these initiatives driving labor standards, but rather labor standards shaping firms' decisions to join one or the other initiative, or neither.
3. The World Justice Project first converts responses for each question to a single number for each country, ranging from 0 to 1. We aggregate these responses for each of these 26 questions to create our measures.
4. These are: Bangladesh, Brazil, Bulgaria, Cambodia, China, Czech Republic, Egypt, El Salvador, Estonia, Guatemala, Hungary, India, Indonesia, Jordan, Malaysia, Mexico, Morocco, Pakistan, Panama, Peru, Philippines, Poland, Romania, Russia, Singapore, Slovenia, South Korea, Sri Lanka, Thailand, Tunisia, United Arab Emirates, Vietnam. Note that this list excludes any countries that are not included in the WJP 2012 data.

APPENDIX

BOX 5A.1　QUESTIONS FROM THE WJP QUESTIONNAIRES REFLECTING TWO DIFFERENT DIMENSIONS OF LABOR STANDARDS: LABOR RIGHTS AND LABOR ENFORCEMENT

WJP Questions Pertaining to Labor Rights

1. General population survey: In practice, workers in [country] can freely form labor unions and bargain for their rights with their employers.
   a. Very likely
   b. Likely
   c. Unlikely
   d. Very unlikely
   e. Don't Know/Not Applicable
2. General population survey: Please assume that a company fires a worker because he/she is promoting the creation of a labor union in a factory, and assume that the worker complains before the relevant authority. Which of the following outcomes is most likely? Choose one single answer:
   a. The worker's complaint is completely ignored by the authorities.
   b. An investigation is opened but it never reaches any conclusions.
   c. The authorities require the company to compensate the worker or reinstate him/her to his/her job.
   d. The company bribes or influences the authorities to ignore the violation.
3. Assume that a company fires a worker because he/she is promoting the creation of a labor union in a factory, and assume that the worker complains before the relevant authority. Which of the following outcomes is most likely?
   a. The worker's complaint is completely ignored by the authorities.
   b. An investigation is opened, but it never reaches any conclusions.
   c. The authorities ensure that the company compensates the worker or reinstates him/her to his/her job.
   d. The company bribes or influences the authorities to ignore the violation.
4. In practice, workers in manufacturing can effectively organize into labor unions.
   a. Very likely
   b. Likely
   c. Unlikely
   d. Very unlikely
   e. Don't Know/Not Applicable
5. In practice, workers in manufacturing can effectively bargain for their rights with their employers.
   a. Very likely
   b. Likely
   c. Unlikely
   d. Very unlikely
   e. Don't Know/Not Applicable

6. In practice, workers in manufacturing can go on strike without fear of reprisals.
   a. Very likely
   b. Likely
   c. Unlikely
   d. Very unlikely
   e. Don't Know/Not Applicable
7. In practice, workers in agriculture can effectively organize into labor unions.
   a. Very likely
   b. Likely
   c. Unlikely
   d. Very unlikely
   e. Don't Know/Not Applicable
8. In practice, workers in agriculture can effectively bargain for their rights with their employers.
   a. Very likely
   b. Likely
   c. Unlikely
   d. Very unlikely
   e. Don't Know/Not Applicable

WJP Questions Pertaining to Labor Enforcement

9. In practice, how long would it take to obtain a decision, or a judgment – starting from the moment the case is filed to the moment a decision or agreement is reached – if the worker uses the following mechanisms? Administrative body:
   a. Less than 1 month
   b. Between 1 month and 1 year
   c. Between 1 and 3 years
   d. More than 3 years
   e   More than 5 years
   f. Don't Know/Not Applicable
10. In practice, after a decision or agreement is reached, how long would it take for the worker to enforce this decision (compel the employer to pay), and collect the payment or compensation if the worker uses each of the following mechanisms? Administrative body decision:
   a. Less than 1 month
   b. Between 1 month and 1 year
   c. Between 1 and 3 years
   d. More than 3 years
   e   More than 5 years
   f. Don't Know/Not Applicable
11. In a case like this, how likely are the following people to request a bribe (or other monetary inducement) from either party to perform their duties or to expedite the process? Labor inspector:
   a. Very likely
   b. Likely
   c. Unlikely

d. Very unlikely
e. Don't Know/Not Applicable

12. Please assume that the manager of a large public hospital in your city requests an illegal payment from a hospital worker in exchange for a promotion, and the worker reports this conduct to the competent authority and provides sufficient evidence to prove it. Which one of the following outcomes is most likely?
    a. The accusation is completely ignored by the authorities.
    b. An investigation is opened, but it never reaches any conclusions.
    c. The manager is investigated and disciplined.

13. Please choose the statement that is closest to your views on how labor authorities respond to the following labor violations: Workplace safety violations:
    a. Very effective (Labor authorities are effective in investigating violations. Negative findings draw prompt corrective action.)
    b. Slightly effective (Labor authorities might start investigations into violations, but are limited in their effectiveness to implement sanctions or corrective actions. They may be slow or unwilling to take on powerful corporations.)
    c. Not effective at all (Labor authorities do not effectively investigate violations.)
    d. Don't Know/Not Applicable

14. Please choose the statement that is closest to your views on how labor authorities respond to the following labor violations: Child labor violations:
    a. Very effective (Labor authorities are effective in investigating violations. Negative findings draw prompt corrective action.)
    b. Slightly effective (Labor authorities might start investigations into violations, but are limited in their effectiveness to implement sanctions or corrective actions. They may be slow or unwilling to take on powerful corporations.)
    c. Not effective at all (Labor authorities do not effectively investigate violations.)
    d. Don't Know/Not Applicable

15. Please choose the statement that is closest to your views on how labor authorities respond to the following labor violations: Forced labor violations:
    a. Very effective (Labor authorities are effective in investigating violations. Negative findings draw prompt corrective action.)
    b. Slightly effective (Labor authorities might start investigations into violations, but are limited in their effectiveness to implement sanctions or corrective actions. They may be slow or unwilling to take on powerful corporations.)
    c. Not effective at all (Labor authorities do not effectively investigate violations.)
    d. Don't Know/Not Applicable

16. Please choose the statement that is closest to your views on how labor authorities respond to the following labor violations: Violations against workers' right to engage in collective bargaining:
    a. Very effective (Labor authorities are effective in investigating violations. Negative findings draw prompt corrective action.)

b. Slightly effective (Labor authorities might start investigations into violations, but are limited in their effectiveness to implement sanctions or corrective actions. They may be slow or unwilling to take on powerful corporations.)

c. Not effective at all (Labor authorities do not effectively investigate violations.)

d. Don't Know/Not Applicable

17. Please choose the statement that is closest to your views on how labor authorities respond to the following labor violations: Violations against workers' freedom of association:

a. Very effective (Labor authorities are effective in investigating violations. Negative findings draw prompt corrective action.)

b. Slightly effective (Labor authorities might start investigations into violations, but are limited in their effectiveness to implement sanctions or corrective actions. They may be slow or unwilling to take on powerful corporations.)

c. Not effective at all (Labor authorities do not effectively investigate violations.)

d. Don't Know/Not Applicable

18. How frequently do people (or private companies) have to pay bribes, informal payments, or other monetary inducements to: Obtain service of process in a labor lawsuit:

a. Almost always

b. In most cases

c. In some cases

d. Almost never

e. Don't Know/Not Applicable

19. How frequently do people (or private companies) have to pay bribes, informal payments, or other monetary inducements to: Expedite the delivery of an occupational health and safety permit:

a. Almost always

b. In most cases

c. In some cases

d. Almost never

e. Don't Know/Not Applicable

20. How likely is a mid-size manufacturing firm to be audited/inspected by the labor authorities as a result of an employee filing a complaint about a safety violation at work?

a. Very likely

b. Likely

c. Unlikely

d. Very unlikely

e. Don't Know/Not Applicable

21. How likely is a mid-size manufacturing firm to be routinely audited/inspected by the labor authorities?

a. Very likely

b. Likely

c. Unlikely

d. Very unlikely

e. Don't Know/Not Applicable

22. How likely are the labor authorities to impose sanctions if occupational safety violations are detected?
    a. Very likely
    b. Likely
    c. Unlikely
    d. Very unlikely
    e. Don't Know/Not Applicable
23. In practice, in your country, the 'Due Process of Law' is respected in administrative proceedings conducted by the following authorities: National labor authorities:
    a. Strongly agree
    b. Agree
    c. Disagree
    d. Strongly disagree
    e. Don't Know/Not Applicable
24. Please choose the statement that is closest to your views on the occupational health and safety conditions in manufacturing sectors in your country:
    a. Most manufacturing firms provide a safe and healthy workplace. Occupational fatalities and injuries are rare.
    b. Manufacturing firms abide by basic safety and health regulations, but many workers still remain exposed to dangerous machinery and harmful chemicals. While fatalities are rare, workplace injuries are common.
    c. Most manufacturing workers work in unsafe and unhealthy conditions. Workplace fatalities and injuries are common.
25. In practice, the prohibition of child labor is effectively enforced.
    a. Strongly agree
    b. Agree
    c. Disagree
    d. Strongly disagree
    e. Don't Know/Not Applicable
26. In practice, the prohibition of forced or compulsory labor is effectively enforced.
    a. Strongly agree
    b. Agree
    c. Disagree
    d. Strongly disagree
    e. Don't Know/Not Applicable

BOX 5A.2   COUNTRIES INCLUDED IN WORLD JUSTICE
            PROJECT 2012 DATA

Albania	Ghana	Peru
Argentina	Greece	Philippines
Australia	Guatemala	Poland
Austria	Hong Kong SAR, China	Portugal
Bangladesh	Hungary	Romania
Belarus	India	Russia
Belgium	Indonesia	Senegal
Bolivia	Iran	Serbia
Bosnia and Herzegovina	Italy	Sierra Leone
Botswana	Jamaica	Singapore
Brazil	Japan	Slovenia
Bulgaria	Jordan	South Africa
Burkina Faso	Kazakhstan	South Korea
Cambodia	Kenya	Spain
Cameroon	Kyrgyzstan	Sri Lanka
Canada	Lebanon	Sweden
Chile	Liberia	Tanzania
China	Macedonia	Thailand
Colombia	Madagascar	Tunisia
Côte d'Ivoire	Malawi	Turkey
Croatia	Malaysia	Uganda
Czech Republic	Mexico	Ukraine
Denmark	Moldova	United Arab Emirates
Dominican Republic	Mongolia	United Kingdom
Ecuador	Morocco	United States
Egypt	Nepal	Uruguay
El Salvador	Netherlands	Uzbekistan
Estonia	New Zealand	Venezuela
Ethiopia	Nicaragua	Vietnam
Finland	Nigeria	Zambia
France	Norway	Zimbabwe
Georgia	Pakistan	
Germany	Panama	

Table 5A.1 Results of models using sample of all countries with World Justice Project data available

DV = WJP Labor Standards	Model 1	Model 2	Model 3	Model 14	Model 5	Model 6	Model 7	Model 8	Model 9	Model 10
Constant	-11.75	44.56 ***	14.24	-13.69	-17.38	-21.38	-12.07	-10.40	-12.27	-5.25
	(8.67)	(8.70)	(12.87)	(8.73)	(10.74)	(15.02)	(8.86)	(8.98)	(8.94)	(7.91)
Democracy	0.30	0.22	0.15	0.26	0.22	0.25	0.29	0.31	0.30	0.26
	(0.24)	(0.25)	(0.24)	(0.24)	(0.26)	(0.25)	(0.25)	(0.24)	(0.24)	(0.25)
Log GDP/Capita	7.06 ***		4.20 ***	6.99 ***	6.86 ***	7.03 ***	7.09 ***	7.14 ***	7.11 ***	7.04 ***
	(0.87)		(1.37)	(0.87)	(0.90)	(0.88)	(0.89)	(0.89)	(0.90)	(0.93)
Log Exports/GDP	3.40	4.03	2.72	3.79	3.48	3.55	3.34	3.18	3.36	
	(2.52)	(2.49)	(2.45)	(2.52)	(2.53)	(2.53)	(2.55)	(2.56)	(2.54)	
Log FDI/GDP	0.30	-0.25	0.52	0.19	0.40	0.26	0.28	0.24	0.34	0.60
	(1.56)	(1.54)	(1.51)	(1.55)	(1.57)	(1.56)	(1.57)	(1.57)	(1.57)	(1.51)
State Capacity		5.65 ***	2.96 ***							
		(0.71)	(1.11)							
Left Party				4.51						
				(3.19)						
Log ILO Conventions					2.01					
					(2.25)					
Log CLS Years						1.79				
						(2.28)				
UN Global Compact							0.32			
							(1.54)			
Labor NGOs								-0.82		
								(1.33)		
Fair Labor Association									0.54	
									(2.03)	

Table 5A.1 Continued

DV = WJP Labor Standards	Model 1	Model 2	Model 3	Model 4	Model 5	Model 6	Model 7	Model 8	Model 9	Model 10
Exports to High-income Countries										1.77
										(1.84)
Exports to Low-income Countries										0.40
										(1.89)
R Squared	0.60	0.58	0.63	0.60	0.60	0.60	0.60	0.60	0.60	0.59
Num. obs.	89	91	89	89	89	89	89	89	89	89

Note: $^{***}p<0.01$; $^{**}p<0.05$; $^{*}p<0.1$.

Table 5A.2   Results of models using sample of developing countries with exports worth over US$1 billion of either garments or electronics in 2011

DV = WJP Labor Standards	Model 1	Model 2	Model 3	Model 4	Model 5	Model 6	Model 7	Model 8	Model 9	Model 10
Constant	-22.22 *	49.51 ***	-22.26	-30.01 **	-19.93	-2.94	-19.58	-20.70	-41.46 **	-25.26 **
	(12.16)	(16.51)	(28.95)	(12.39)	(16.84)	(24.34)	(11.83)	(13.35)	(15.06)	(10.90)
Democracy	0.17	0.35	0.17	0.18	0.20	0.30	0.21	0.17	0.20	-0.10
	(0.29)	(0.33)	(0.30)	(0.28)	(0.33)	(0.32)	(0.28)	(0.30)	(0.28)	(0.29)
Log GDP/Capita	8.58 ***		8.58 ***	8.81 ***	8.75 ***	8.65 ***	8.75 ***	8.55 ***	11.22 ***	9.22 ***
	(1.83)		(2.99)	(1.76)	(2.05)	(1.84)	(1.77)	(1.87)	(2.19)	(1.67)
Log Exports/GDP	1.01	0.16	1.01	2.56	0.60	-0.38	0.48	0.88	-0.47	
	(3.67)	(4.88)	(4.32)	(3.62)	(4.26)	(3.99)	(3.56)	(3.76)	(3.56)	
Log FDI/GDP	4.65	5.22	4.65	2.79	4.72	5.57 *	5.77 *	4.69	4.40	5.30 *
	(2.98)	(3.49)	(3.09)	(3.03)	(3.06)	(3.16)	(2.95)	(3.04)	(2.83)	(2.69)
State Capacity		6.23 ***	0.00							
		(1.96)	(2.78)							
Left Party				8.04 *						
				(4.38)						
Log ILO Conventions					-0.68					
					(3.37)					
Log CLS Years						-3.09				
						(3.38)				
UN Global Compact							-4.05 *			
							(2.36)			
Labor NGOs								-0.51		
								(1.69)		

Table 5A.2 Continued

DV = WJP Labor Standards	Model 1	Model 2	Model 3	Model 4	Model 5	Model 6	Model 7	Model 8	Model 9	Model 10
Fair Labor Association									4.82 *	4.87 *
									(2.43)	(2.66)
Exports to High-income Countries										
Exports to Low-income Countries										−5.63 **
										(2.71)
R Squared	0.67	0.56	0.67	0.71	0.67	0.68	0.70	0.67	0.71	0.73
Num. obs.	31	31	31	31	31	31	31	31	31	31

Note: ***$p<0.01$; **$p<0.05$; *$p<0.1$.

Table 5A.3 Results of models using sample of all countries with World Justice Project data available

DV = WJP Labor Rights	Model 1	Model 2	Model 3	Model 4	Model 5	Model 6	Model 7	Model 8	Model 9	Model 10
Constant	25.63 **	60.10 ***	50.23 ***	24.44 **	7.58	−11.23	24.74 **	28.61 **	27.46 **	32.71 ***
	(11.13)	(10.84)	(16.84)	(11.31)	(13.43)	(18.70)	(11.36)	(11.47)	(11.44)	(9.91)
Democracy	0.65 **	0.54 *	0.51	0.63 **	0.40	0.46	0.62 *	0.68 **	0.64 **	0.53 *
	(0.31)	(0.31)	(0.31)	(0.31)	(0.32)	(0.31)	(0.32)	(0.31)	(0.31)	(0.31)
Log GDP/Capita	4.12 ***		1.41	4.08 ***	3.46 ***	3.99 ***	4.20 ***	4.30 ***	3.94 ***	3.18 ***
	(1.12)		(1.79)	(1.12)	(1.13)	(1.09)	(1.14)	(1.13)	(1.15)	(1.17)
Log Exports/GDP	−1.14	−1.21	−1.78	−0.90	−0.86	−0.55	−1.28	−1.63	−1.01	
	(3.24)	(3.10)	(3.20)	(3.27)	(3.16)	(3.16)	(3.27)	(3.26)	(3.25)	
Log FDI/GDP	−0.73	−0.89	−0.52	−0.80	−0.40	−0.89	−0.77	−0.86	−0.87	−0.59
	(2.00)	(1.91)	(1.97)	(2.01)	(1.96)	(1.95)	(2.01)	(2.00)	(2.02)	(1.89)
State Capacity		3.68 ***	2.80 *							
		(0.88)	(1.46)							
Left Party				2.76						
				(4.13)						
Log ILO Conventions					6.44 **					
					(2.82)					
Log CLSYears						6.86 **				
						(2.84)				
UN Global Compact							0.89			
							(1.97)			
Labor NGOs								−1.82		
								(1.70)		

89

Table 5A.3 Continued

DV = WIP Labor Rights	Model 1	Model 2	Model 3	Model 4	Model 5	Model 6	Model 7	Model 8	Model 9	Model 10
Fair Labor Association									−1.91	
									(2.59)	
Exports to High-income Countries										2.50
										(2.30)
Exports to Low-income Countries										−4.38 *
										(2.37)
R Squared	0.30	0.32	0.33	0.30	0.34	0.34	0.30	0.31	0.30	0.32
Num. obs.	89	91	89	89	89	89	89	89	89	89

Note: $***p<0.01; **p<0.05; *p<0.1$.

90

Table 5A.4 Results of models using sample of developing countries with exports worth over US$1 billion of either garments or electronics in 2011

DV = WJP Labor Rights	Model 1	Model 2	Model 3	Model 4	Model 5	Model 6	Model 7	Model 8	Model 9	Model 10
Constant	21.60	55.54***	30.85	13.11	1.94	24.21	21.80	27.94*	20.61	14.08
	(14.74)	(17.55)	(35.03)	(15.21)	(19.58)	(29.99)	(15.15)	(15.86)	(19.63)	(11.97)
Democracy	0.68*	0.76**	0.69*	0.69*	0.43	0.70*	0.69*	0.70*	0.69*	0.25
	(0.35)	(0.35)	(0.36)	(0.34)	(0.39)	(0.40)	(0.36)	(0.35)	(0.36)	(0.31)
Log GDP/Capita	3.78		2.95	4.03*	2.31	3.79	3.79	3.66	3.91	5.10**
	(2.22)		(3.62)	(2.16)	(2.39)	(2.27)	(2.27)	(2.22)	(2.85)	(1.84)
Log Exports/GDP	-1.32	-2.38	-2.09	0.37	2.19	-1.51	-1.37	-1.85	-1.40	
	(4.45)	(5.19)	(5.23)	(4.44)	(4.96)	(4.91)	(4.56)	(4.47)	(4.64)	
Log FDI/GDP	2.40	2.80	2.60	0.38	1.81	2.53	2.49	2.58	2.39	3.85
	(3.61)	(3.71)	(3.74)	(3.72)	(3.56)	(3.89)	(3.78)	(3.61)	(3.69)	(2.96)
State Capacity		3.13	0.98							
		(2.09)	(3.37)							
Left Party				8.76						
				(5.38)						
Log ILO Conventions					5.82					
					(3.92)					
Log CLS Years						-0.42				
						(4.16)				
UN Global Compact							-0.31			
							(3.02)			
Labor NGOs								-2.14		

Table 5A.4 Results of models using sample of developing countries with exports worth over US$1 billion of either garments or electronics in 2011

DV = WJP Labor Rights	Model 1	Model 2	Model 3	Model 4	Model 5	Model 6	Model 7	Model 8	Model 9	Model 10
Fair Labor Association									0.25	
								(2.01)	(3.17)	
Exports to High-income Countries										5.16 *
										(2.92)
Exports to Low-income Countries										−10.36 ***
										(2.98)
R Squared	0.28	0.26	0.28	0.35	0.34	0.28	0.28	0.31	0.28	0.52
Num. obs.	31	31	31	31	31	31	31	31	31	31

Note: $***p < 0.01; **p < 0.05; *p < 0.1$.

Table 5A.5   Results of models using sample of all countries with World Justice Project data available

DV = WJP Labor Enforcement	Model 1	Model 2	Model 3	Model 4	Model 5	Model 6	Model 7	Model 8	Model 9	Model 10
Constant	−28.88 ***	37.05 ***	−2.13	−31.28 ***	−29.02 **	−26.16 *	−28.88 ***	−28.11 ***	−30.36 ***	−22.50 ***
	(9.04)	(9.33)	(13.43)	(9.05)	(11.24)	(15.70)	(9.23)	(9.37)	(9.28)	(8.24)
Democracy	0.14	0.07	−0.01	0.10	0.14	0.15	0.14	0.15	0.15	0.15
	(0.25)	(0.26)	(0.25)	(0.25)	(0.27)	(0.26)	(0.26)	(0.25)	(0.25)	(0.26)
Log GDP/Capita	8.35 ***		5.41 ***	8.27 ***	8.35 ***	8.36 ***	8.35 ***	8.40 ***	8.50 ***	8.74 ***
	(0.91)		(1.42)	(0.90)	(0.94)	(0.91)	(0.93)	(0.92)	(0.93)	(0.97)
Log Exports/GDP	5.64 **	6.57 **	4.94 *	6.13 **	5.64 **	5.60 **	5.64 **	5.52 **	5.54 **	
	(2.63)	(2.67)	(2.55)	(2.61)	(2.64)	(2.65)	(2.65)	(2.67)	(2.64)	
Log FDI/GDP	0.65	−0.06	0.88	0.52	0.65	0.66	0.65	0.61	0.76	1.03
	(1.62)	(1.65)	(1.57)	(1.61)	(1.64)	(1.63)	(1.64)	(1.64)	(1.64)	(1.57)
State Capacity		6.52 ***	3.05 **							
		(0.76)	(1.16)							
Left Party				5.58 *						
				(3.31)						
Log ILO Conventions					0.05					
					(2.36)					
Log CLS Years						−0.51				
						(2.38)				
UN Global Compact							0.00			
							(1.60)			
Labor NGOs								−0.47		

93

Table 5A.5 Continued

DV = WJP Labor Enforcement	Model 1	Model 2	Model 3	Model 4	Model 5	Model 6	Model 7	Model 8	Model 9	Model 10
Fair Labor Association								(1.39)	1.55	
									(2.11)	
Exports to High-income Countries										1.56
										(1.91)
Exports to Low-income Countries										2.66
										(1.97)
R Squared	0.65	0.62	0.68	0.66	0.65	0.65	0.65	0.65	0.65	0.64
Num. obs.	89	91	89	89	89	89	89	89	89	89

Note: ***$p < 0.01$; **$p < 0.05$; *$p < 0.1$.

Table 5A.6 Results of models using sample of developing countries with exports worth over US$1 billion of either garments or electronics in 2011

DV = WJP Labor Enforcement	Model 1	Model 2	Model 3	Model 4	Model 5	Model 6	Model 7	Model 8	Model 9	Model 10
Constant	-42.27 *** (13.59)	46.42 ** (19.27)	-47.60 (32.33)	-49.92 *** (14.06)	-30.12 (18.49)	-15.27 (26.94)	-38.51 *** (12.72)	-42.65 *** (14.95)	-69.46 *** (16.01)	-43.28 *** (12.92)
Democracy	-0.07 (0.32)	0.17 (0.38)	-0.07 (0.33)	-0.06 (0.32)	0.09 (0.36)	0.11 (0.36)	-0.01 (0.30)	-0.07 (0.33)	-0.03 (0.29)	-0.27 (0.34)
Log GDP/ Capita	10.77 *** (2.05)		11.25 *** (3.34)	11.00 *** (2.00)	11.68 *** (2.25)	10.87 *** (2.04)	11.01 *** (1.90)	10.78 *** (2.09)	14.50 *** (2.33)	11.09 *** (1.98)
Log Exports/ GDP	2.13 (4.11)	1.45 (5.70)	2.57 (4.83)	3.65 (4.11)	-0.04 (4.68)	0.18 (4.41)	1.37 (3.83)	2.16 (4.21)	0.03 (3.79)	
Log FDI/GDP	5.52 (3.33)	6.16 (4.07)	5.41 (3.45)	3.70 (3.44)	5.89 * (3.36)	6.81 * (3.49)	7.12 ** (3.17)	5.51 (3.40)	5.17 * (3.01)	5.80 * (3.19)
State Capacity		7.60 *** (2.29)	-0.57 (3.11)							
Left Party				7.88 (4.97)						
Log ILO Conventions					-3.60 (3.70)					
Log CLS Years						-4.33 (3.74)				

Table 5A.6 Continued

DV = WJP Labor Enforcement	Model 1	Model 2	Model 3	Model 4	Model 5	Model 6	Model 7	Model 8	Model 9	Model 10
UN Global Compact							-5.77 **			
							(2.54)			
Labor NGOs								0.13		
								(1.89)		
Fair Labor Association									6.81 **	
									(2.58)	
Exports to High-income Countries										4.86
										(3.15)
Exports to Low-income Countries										-3.52
										(3.22)
R Squared	0.72	0.60	0.72	0.75	0.73	0.74	0.77	0.72	0.78	0.75
Num. obs.	31	31	31	31	31	31	31	31	31	31

Note: $^{***}p<0.01$; $^{**}p<0.05$; $^{*}p<0.1$.

96

6. The United States in the struggle for labor standards

The United States exemplifies an instance of the erosion of domestic labor rights and protections once seemingly securely won. By the second half of the twentieth century, a combination of worker organization and government action had eliminated sweatshops (spurred in part by new information revealed by the 1911 Triangle Shirtwaist Factory fire), secured a high standard of health and safety at the workplace, and guaranteed numerous other labor rights and protections. Union density in the private sector was at its peak, and so was the power of organized labor politically and economically. The New Deal legislation under President Franklin Roosevelt in the 1930s, along with subsequent laws, ensured a steady eradication of the worst forms of job discrimination. The United States was always uneven in the distribution of labor rights, given that the South and mountain West successfully resisted unionization and that many states had – and still have – minimum wages below the poverty line. However, beginning in the 1980s (and, by some accounts, the 1970s), a decline in job security, benefits, and protections for worker organization became increasingly evident (Levi, 2003; Goldfield and Bromsen, 2013; Lichtenstein, 2013). By the 1990s, sweatshops reappeared.

While US workers are generally better off than their counterparts in developing countries, the United States is a case of rollback of hard-won labor victories, rights, and protections. It is a reminder that changes in the balance of power and alignment of interests within and across clusters do not always signal improvements in labor rights; indeed, some changes have the opposite effect. Simultaneously, the United States is the location of some of the most forceful and successful instances of campaigns to raise labor standards in global supply chains elsewhere in the world. This chapter sets out to explain why the alignment of interests is so different and has such different consequences for labor rights in the United States and in developing countries.

THE ROLLBACK OF LABOR STANDARDS

The United States is a case in which labor, beginning effectively in the 1930s, was able to coordinate with allies and win support of government in order to establish the right to union representation, collective bargaining, fair labor standards, and occupational health and safety (Katznelson, 2013; Lichtenstein, 2013).

Business

One consequence, from which business initially benefitted, was the end to employer–worker violence that endangered human lives and the increased productivity of American labor (Levi et al., 2014). Indeed, American productivity is still among the highest in the world. Over time, however, business became even less sanguine with the increased power of labor expedited by the new arrangements. Business subsequently engaged in two kinds of practices to undermine the economic and political power of unions specifically and workers more generally. Most evidently, it fought back politically to reduce regulatory control by changing laws, eviscerating enforcement, and defaming unions. In the process, it often won allies in government and among consumers. Second, business evolved in ways that significantly decreased direct employment of its workers. David Weil, an economics professor at Boston University and currently the Department of Labor's Administrator, Wage and Hour Division, documents the rise of the 'fissured workplace' and notes, 'By shedding employment to other parties, lead companies change a wage-setting problem into a contracting decision' (Weil, 2014, p. 4). The brand model of relatively little direct employment has increasingly become the practice of corporations and companies providing services as well as products: hotel employees may wear uniforms with the hotel insignia but actually are paid by contracting firms, as are those who appear to be employees of cable companies or of Microsoft. The end result in the United States is not only a decline in union density and a decrease in worker power but also a significant reduction in worker rights, privileges, and benefits.

The combination of the shift from manufacturing to brand supply chains and from direct employment to indirect contributed to the transformation in the alignment of interests. The brand model contributed to the loss of leverage by workers and their allies vis-à-vis employers. Business power gained an additional boost with the ideological shift that took place during the presidency of Ronald Reagan, 1981–88. Since the

1930s, the federal government, for the most part, protected labor standards; Reagan changed policy while also reinforcing beliefs that were in the interest of business. The first was among workers; they lost confidence that government was a reliable ally. The second was among the public; many citizens came to believe that unions were a detriment to the economy rather than a source of productivity and a force for equality. In the 2000s the Tea Party conservatives, backed by many wealthy donors from the business community, further reinforced negative public and legislative beliefs about unions.

Government

Business may be a key initiator of the rollback of labor rights, but government is the pivotal actor; it is government that determines both what the laws are and how well they are enforced. Indeed, the shift in the alignments of so many actors in government is a large part of the explanation for the weakened labor case and effectiveness.

The regulatory framework established by government in the 1930s included the Fair Labor Standards Act (FLSA) and the National Labor Relations Act (NLRA), both designed to give workers increased power vis-à-vis employers. With the Taft-Hartley Act of 1947, the unions lost some of their strategic capacity. The restrictions on secondary boycotts significantly reduced the ability of unions to rely on each other for support during strikes. 'Right to work' laws (the misnomer applied to laws that gives workers the 'freedom' to decline union membership although represented by unions in negotiations) means that beneficiaries of union contracts can opt out of paying dues once states pass the enabling legislation. Virtually all of the Southern states immediately did once Taft-Hartley became law. By the 1950s, it was even harder for unions to organize, win strikes, and sustain themselves than it had been in the late 1930s.

The Thatcher Revolution, embodied in the United States in the policies and rhetoric of President Ronald Reagan, initiated a new set of beliefs about the appropriate role and size of government. Recessions have reinforced the related beliefs that government cutbacks are essential to stimulate growth and that unions impede growth. Of course, not everyone buys into supply-side economics or credits the policies of austerity as the best means for enhancing economic development (see, e.g., Blyth, 2013). However, many presidents, legislators, governors, and Supreme Court justices have – and do – with the result that fewer and fewer government actors see their interests aligned with organized labor or labor rights activists.

Perhaps as importantly, with direct employment in firms giving way to indirect employment, the federal regulatory framework became increasingly ineffective (Weil, 2014). The laws were designed with the presumption of a clear and direct employment relationship, and administrators often have difficulty adapting the law to the complex set of employment relationships that have evolved.

Until the 1930s, much of government generally sided with business in conflicts between employers and unions. The New Deal transformed that set of alignments, but the combination of ideological shifts and business power has shifted the alignments once again. Today government actors are more likely to be allies of business than labor. Business has always exercised its muscle to protect its prerogatives and power, but its arguments now fall on responsive ears among the majority of congressmen and women and among legislators and governors in the South and Southwest, and, more recently, parts of the Midwest. The 'big-box' stores (Wal-Mart, Target, K-Mart) actively campaign to maintain low labor standards or to reduce them further. Feeling the double pinch of economic recession and outsourcing, US domestic firms lobby for protection.

Starting with Reagan and intensified by the Tea Party, an ideological and regulatory shift has occurred. Supreme Court decisions reduce union rights and privileges and undermine union protections. Congress obstructs the effective implementation power of bureaucracies such as Occupational Safety and Health Administration (OSHA) and the National Labor Relations Board (NLRB), and an increasing number of state governments are passing 'right to work' laws. The 2013 explosion at the West Fertilizer Company in Texas, where there had been no inspection in almost two decades, is a demonstration of OSHA's ineffectiveness. The meat, mining, and many other industries have experienced serious declines in safety, and environmental and chemical health issues at the workplace have become more pervasive. Many scholars are now documenting these problems in the United States, as well as considering changes over time and comparisons with other countries (Mendeloff, 1979; Rosner and Markowitz, 1994; Blanc, 2009; Vogel, 2012). The NLRB, always hamstrung by inefficiencies and politics (Cooke et al., 1995; Gould, 2001; Levi et al., 2009), nearly ceased to exist in the early years of Obama's second term because of Republican Party refusal to approve Presidential appointments.

The shifts in the alignment between government and labor have not been uniform, however. Divergent perspectives and interests among various agencies and branches of government produce conflicts within government and provide multiple points of leverage for those trying to influence government. A transformation in the political will and capacity of the federal government and many previously labor-friendly states results in a growing divide in the alignment of interests between labor and government, even when elected officials and legislators are members of the Democratic Party.

To understand this shift requires some consideration of the shifting alignment of interests and coordinating capacity within the worker and consumer clusters.

Workers and their Allies

Among those pressuring the government to uphold labor rights and protections, including facilitating unionization, are labor unions and labor activists, segments of the Democratic Party, and some agencies and other government officials. The links between the Democratic Party and organized labor were once quite strong (Greenstone, 1977; Dark, 2000, 2001; Francia, 2006; Warren, 2010). However, as union density declines and as unions go on the defensive against the passage of new 'right to work' laws, labor's political clout deteriorates. Even though labor could still arguably form the biggest voting bloc in the country and certainly for the Democratic Party, Democrats no longer make the concessions they once did. This may be because the unions and their confederations have not done a good job of mobilizing those votes, or it may be that labor is far more heterogeneous politically than it once was (à la the defection of traditional Democratic voters to Reagan). Perhaps the explanation (Zlotnick, 2014) is that the Democratic Party knows the unions have nowhere else to go, making political consideration less likely, given the Republicans' large stride to the right.

The National Labor Relations Act of 1935 and the restrictive Taft-Hartley Act of 1947 are the lynchpins of the regulatory framework under which unions in the United States operate. We have already noted the detrimental effects on unionization with the prohibition of secondary boycotts and the legalization of 'right to work' laws. As importantly, agricultural workers, domestic workers, and various supervisory workers (a category enlarged by judicial decisions) are not covered; their efforts to unionize remain unprotected. One consequence is the development of new community-based organizing strategies (Fine, 2006; Eidelson, 2013), which – at least so far – have had little effect on the statistics on union density.

Adding to the problems confronting organized labor are shifts in economic structure. Manufacturing was a stronghold of US unions, but

102 Labor standards in international supply chains

jobs in that sector have significantly declined. Although the auto companies and the aircraft industry are once again hiring, often the jobs are created in states with low union density and right to work laws. Boeing is locating factories in South Carolina, for example, and many auto companies moved to the South. Even those companies that are open to unions confront workers who believe that unions are a problem rather than a solution: in 2013 in Tennessee those employed by Volkswagen, a pro-union corporation, rejected United Auto Worker representation. An additional effect is the creation of a two-tier system in which those most recently hired by unionized companies have fewer benefits and lower wages (Goldfield and Bromsen, 2013).

The impassioned opposition of so many American unions and workers to outsourcing reflects the high degree of economic insecurity of those facing unemployment. The United States is a country in which workers bear the risk. The government provides little in the way of unemployment insurance and virtually no support for retraining or relocation. There are some corporations that offer one or the other or both, but these, too, are few and far between – and rapidly becoming even farther and fewer between. For example, the major auto companies used to provide health insurance, pensions, and other benefits; long-term workers are experiencing cutbacks in these programs, and new workers may not get any of these benefits. Moreover, there is increasing evidence that those who lose jobs not only have difficulty finding new jobs but also are likely to be paid less at their next job than they were at their former placement (Farber, 2007).

The change in the structure of jobs (Silver, 2003; Freeman, 2007; Reich, 2008) also contributes to the increased inequality in the United States, generating jobs at the top end of the spectrum, that is, in the technology, finance, and knowledge industries, and jobs at the lowest end, that is, home health care, janitorial services, restaurant and hotel work. There is less and less in between.

Unions and workers tend to use xenophobic rhetoric to describe the structural changes Americans are experiencing. They define jobs as belonging to Americans. Immigrants and foreign workers are 'taking' American jobs. Outsourced jobs are described as lost, terminated, and destroyed. The increasing weakness of the labor movement adds to workers' frustration. Unions lack the economic clout with employers and the political clout with government to ensure that they are compensated for job loss. Instead, they do all they can to insist that jobs stay in the United States. They resist free trade agreements such as NAFTA (North American Free Trade Agreement), CAFTA (Central American Free Trade Agreement), and most recently with Colombia. They initiate 'Buy

American' campaigns with websites listing where and how to purchase approved goods.[1] The well-documented nationalism of such strategies (Frank, 2000) is no deterrent, given the focus of most unions on keeping 'our' jobs in the United States.

Such activity only confirms the beliefs of brands, other firms, and many politicians that unions are unable to adapt to changing market and technological conditions, that they impede progress and economic growth. Further, it reinforces the beliefs of the groups fighting for labor rights abroad that American unions are not always reliable allies in that struggle. Indeed, the only reliable union allies have been groups, such as Jobs With Justice, that the labor movement itself has generated.

The US labor movement has not developed a model and movement to deal with the structural changes affecting workers worldwide. However, while most unions sound increasingly protectionist and xenophobic, the labor movement is far from homogeneous in attitude. A more internationalist and encompassing spirit does motivate some unions and labor leadership. The International Longshore and Warehouse Union (ILWU) (Ahlquist and Levi, 2013; Ahlquist et al., 2014), the Communication Workers of America (CWA), and other select unions argue for a larger social justice agenda that extends beyond the material interests of their own members. Most notably, the AFL-CIO (American Federation of Labor-Congress of Industrial Organizations), the large federation of American and Canadian unions, called for amnesty of undocumented workers in 2000 and was a driving force behind the Immigrant Rights Freedom Ride in 2003 (Levi et al., 2007, p. 527). On the same website that encourages the purchase of union-made products are a long list of documentaries and books that speak to the problems foreign workers are confronting. Throughout the AFL-CIO website are discussions of the need to support the organizing efforts and other demands by workers everywhere who are exploited by international corporations.

The development by parts of the US labor movement of a more nuanced approach to international structural change is most evident around fair trade issues. Some American unions are part of a large and encompassing coalition that includes not only workers' groups but also a wide variety of environmental, human rights, religious, consumer, and other civil associations. Union participation in the WTO protests, discussed below, is one indicator.

Unions continue to engage in support of international labor rights. Support by the AFL-CIO and its competitive federation, Change to Win, of immigrant rights and of Core Labor Standards for workers throughout the world reflects two very different factors that, at the moment, are pushing in the same direction. The first is the efforts of the leadership to promote their organizations as inclusive of the diversity of interests in the labor movement. The second is the recognition of the need for a more sophisticated protectionism if American workers are to gain allies in their political efforts to maintain high levels of employment and good jobs. By requiring that the US government demand that its trading partners meet the ILO (International Labor Organization) Core Labor Standards, the union movement can both level the playing field while supporting workers' movements internationally. Such a requirement is actually incorporated into US law, passed by Congress in the 1980s.

Motivated primarily by economic interest, American unions participate in new alliances with civil associations in the United States and with worker groups internationally. In the process of coordinating and developing effective campaigns, and of becoming part of a wider and more encompassing coalition, the union leadership – and at least some members – have come to value social justice goals that may require them to make some sacrifice of their narrower economistic goals. They have begun to worry about environmental degradation, the protection of immigrant workers, and the abuses of rights in the United States as well as in the rest of the world. While the wage and hour gains once exclusively emphasized remain a primary goal, changed economic circumstances have combined with new organizational alliances to promote a broader notion of interest, at least among a small part of the workforce.

Consumers

American consumers are also increasingly anti-union. Robert Reich (2008, p. 127) notes:

> The problem is that the choices we make in the market don't fully reflect our values as citizens. We might make different choices if we understood and faced the social consequences of our purchases or investment and *if* [his emphasis] we knew all other consumers and investors would join us in forbearing from certain great deals whose social consequences were abhorrent to us ... Lonely forbearance can be the last refuge of a virtuous fool.

Consumers have a divided brain. As purchasers, price tends to swamp other concerns such as the extent to which the goods are produced under fair labor conditions, be it in the United States or abroad. As citizens, working class and poor voters generally supported the Democratic Party. However, as exemplified by the Wisconsin and other state efforts to reduce union prerogatives, the beliefs of many citizens – even those once socio-economically working class – have changed about unions; more and more voters appear to believe that unions, especially the public sector unions, have privileges that are hurting consumers, government service recipients, and the economy as a whole (Ahlquist, 2012).

One domain in which there is some evidence of consumer support of workers is in relation to 'big-box' stores, especially Wal-Mart. There are instances of local resistance to the location of Wal-Mart stores and other firms perceived as a threat to local businesses and their employees (Warren, 2005; Lichtenstein, 2006, 2010). Since the early 2000s, campaigns have developed in several states to compel Wal-Mart to pay its fair share of health costs rather than rely on Medicare for its employees. The initiators are usually the United Food and Commercial Workers (UFCW) International Union, but at least in some states (e.g., Washington, Maryland, and California) it attracts consumers, legislators, and other businesses into the coalition.

THE ALIGNMENT OF INTERESTS ON LABOR RIGHTS IN GLOBAL SUPPLY CHAINS

Due to the global transformations brought about by the brand model, increasingly few of the workers in global supply chains actually live or work in the United States. At the same time, given the changing beliefs about labor unions in the United States, American supporters of labor rights are now more likely to function as allies of mistreated workers abroad than of those employed in their own country. Some unions, as we have seen, have become more internationalist in their activities, although sometimes this is to advance a sophisticated protectionism rather than out of real concern for global workers. Consumers appear to find fair trade more salient than safeguarding domestic unions. Government struggles to find its proper role.

There remain, however, numerous ways in which businesses and brands affect, and are affected by, the shifting alignments of interests among the clusters in the United States. First, corporate decisions contribute to the major shift of jobs overseas and thus to the politics surrounding outsourcing. The rhetoric of protectionism tends to dominate the debate. Second, as the brands and large corporations contract out more of the work, they are reducing their costs, increasing their profits, and simultaneously exerting an overall downward pressure on wages and benefits, even for domestic work. Third, the United States is still the largest market for brand goods, which makes it the home of many of the campaigns demanding proactive behavior by brands in support of labor rights. Fourth, as employment opportunities become more tentative or actually decrease, the demands of consumers for cheaper goods increases.

These phenomena all occur within the context of the rollback of American labor rights and arguably contribute to further union decline. Simultaneously, they create new opportunities for campaigns to protect workers overseas.

Campaigns in Support of Better Labor Practices

In the earlier discussions of Levi-Strauss, Nike, and Apple, we documented some of the effects of activists and their power to tarnish brand reputations and pocketbooks. More generally, 'sweat-free' and 'fair trade' products have captured the imagination of the American public, or at least enough of the public to have some small impact on brands and on government. Several large corporations, including Nike and Wal-Mart, have changed their practices in response to the large-scale campaigns directed against them (Locke et al., 2007b, 2009; also see our other case study chapters). To the extent that there has been corporate response, however, it has been to consumer pressure as much or more than to union demands. Civil society associations and NGOs have had a significant influence, including encouraging some of the labor movement to begin to reassess how best to react. Upholding decent labor standards internationally serves the economic interests of unions in leveling the playing field in the competition for work and by improving the image of American unions with workers they hope to organize in the United States. At the same time, it demonstrates a commitment to an international social program. However, the major impact has been on the brands.

The contemporary global justice campaigns began in the 1990s. One of the high points in raising general public awareness were the protests against the WTO Ministerial that led to the 'Battle of Seattle' in November and December of 1999 (Smith, 2001). Opposition intensified to the increasing concentration of economic power no longer subject to national regulation and the increasing imbalance of incomes and wealth – within countries and among countries. The individuals and groups who assembled shared a common feeling that the only alternative was to go out on the streets. No other option seemed viable. Almost all participants expressed a loss of citizen power at the national but also at the regional and local levels.

The coalition in Seattle was composed of environmentalists, faith-based organizations, farmers, anarchists, human rights groups, and organized labor, among others (Levi and Murphy, 2006). The demands included inhibiting environmental degradation, alleviation of Third World debt, and restrictions on genetic modification of food, but the dominant concerns were with labor rights as human rights and with democratic accountability. 'Fair trade' became the summary term for expressing these aspirations.

Organized labor was a major participant in the WTO protests. For some unions and workers, the motivations might well have been – and could certainly be interpreted as – protectionist. For others it also involved a larger strategy of inhibiting what they perceived as a 'race to the bottom' for all. But there were also many who possessed a real commitment to international labor solidarity (Levi and Olson, 2000; Ahlquist and Levi, 2013). The choice of the WTO as a target of protest reflected this commitment. Throughout the planning and certainly in the meetings of the International Confederation of Free Trade Unions (ICFTU), a meeting that took place in Seattle a few days before the protest, there was discussion of the ineffectiveness of the ILO in enforcing the Core Labor Standards and of the failure of the United States to enforce the standards through its trade agreements. The WTO was perceived as another possible mechanism for enforcement of labor codes. It was also, of course, the symbol of free trade and of decisions made among finance ministers without concern for national democratic processes or voices.

The protests made little difference in terms of the operations of the WTO. The coalition did close down the Ministerial for a day, and it did have the effect of ensuring that future meetings would be held in places far less accessible than Seattle. The 2001 Ministerial met in Doha.

The protests had a large impact on mobilization for fair trade, however. They stimulated large-scale protests that subsequently took place around the world, most notably in Italy. Other citizenship actions and protests, based in consumer as well as political rights, began to have some impact (Tarrow, 2000, 2005). With 9/11, such protests became nearly impossible; security became far more intense. The campaign tactics morphed, but the campaigns did not stop.

Since the late 1990s, there have been a number of consumer-driven campaigns. Fair trade coffee has succeeded in creating a large niche market and demand for coffee produced by cooperatives, whose workers are paid and treated according to Core Labor Standards (Levi and Linton, 2003), and there have been relatively successful campaigns around other foodstuffs and products (Raynolds et al., 2007). To the extent there have been successes in these and in the apparel industry, the pressure has come more from collective than individual purchasing power. In her influential account of the problems with labeling, including Rugmark in India, Gay Seidman (2007, p. 7) notes that successful campaigns 'have invariably worked through more organized consumer pressure – through church groups, universities, and major stockholders'. As we shall see in the case study of Honduras (Chapter 7), the decisions of institutional purchasers, specifically universities, can have major impacts on brand decisions.

Among the most important players in the US-based campaigns directed at improving labor rights in apparel and footwear internationally are the United Students Against Sweatshops (USAS), founded in the late 1990s, and the Worker Rights Consortium (WRC), which began in 2000. Both are allies of international workers and, on some important occasions, American workers. Both were involved in revealing the abuses in the Russell supply chain in domestic plants in the United States. USAS spearheaded the campaign on behalf of American workers employed by Sodexo, and they press for the organization of unionized campus workers.[2]

USAS and the WRC have long played and continue to play an important role in affecting the rewards and punishments for brand responses to labor rights among their suppliers and subcontractors in countries throughout the world, including, as we shall see, Honduras, Bangladesh, and China. USAS has branches on a large number of the American university and college campuses, and the WRC is subscribed to by universities to serve as a whistle-blower concerning abuses by its licensees, those brands and firms who put the university logo on sweatshirts, mugs, and so on. Driven by strong ethical commitments, USAS and WRC have proved effective in publicizing labor abuses and pressuring consumers, particularly universities, to use their influence effectively. Universities are not only purchasers, but they can also act to verify the credibility of USAS and WRC information about abuses and use their moral position to persuade other consumers to reconsider their buying decisions.

Government Response

Fear of the economic consequences of outsourcing helped propel President Bill Clinton, his Secretary of Labor Robert Reich, and other governmental leaders to seek new means to enforce labor standards internationally. This move by the Clinton administration intersected with the largely student-led movement to end sweatshops on foreign shores and, more recently, in the United States itself, where they have significantly re-emerged. Sweatshops were among the principal targets of the nineteenth- and early twentieth-century industrial labor movements. By mid-twentieth century, their elimination seemed certain in the advanced democratic world, but they were omnipresent in the developing countries where major firms were subcontracting work.

In 1996 the Clinton administration convened the Apparel Industry Partnership (AIP), led by Labor Secretary Robert Reich and composed of representatives of industries, NGOs, and unions. Its first job was to develop a code of conduct, which it did in 1997. From these negotiations emerged the Fair Labor Association (FLA), charged with devising and providing a means for independent monitoring of factories. China immediately became the subject of debate within the FLA:

> The nonindustry members have proposed that in any country that does not allow employees freedom of association and collective bargaining, employers shall nonetheless take steps to ensure that those rights can be exercised. This proposal says that if, despite such efforts, no participating company can demonstrate progress in guaranteeing its employees those rights, then the Fair Labor Association can determine that producing garments in that country is inconsistent with the code of conduct. (Greenhouse, 1998)

The target was obviously China, given the role in the debate of UNITE (the Union of Needletrades, Industrial and Textile Employees),[3] the largest apparel union in the United States and a union that expressed serious concern about moving work to countries – especially China – where labor rights were not respected. The proposal raised the ire of industry members of the FLA, eager to maintain or establish factories in China.

The corporate response fueled union and NGO skepticism about the FLA and the seriousness of its monitoring efforts. The WTO protests in 1999, followed by student protests that emerged on campuses across the United States in 2000 (Featherstone, 2000; Esbenshade, 2004), led to the creation of a second organization, the Worker Rights Consortium (WRC), to serve as a watchdog and 'fire alarm' on labor standard violations. Today, the two organizations often work together in a division of labor. However, the leaders of both the FLA and WRC, as well as many of those most concerned about facilitating the production of sweat-free products, have become increasingly disenchanted with the monitoring model (Locke, 2013). Consequently, a range of alternatives is currently under exploration, including in Bangladesh (see Chapter 8).

In 2011, President Barack Obama notably met with the leaders of Silicon Valley to try to persuade them to relocate factories in the United States. His impact was marginal, as exemplified by Apple's decision to produce a small number of computers domestically indicates, but his resort to moral suasion reveals how few rewards and punishments the Federal government has available to shape the production decisions of the brands. Nor does it have any significant power in relationship to the tax homes of the brands, although there have been increasing efforts by the judiciary, legislature, and executive in recent years to require brands based in the United States to actually pay taxes in the United States.

During the 2012 American Presidential debates CNN's Candy Crowley asked candidates Mitt Romney and President Obama if there was any way to convince a 'great American company' like Apple to bring manufacturing back to the United States. President Obama answered, 'there are some jobs that are not going to come back because they're low-wage, low-skill jobs' (Goldman, 2012a). While some were skeptical of President Obama's answer, many agreed and noted that going overseas for production is really the only option for companies like Apple, not only because of cost but also because of the speed and flexibility that many of the mega-suppliers, such as Foxconn, have developed (Duhigg and Bradsher, 2012).

The California Transparency in Supply Chains Act of January 2012 represents a different kind of government response. Retailers and manufacturers doing business in California must, at a minimum, disclose the extent to which the retailer, seller or manufacturer does each of the following:

1. Engages in verification of product supply chains to evaluate and address risks of human trafficking and slavery. The disclosure shall specify if the verification was not conducted by a third party.
2. Conducts audits of suppliers to evaluate supplier compliance with company standards for trafficking and slavery in supply chains. The disclosure shall specify if the verification was not an independent, unannounced audit.
3. Requires direct suppliers to certify that materials incorporated into the product comply with the laws regarding slavery and human trafficking of the country or countries in which they are doing business.
4. Maintains internal accountability standards and procedures for employees or contractors failing to meet company standards regarding slavery and trafficking.
5. Provides company employees and management, who have direct responsibility for supply chain management, training on human trafficking and slavery, particularly with respect to mitigating risks within the supply chains of products (California, 2010).

While the Act only regulates disclosure and not practice, it does provide opportunities for injunctive relief by the California Attorney General against companies or corporations in violation of the Act. Moreover, the law provides opportunities for activists in California to lobby for full disclosure of the labor practices of corporations.

California is, not unusually, an outlier in the US context. Nonetheless, there is a well-documented 'California effect' in environmental regulation, where the high environmental standards required by a large Californian export market led to the introduction and implementation of strict environmental regulations for firms wanting to export cars to California (Vogel, 1995). The regulations then spread to other parts of the world; it became more efficient for auto manufacturers to meet California's standards for all production than to employ different procedures for different export markets. There is some hope that the Just Supply Chains Act will create a 'California effect' for labor rights, as factories comply with the requirements of the Act to avoid having their products excluded from the large California market.

Business Response

The campaigns against their practices appear to evoke efforts from brands and other businesses to improve their public images when there is likely to be a profitability problem. The corporate rhetoric has begun to shift. It is no longer a question of 'training your own replacement', and there is increasing avoidance of words such as 'outsourcing' and 'offshoring'. Several brands are considering or have even begun to locate new production facilities in the United States, particularly given that the cost of production has risen elsewhere while declining in the United States (partially because of the weakening of unions and labor rights). Apple and Levi Strauss are among them.

Some brands, for example, Nike, once clearly antagonistic to labor rights and certainly to unions, have become better employers domestically and more active in the support of labor protections among their subcontractors overseas (Locke, 2013). Others, such as Apple, have poured considerable resources into improving their supply chains. The change is at least partially an effect of well-publicized campaigns for labor rights that have tarnished (or they fear will tarnish) their reputations and, thus, share of the market. Norms and corporate culture may also play a role, at least in some notable instances such as Patagonia and Timberland among the brands and Costco among the 'big-box' stores (Greenhouse, 2008). As we have seen in the case of Knights Apparel, a moral commitment by the CEO who also has a good business plan produces a very different set of corporate practices than a company that places a low value on worker well-being and a corresponding high value on squeezing every bit of profit possible.

THE CURRENT ALIGNMENT OF INTERESTS AND POINTS OF LEVERAGE

At this moment (fall of 2014), the prognosis for labor rights in the United States is poor. Unions are in decline, and their effective allies are few. The regulatory framework protecting labor rights has weakened substantially. US unions have few points of leverage to use to help them revive. Most businesses are actively hostile to labor organization, and state governments are increasingly shifting in that direction. The Democratic Party cannot deliver on the few promises it makes to labor, given the current gridlock in Congress. The bureaucracies that might support labor rights have become relatively impotent, as a result of the contemporary anti-union ideology combined with the failure of laws to keep up with changes in the nature of employment. The most effective NGOs, like USAS, WRC, and FLA, focus largely on international workers – albeit in American-based supply chains.

Where there has been movement towards improved labor standards is in global supply chains. American allies of supply chain workers have opportunities for leverage with the brands, given the large size of the American consumer market. Some government agencies also have potential leverage if their officials have the will to enforce trade laws and other laws on the books, but seldom these days do government officials have the necessary incentives or capacity.

Student and consumer groups have the motivation out of ideological commitment. In the case of NGOs, such as FLA and WRC, there is a combination of ethical motivations and material ones: their jobs and contributions to the organization depend on some degree of demonstrated effectiveness. When activists appeal to corporate codes and international norms, they sometimes win an audience within bureaucracies, among some subset of the American consumers, and with institutional purchasers, both university and government. When these regulators and consumers act, the brand is put at risk. Reputational fears and public shaming motivate some, perhaps most, of the change in corporate practices. Information is also an important means of exercising leverage, and this is a significant part of what the best NGOs and researchers provide. Corporate recognition of the problems in supply chains and of failures to rectify them is also a motivator, at least to some corporate officials, particularly when recognition is combined with an understanding that improvements in conditions might also increase productivity and product quality.

NOTES

1. See, for example, Buy American (2014) and AFL-CIO (2014a). The latter emphasizes union-made products rather than American per se, but nearly all the goods sold are in fact American or Canadian.
2. Both USAS (http://usas.org/) and WRC (http://www.workersrights.org/) have informative websites about their practices, policies and campaigns.
3. In 2004 UNITE merged with the Hotel Employees and Restaurant Employees (HERE) to form UNITE HERE!

7. Apparel production in Honduras: a case of cross-cluster alignment

Honduras is home to one of the world's most repressive labor regimes. Honduran labor activists are routinely intimidated, threatened, and assassinated for their efforts to improve working conditions in the country. Between 2009 and 2012, 31 trade unionists were assassinated and over 200 injured in violent attacks (United States Department of State, 2013; AFL-CIO, 2014b). In addition, the American Federation of Labor-Congress of Industrial Organizations (AFL-CIO) reports that some 52 rural workers have been killed in confrontations with landowners and the government (AFL-CIO, 2014b). San Pedro Sula, Honduras' apparel and manufacturing capital, is plagued by violent crime and ongoing insecurity. The economic situation for many ordinary Hondurans is one of poverty and unemployment. The per capita GDP in Honduras at the time of the two campaigns we examine in this chapter (2007–10) was between US$1731 and US$2026 (World Bank, 2013). Most recent available data on employment estimates 5.7 percent of the young (15–24 years old) male labor force remains unemployed (World Bank, 2014) but this figure obscures an enormous number of workers who are considered to have 'vulnerable employment' situations, which in Honduras in 2010 was an estimated 53 percent of workers (World Bank, 2013). The Honduran economy is not only significant as an example of how workers leverage alignment and misalignment within and between clusters of actors but also because the Honduran economy is inextricably linked with the US economy as the United States is a primary export destination for Honduran goods.

Despite organizing in a context of high unemployment and economic hardship as well as a consistently repressive labor regime, some Honduran workers in the apparel sector have campaigned to improve their living and working conditions and won. In this chapter, we focus on two specific campaigns against global apparel brands by workers and their allies to leverage the increased alignment between local workers' organizations, local labor activists, international labor activists, and end consumers against global apparel brands. The strategies employed by the worker and consumer clusters were sufficient in the two cases we present to result in limited but important wins for Honduran workers. Although these victories were limited in their capacity to bring about long-term or systemic change, they offer valuable insights into the conditions under which businesses can be persuaded to act against their perceived material interests to redress workers' grievances. We show that despite some internal disagreements within each of the clusters, over the course of both campaigns the brands' calculations of the punishments and rewards associated with different courses of action compelled them to provide direct compensation to workers.

The first campaign we analyze began in 2011. Illegally terminated apparel factory workers at a factory that supplied for Nike, Inc. initiated the campaign. The result of the campaign was a compensation and priority-rehiring package for the terminated workers that amounted to almost US$2 million. The second campaign we analyze began in the same year, when another factory owned by the apparel brand Russell Athletics was closed due to workers' efforts to unionize. After a protracted international campaign against Russell Athletics, Russell opened a new factory in the San Pedro Sula area and re-employed a number of the workers fired at the previous factory with guarantees that workers' collective bargaining rights would be protected. While concessions by firms to workers at the bottom of global supply chains have been few and far between, analyzing specific instances in which concessions have been made allows us to better understand the ways in which alignment and misalignment within and among clusters of actors both facilitate and obstruct the interests of workers. In the remainder of this chapter, we first outline who the important actors are in the Honduran case and then trace in detail the Nike and Russell campaigns to demonstrate how workers leveraged a moment of greater alignment between themselves and end consumers to win concessions from global brands.

THE GOVERNMENT

Honduras is the third most impoverished nation in the Western hemisphere, with development challenges that include an estimated poverty rate of 64 percent, an infant mortality rate of 34 per 1000, chronic malnutrition (33 percent of children under five years), an average adult education level of 5.3 years, and rapid deterioration of water and forest resources (Sullivan, 2006). Honduras has also long been considered one of the most labor-repressive countries in the world. The country has also been plagued by violent crime and political instability since its

independence in 1821 (Gutiérrez Rivera, 2010). Over the past two
decades, the situation has deteriorated further. In 1998, Hurricane Mitch
devastated the country, compounding an already volatile political climate.
In addition to the enormous loss of life, an estimated 70 percent of the
country's infrastructure, including roads and bridges, was destroyed
(NOAA, 2011).

Corruption, homicide, gang-related crimes, and drug trafficking are all
significant characteristics of Honduran politics. In 1999, the United
National Office on Drugs and Crime reported 2563 intentional homicides
in Honduras. In just ten years the count tripled to 6239, with over 80
percent caused by firearms (Gutiérrez Rivera, 2010) (United Nations
Office of Drugs and Crime, 2014). Mexican drug cartels – particularly
Sinaloa and Los Zetas – have employed Honduran Mara Salvatrucha
(also known as Mara or MS-13) gang members for intimidation and drug
trafficking. The cartels are also a major source of illegal weapons and
money laundering activities.

Against this background of dysfunction and violence, the Honduran
state has consistently tried to repress a labor movement from emerging
for both political and economic reasons. The state is closely linked with
major businesses and business owners and has, therefore, adopted the
view that economic development is best served by attracting foreign
brands to contract with supplier factories in Honduras. In order to make
Honduras an attractive locale for investment and manufacturing, a stable
and docile workforce is necessary. Given the overall climate of fear and
high unemployment in Honduras, most workers in the manufacturing
sector are uninformed of their workplace rights, uneducated about the
codes of conduct their employers have agreed to meet as suppliers of
international brands, and unorganized. Those workers that are organized
into unions have organized themselves often at great personal risk with
support from dedicated labor activists at the grassroots level.

As a result of the agricultural background of former Honduran
President Carlos Roberto Flores (1998–2002), rural elite landowners have
been the primary beneficiaries of social and economic policy since he
came into office. While rural elites continued to amass power and
resources from 1998 to 2008, rural elite entrenchment was solidified in
2009 when a coup ousted Honduran President Manuel Zelaya. Many
speculate that Zelaya lost support of the Honduran elite after raising the
minimum wage in 2008 (Taylor Robinson and Ura, 2010) (Wikileaks,
2014a). This 60 percent increase in minimum wage was widely con-
demned by the business community. Business leaders and even mayors
claimed that they were forced to lay off workers to be able to meet the
new payroll costs. Recent media reports indicate that 180 000 jobs were

lost last year because of the combined effects of the global economic crisis, the steep wage hike, and the political crisis (Wikileaks, 2014b).

In 2006, Honduras also joined the Central American Free Trade Agreement (CAFTA), which liberalized trade between the United States, Costa Rica, the Dominican Republic, El Salvador, Guatemala, Honduras, and Nicaragua. CAFTA eliminates all tariffs on 80 percent of US manufactured goods and, at least theoretically, strengthens regulatory standards and environmental protections (see Central American Free Trade Agreement, 2004 for the full text). In CAFTA countries, US companies are treated as domestic firms for the purposes of taxation.

Although many expected that tax-free imports resulting from CAFTA would lead to a loss of jobs among Honduran workers in the immediate term, CAFTA proponents suggest that linkages to the global economy will outweigh short-term insecurity. They expect income losses to be modest. As farmers transition to crops that can be exported to the United States (Schalch, 2005). Another recent study by the International Food Policy Research Institute (IFPRI; Morley et al., 2008) shows that trade liberalization under CAFTA has had a positive effect on growth, employment, and poverty, but the effect is small.

CAFTA has ultimately led to increased foreign investment in Honduras, including the apparel sector. From the perspective of workers' rights, the continuing reliance of the Honduran economy on jobs that require only basic education does little to motivate the state to increase investments in education. Moreover, many *maquilas* (the Spanish word for factories) are located in export processing zones (EPZs) where workers have fewer collective bargaining and associational rights.

Although the apparel industry has expanded rapidly in Honduras over the past 30 years, it has also had a period of contraction. Due to the reliance of the Honduran economy on exports to the United States, the Honduran *maquila* industry contracted as a result of the 2008 financial crisis and subsequent economic downturn. Reports estimate that orders in the *maquila* sector declined about 40 percent and 30 000 workers lost their jobs in 2008/09 out of a pre-crisis workforce of 145 000. As of 2010, over one-third of the Honduran workforce was considered either unemployed or underemployed (United States Department of State, 2013; World Bank, 2013).

BUSINESSES

Throughout the 1980s and 1990s manufacturing became increasingly important to the Honduran economy. In 1993, approximately 10 percent of the Honduran labor force was engaged in the country's manufacturing sector. While small-scale manufacturing and production for the domestic market was hit hard during this period, a number of Asian-owned assembly industries sprang up in the free trade EPZs established by the government along the Caribbean coast. These factories drew thousands of job seekers to the new population centers of San Pedro Sula, Tela, and La Ceiba. By the 1990s, Honduras was the third largest exporter of apparel and textiles to the United States in the world and the largest exporting country of apparel and textiles in Central America (AFL-CIO, 2014). In 2006 around 11 percent of Honduran households were economically dependent on a family member employed in an apparel-producing *maquila* (Bussolo et al., 2008), and approximately 25 percent of the female labor force in the country was employed by *maquilas*.

WORKERS

The primary sources of labor and employment law can be found in the Labor Code, the Social Security Law, the Minimum Salary Law and the Minimum Salary Agreement (Government of Honduras, 1959; Padilla, 2012). The institutions responsible for labor law implementation, oversight, and enforcement are the Department of Justice, the Ministry of Labor, and the Social Security Institute. The Honduran labor code stipulates that written contracts are required for permanent employees.[1] However, many *maquila* workers are employed using short-term contracts, which exempt employers from providing them with written contracts. The Labor Code also stipulates that the maximum working time per week is 44 hours and entitles workers to overtime pay to the value of 125 percent – 175 percent depending on the shift worked. The Labor Code provides for the right to a period of leave for each year of continuous work and paid leave for national holidays (Government of Honduras, 1959).

While Honduras has a relatively strong legal framework protecting the rights of apparel workers, there is a severe shortage of factory inspectors who can investigate the working conditions of the hundreds of *maquilas*. Moreover, the majority of *maquila* workers are women, who face particular challenges in the workplace, including sexual harassment, denial of maternity leave, and forced pregnancy tests.

THE CAMPAIGNS AGAINST RUSSELL ATHLETICS AND NIKE BRANDS

This chapter focuses on two campaigns by workers and their allies that brought end consumers of apparel into greater alignment with workers to pressure apparel global apparel brands Nike, Inc. and Russell Athletics to uphold labor rights in their global supply chains. We analyze how, over the course of the campaigns, changing incentives and beliefs led Russell and Nike to alter their behavior in some instances and not in others. These patterns demonstrate that the alignment of workers and their allies with end consumers, particularly institutional consumers such as universities, can effectively increase the power of workers even in conditions where the interests of suppliers have captured the state. In the campaign against the Nike brand by workers in the Hugger and VisionTex factories, the result of the campaign was a commitment by Nike to pay the workers their severance pay, as well as provide a year of health insurance coverage, prioritize re-hiring the workers in Nike supplier factories, and provide a retraining program. In the campaign against the Russell brand by workers in the Jerzees de Honduras and Jerzees Choloma factories, the result of the campaign was the re-opening of a union-friendly factory and the rehiring of some of the previously terminated workers. These victories were indeed limited to workers in specific firms and do not signal a more systemic shift in the labor rights environment in Honduras. However, the cases do provide insight into the conditions under which the incentives of global brands and beliefs about the rewards and punishments associated with violating workers' rights can be brought into alignment with the interests of workers. In the following sections, we show how workers and their allies were able to bring the interests of consumers into line with their own.

The Russell Athletics Campaign

The campaign against Russell Corporation, a subsidiary of Fruit of the Loom, began in late 2008. Russell was accused of a series of labor violations in two factories it owned and operated in the Indhelva free trade zone near San Pedro Sula, Honduras. Together the two factories employed approximately 1800 workers. Factory employees claimed that managers had conducted a two-year campaign of employee intimidation and had fired 145 union supporters in 2007. Following increased activism by disgruntled employees Russell shut down the Jerzees de Honduras factory in 2009. The corporation claimed that the factory was shut down out of economic necessity. However, it was apparent to many factory employees, monitoring organizations, and labor rights NGOs that the firing of labor organizers and the subsequent factory closure was in direct response to attempts by workers to unionize. The right to unionize is explicitly protected under Honduran law, as well as under regional and international law and in the codes of conduct of many of the universities that purchase apparel from Russell. In November of 2009, Russell Athletics reached a multi-part settlement with a national labor union representing the interests of the terminated workers. In response to union demands, the settlement specified that Russell would establish a unionized apparel factory of 'substantial size' called Jerzees Nuevo Dia, which would offer employment to former Jerzees de Honduras employees.

At the beginning of the campaign, following the termination of 145 union workers and the subsequent factory closures, workers from Jerzees de Honduras and Jerzees de Choloma brought the issue to the attention of their union, the Central General de Trabajadores (CGT Honduras). CGT Honduras filed third-party complaints on behalf of workers at the factories with the US-based Worker Rights Consortium (WRC) and the Fair Labor Association (FLA) on the grounds that labor protections enshrined in the codes of conduct of Russell's institutional purchasers had been violated. In response to these complaints, both the WRC and the FLA immediately sent investigators to collect evidence on the alleged violations. The WRC and the FLA are responsible for monitoring labor grievances in factories supplying their members (in the case of the FLA) or of member universities who are end consumers of goods (in the case of the WRC).

WRC and FLA representatives conducted interviews with employees, government officials, and apparel industry representatives and analyses of documentary evidence. Throughout the investigation, Russell maintained that the factory closures and terminations resulted from the decline in the market for fleece products and subsequent oversupply. However, a 2008 WRC report notes that in March 2008, a Jerzees de Honduras supervisor claimed: 'this factory is going to close because of the union ... The workers will starve because they got involved with a union' (Worker Rights Consortium, 2008). In similar statements, the WRC reports that the facility's general manager stated, 'the plant has high efficiency, but unfortunately, because of a union, the factory may close', and Russell's regional head of human resources claimed that: 'There is a group that is a group of anti-social people who are forming a union ... but we are not going to accept this in the factory' (ibid.).

Workers claimed that the closure of Jerzees de Honduras and Jerzees Choloma by the Russell Corporation unlawfully deprived employees of the livelihoods on which they depended for survival and violated protections enshrined by law concerning rights to freedom of association. The reports caused the FLA to place Russell under 'special review,' which is the highest level of sanction that the FLA can take against a member company. The WRC also collected credible evidence that the exercise of associational rights was a significant factor in Russell's decision to close the factory. The WRC noted that factory closure and the termination of its employees on these grounds explicitly violated the codes of conduct of many of Russell's institutional purchasers.

Through links with the WRC, FLA, and AFL-CIO, workers from the Jerzees de Honduras and Jerzees de Choloma factories connected with other NGOs and student groups in the United States. One worker from Jerzees de Honduras noted in an interview that the terminated workers attended conferences with students and embarked on a tour of US universities to explain the working conditions at the factory, the reasons for the closures, the violations of Honduran law, and the anti-union sentiment in the factory before its closure (SITRAJERZEESH, 2011). In a tour organized by AFL-CIO and the student group, United Students Against Sweatshops (USAS), representatives from Jerzees de Honduras visited the campuses of the University of Maryland, Georgetown, Cornell, Rutgers, Columbia, University of Wisconsin-Madison, University of Michigan-Ann Arbor, University of Indiana, and University of Minnesota, among others. On this trip, they also attended a conference organized by AFL-CIO and USAS. One Jerzees de Honduras representative stated:

> We had good response at all the universities. Our testimony was important to them. We were told that some schools were demanding their school cut the contract with Russell … We asked for our jobs back and asked for the factory to be opened again … Over 100 contracts between universities and Russell were cut. We recognized the economic impact of our efforts was significant. We also found out through our collection of evidence that the factory, at the same time that it was closing, was making pacts with other factories. Evidence was really important in this case. We also recognized all the international pressure on Russell. There were efforts from students at Canadian universities as well as in the US. (Ibid.)

In the case of Russell, the WRC and USAS were incredibly active in pushing the issue of labor violations to the forefront of university agendas. US universities acted as a critical consumer group in each of the Honduran cases, as one of the key institutional purchases of apparel made in Central American factories. As a result, campus organizing and mobilizing of support was important for keeping the issue alive and salient and placing pressure on university administrators. One terminated worker said in an interview: 'Cooperation between CGT and international organizations made the difference in this case' (ibid.).[2]

Interviewees described the cascade effect that compelled universities and university administrators to respond to the Russell campaign. The fact that USAS coordinated a highly organized, multi-campus effort to keep the Russell issue on the agenda of senior university administrators was a key factor in many universities' decisions to de-license or decline to renew their contracts with Russell. Sustained USAS activism across the country meant that once the alleged violations had been confirmed by monitoring organizations and NGOs and were found to clearly violate the codes of conduct of many universities, the violations became difficult for trademarks and licensing offices to ignore. Once a few universities took the decision to de-license Russell, others followed suit. Multiple interviewees involved in the Russell campaign observed that senior administrators were wary of being the first school to cut a contract. Once others have de-licensed, however, senior administrators are more inclined to take alleged labor violations seriously. Alex Bores, student activist at Cornell, comments: 'There's always the question of "no other school's done it, why should we?" Then once a few schools have cut, and said it's violating the contract, [the question is] why are we still with them if other schools [have cut]?' (Bores, 2011).

Other interviewees emphasized the importance of university activism in labor rights campaigns against global brands. Lynda Yanz, Executive Director of Maquila Solidarity, observes:

> The thing with universities that's so important, and again it's much more important in the US, is this leverage related to sports teams and brand recognition. You have huge deals that are being made, and money that is generated in the US, that relates to licensees at universities. That's an incredible pressure point. (Yanz, 2011)

After 100 universities severed contracts with Russell, Russell had little choice but to rethink its policy on the Jerzees de Honduras issue. Bores observes:

> With Russell I really think the workers, the students, everyone who was working on this, really actually hit them in their wallets. They [Russell] went from being the eighth most popular collegiate licensee to the twentieth in the course of the campaign. They were dropped by a major retailer ... There is no way it could get done with just people working in Honduras or just students working in the United States. It was the fact that Russell was getting bombarded from all over that changed it. (Bores, 2011)

Under intense pressure from its institutional purchasers, the Russell Corporation eventually reached a multi-part settlement with CGT. The settlement specified that Russell would establish a unionized apparel factory of 'substantial size' called Jerzees Nuevo Dia, which would offer employment to all former Jerzees de Honduras employees (Worker Rights Consortium, 2010). Ultimately around 800 workers were re-employed (Worker Rights Consortium, 2011; United Students Against Sweatshops, 2012).

A union, SITRAJERZEESH, organized at the new factory, and Russell agreed to create a training program that would help establish a culture of respect for freedom of association. Part of that effort also included hiring an ombudsman and offering mediation for workplace disputes. Russell also agreed to establish a workers' welfare fund to provide assistance to displaced workers. In May 2011, Russell and SITRAJERZEESH signed a collective bargaining agreement, resulting in the hiring of an additional 250 workers at Jerzees Nuevo Dia, as well as a 19.5 percent wage increase, free transportation to and from the worksite and lunches (which workers had previously had to pay for themselves). Russell also made a significant investment in new machinery that increased production efficiency. Each individual's wages depended on the number of apparel pieces she or he produced per day, thus, the investment in more efficient machinery also resulted in a wage increase for workers. The WRC writes:

> These successful negotiations constitute full implementation of two critical components of the accord Russell signed with [CGT] and of the company's remediation agreement with the WRC: 1) the obligation of Russell to bargain in good faith with the Jerzees Nuevo Dia workforce, and 2) the obligation to rehire, over time, all of the former employees of Jerzees de Honduras. There are roughly 200 of these workers, out of the initial group of over 1200, who were never re-hired; under the new contract, all of these workers were promised jobs at Jerzees Nuevo Dia. (Worker Rights Consortium, 2011)

The Russell case shows that mobilization by workers in Honduras and their allies in the United States played a critical role in shifting the incentives of a key consumer group: universities as institutional purchasers. In this specific case, workers and their allies were able to bring the interests of consumers into line with their own, and exert pressure – in the form of threatening to cut contracts with global brands – to shift the incentives of firms to protect and uphold the rights of workers. Kathy Hoggan, Director of UW Trademarks and Licensing and a member of ACTL, explains:

> I spoke at a Fair Labor Association board meeting with the Russell representative Stan Blankenship, June of this year, and he explained that there was

still about 30 percent [of schools] that had not reinstated their licenses, and [Russell's] business is still suffering greatly. There is concern that they will never recapture the business to the level that they were prior to this incident. (Hoggan, 2010)

Significant alignment within the consumer cluster, complemented by cross-cluster alignment between workers and consumers, were critical to obtaining the outcomes observed. Without this, it is unlikely that pressure could have been leveraged effectively to change the beliefs and incentives of the Russell Corporation.

The Nike, Inc. Campaign

In January 2009, just a few months after the closure of the Jerzees de Honduras factory, two factories, Hugger and VisionTex, in a manufacturing zone close to San Pedro Sula, declared bankruptcy and closed for business. As a result of the factory closures, 1800 employees were terminated. The bankruptcy of Hugger and VisionTex was a direct consequence of Nike, Inc.'s decision to no longer order from either of the two supplier factories because Nike was a major buyer in both factories. Over the next 18 months a campaign by workers, local and international NGOs and activists, as well as end consumers of Nike apparel, succeeded in changing Nike's calculus. In July of 2010, in an unprecedented move, Nike announced a compensation and priority-rehiring package for the terminated Hugger and VisionTex employees with a value of approximately US$2 million.

The campaign against Nike began following the closure of Hugger and VisionTex when workers at the factories communicated their grievances to CGT. The local campaign to help workers obtain their compensation was coordinated by CGT representative Evangelina Argueta who, immediately upon learning of the factory closures, communicated the workers' grievances to the WRC. Scott Nova, Executive Director of the WRC, reports, 'We learned of the problems at Hugger and VisionTex from the CGT ... essentially on the day that the factories were closed and we immediately notified Nike of the problem' (Nova, 2011). The WRC then conducted an independent investigation into the allegations by interviewing the workers at the former Hugger and VisionTex factories and auditing available financial documents from the factories.

At the same time CGT was in communication with the WRC, the union also filed a lawsuit in the Honduran courts. However, the Hugger and VisionTex factory owners fled Honduras. Honduran law is clear that workers are due terminal compensation even in the case of bankruptcy.

Yet without factory owners to pressure, the Honduran legal system could do little to remedy the situation other than mandate valuable equipment remaining in the factories be sold off and that the proceeds go toward compensating workers. The CGT originally assessed the amount owed to workers at Hugger to US$2 030 360 and US$571 896 at VisionTex. A total of US$425 990 was raised through liquidation of factory assets.

Although the sale of factory equipment provided some compensation for workers, much of what was legally owed the workers was left unpaid. Given the unsatisfactory outcome of the legal proceedings against the supplier factory owners, workers and their allies then began to focus on Nike. CGT maintained that because the owners of the factories had declared bankruptcy, Nike should be financially liable for the unpaid wages and benefits. However, Nike adamantly denied legal or financial responsibility and claimed that attention should instead be directed toward the owners of Hugger and VisionTex.

After the WRC had concluded its investigation in Honduras, the report was passed on to its member universities as well as to USAS (Worker Rights Consortium, 2009). Trademarks and licensing offices (the offices that are typically responsible for reviewing compliance of university branded products with university codes of conduct) at universities around the country reviewed the WRC report and passed on the information to relevant administrators. Through a combination of student activism and discussions among various trademarks and licensing offices, administrators from universities holding Nike contracts quickly became aware of the issues facing the former Hugger and VisionTex employees.

The WRC and USAS worked hard to mobilize support from a diverse body of students not ordinarily engaged in labor issues and to apply pressure to university administrators to prioritize a resolution of the labor rights violations in Nike's supply chain. Student activists conducted educational events and awareness-raising activities at campuses across the country to overcome collective action problems and raise support for the terminated Hugger and VisionTex employees. They did so by initiating public letter-writing campaigns and protests at multiple universities that urged senior university administrators to sever contracts with Nike. The campaigns received a great deal of press coverage in campus-wide publications and in local news. Realizing that the violations had turned into a major issue for students and the media, senior administrators began to take student demands more seriously. A diverse group of actors on various campuses – including students, faculty, administrators and trademarks and licensing personnel – began to work as a loose coalition toward alleviating the problems faced by the terminated workers in Honduras and aligning the interests of the consumer group with the aggrieved workers. In response to increased pressure and media attention, Nike agreed to meet with the WRC to discuss concerns over its obligations to formerly subcontracted employees.

Following mounting student pressure and the deliberations of many trademarks and licensing committees, late in 2009 several universities threatened to let their contracts for collegiate licensed apparel with Nike expire if no progress was made towards a settlement with CGT. In the months that followed, the University of Wisconsin-Madison, Cornell University, and Brown University terminated their contracts with Nike. University of Washington (UW) President Mark Emmert issued a statement saying that UW would do the same if no resolution to the issue were forthcoming. Lynda Yanz, of Maquila Solidarity, explains the importance of university contracts with Nike during the campaign:

> [Maquila Solidarity] certainly sees that universities and institutional buyers and universities being amongst the largest, have a critical role to play in [labor rights campaigns] and, in our view, at least at present, much more important than individual consumers ... The thing with universities that's so important is ... this leverage related to sports teams and brand recognition ... the threat and bad publicity linked to Nike on campuses is quite important as a pressure point. (Yanz, 2011)

While Nike consistently denied any legal or contractual obligations to pay severance to the terminated employees, the pressure placed on the brand from a key consumer group (universities) made it difficult for Nike to reject CGT's demands out of hand. Finally, in July 2010, after private negotiations between CGT and Nike, Nike agreed to a settlement of almost US$2 million. The settlement package included an approximately US$1.5 million emergency fund to compensate the workers who had not received their severance pay as well as healthcare benefits and a job training program (for the purposes of finding future employment) for former Hugger and VisionTex employees. Nike consistently maintained that it was under no legal obligation to reach the settlement but rather that the settlement was a gesture of goodwill and served as a relief fund for terminated employees.

Many of those interviewed for this chapter observed that Nike feared that the sequence of events that occurred in the Russell case would be replicated in the Nike case. Once four schools formally threatened to allow their contracts to expire it seemed likely that a number of others would follow suit. This cascade effect would have posed a considerable threat to Nike's business and reputation that would have been difficult to recover from. Mike Powers, responsible for Trademarks and Licensing at Cornell University, observed:

As I recall [in the Russell campaign], we were something like the twelfth school to pull the license. Ultimately, I think there were about 120. Russell at that point really finally did do an about-face and solve the problems. It's interesting because I really think that the speed with which Nike reacted to all this, was from their experience in watching what happened with Russell. I think they figured once the domino effect started to happen, and once one school pulled their license, the handwriting was on the wall. This is not really a huge financial issue for companies of that size. The American sportswear market, we make up something like 5 to 10 percent [colleges and universities], so it's really dust in the overall scheme of things. It's very harmful to them from a public relations point of view to have a big issue in the public eye. (Powers, 2011)

Despite Nike's careful language that avoided setting a precedent that would obligate them to take responsibility for all subcontractors' labor violations in the future, activists involved in the campaign were excited about the settlement. University of Washington professor and former Trademarks and Licensing committee member Angelina Godoy noted:

To be honest, this is the kind of case I would've fought five years ago but I would never have believed it could be winnable ... I would never have thought that we would have this kind of a victory ... and I think you can't separate it from the other big victories, especially the Russell case – this is kind of building on other important precedents, it's not something that came out of the sky. (Godoy, 2010)

University of Washington President Mark Emmert stated that he hopes that the outcome will 'empower Nike to hold its competitors to a higher standard' (Emmert, 2010).

Student representative to the University of Washington's Advisory Committee on Trademarks and Licensing Andrew Schwartz also struck a positive tone in his reflection on the resolution of the Nike case:

Universities should feel emboldened, they have a lot of power. Students have the final power ... [our Student Labor Action Project]'s slogan is 'All we do is win' and we did, all we did is win ... This is precedent setting because we were able to interpret the code. We were actually able to make the code a living, active document. (Schwartz, 2010)

UW advisory committee member Norm Arkans points out, however, that:

No university on Earth can do this on its own. The collective will and power of universities through consortiums have been what [how] we've been able to do what we have. . .we rely on both the FLA, WRC, and some of the NGOs that are in this business that are monitoring compliance with codes of conduct. We rely on them to bring problems to light. (Arkans, 2010)

A NEW EQUILIBRIUM? BEYOND THE RUSSELL AND NIKE CAMPAIGNS

As a result of the Nike and Russell campaigns, the economic well-being of specific workers improved in the aftermath of negotiated settlements involving compensation and re-employment. While domestic legal protections, as well as rights enshrined in corporate and institutional codes of conduct, provided the tools around which workers and unions could mobilize, union successes in these cases depended on bringing the interests of end consumers, and ultimately global brands themselves, into greater alignment with the interests of workers.

This proceeded in three stages. First, workers, through their unions and NGO allies, sought the support of student activists and ethical consumers embedded within a powerful group of institutional purchasers: American universities. The loose alignment of interests between workers and end consumers in these cases meant that student pressure, channeled through university trademarks and licensing offices, eventually succeeded in threatening the profits and reputation of global brands. As a result of the new alignment between workers and end consumers, key stakeholders were able to gain some leverage over global brands by changing their beliefs and interests. Executives at Russell and Nike believed that they needed to address the concerns of their subcontracted Honduran workers to avoid losing business. In the Nike case, this changed alignment and also caused ruptures within the business cluster as Nike initially sought to pressure its supplier factories into addressing worker demands. It was only when this failed, that Nike itself showed some willingness to assume responsibility.

The documentation of positive outcomes in these particular cases suggests conditions under which labor rights campaigns and transnational advocacy movements can result in improved working conditions and increase respect for labor standards. Despite the failure of weak governments to implement or enforce labor laws, as well as considerable resistance from global brands, labor unions and workers enlisted the support of end consumers to shift the incentive structures of global brands and significantly improve conditions for workers at the bottom of the supply chain. It is evident that in the face of mounting consumer pressure, communication and collective action among worker representatives, institutional purchasers and corporate social responsibility offices can be effective.

However, it is highly unlikely that these cases are indicative of broader change. In each case, after early legal claims did not produce the desired results, the Honduran state was bypassed almost entirely. Furthermore, while specific workers involved in these cases received compensation or re-employment, this is hardly evidence of systemic change. The vast majority of labor violations in Honduras remain unaddressed. Violations are either never reported or, in the few cases where grievances are filed, they are far more likely to be met with resistance and failure than in support from transnational allies.

It is also important to note that even the successes in the campaigns we have highlighted in this chapter have proved difficult to sustain. As of 2011 when fieldwork for these case studies was conducted in Honduras, only some of the workers who went through vocational retraining were ever re-hired. Moreover, reports indicate that, although freedom of association is intact at the SITRAJERZEESH factory, union repression has continued in other Russell-owned factories. The problems enforcing the settlement between workers, the union, and the brands demonstrate the continued misalignment between the interests of workers and the interests of brands when consumers are no longer scrutinizing apparel supply chains.

Long-term and sustained improvements to working conditions at the bottom of global supply chains require an effective state apparatus. It is evident that workers and their allies can only do so much when their efforts are not supported by effective government regulation. In the absence of government support, an incredible burden is placed on under-resourced unions, NGOs, and activist groups who have little power to alter incentive structures in any systemic way.

CONCLUSION

The case of universities as institutional purchasers illustrates the ways in which the interests of different stakeholders within the consumer cluster can be aligned with one another and with workers to exert pressure on global brands to improve workers' rights. In the cases of both Russell and Nike, alignment between workers and consumers changed the incentives of the corporations, who believed that their business interests and reputation would be threatened by failing to take worker grievances seriously.

However, problems associated with the implementation of training and priority rehiring, as well as continued allegations of violations in factories associated with both brands, lead us to believe that this victory was short-lived. While the interests of consumers and workers were aligned under very specific sets of conditions, these actors were unable to fundamentally alter the incentive structures of brands and suppliers in the longer term. Brands and suppliers remain motivated by material incentives and continue to believe that low cost of production largely outweighs the rewards associated with devoting serious attention to labor issues.

NOTES

1. Exceptions to the law on formal employment contracts are made in cases of domestic service, incidental or temporary work not exceeding 60 days, work for which the value does not exceed 200 lempiras and farming or ranching, unless in the case of industrial or commercial enterprises from agriculture or livestock.
2. Notes and transcripts for all interviews conducted by the authors of this book and consulted for Chapter 7 can be found at the Brand Responsibility Project website: http://depts.washington.edu/brandrp/transcripts.html.

8. Apparel production in Bangladesh: opportunity amidst tragedy?

Bangladesh is a semi-competitive democracy that has struggled to shift its over-populated, under-skilled agricultural workforce into the industrial sector. Two major political parties and intermittent military rule have monopolized political power since independence. The most successful export-oriented industry in Bangladesh has been the apparel industry. Abuses in the apparel sector have been the subject of international scrutiny, particularly after the Rana Plaza disaster in 2013, but other sectors, such as the ship-breaking industry, have also been spotlighted in labor rights reports as being rife with poor labor practices. The nature of political competition between the two major political parties in Bangladesh as well as high levels of bureaucratic corruption are two of the key factors that shape material incentives for firms and workers in Bangladesh in the area of labor rights. The result of the existing political equilibrium has been poor working conditions, including several major factory fires and building collapses that have made headlines worldwide.

Although there have been many factory fires and accidents resulting in the injury and death of apparel workers in Bangladesh, it is the collapse of Rana Plaza, an eight-story commercial building in Dhaka housing apparel-producing facilities, that disrupted the existing equilibrium and has presented a political opportunity for workers and their allies to intervene in the poor working conditions in global apparel supply chains that source from Bangladesh. Rana Plaza has become shorthand for the horrors of sweatshops much in the way the Triangle Shirtwaist Factory Fire in the United States became shorthand for the same problem over 100 years ago. Rana Plaza has infamously been named the most deadly apparel factory accident ever recorded leaving 1129 dead and 2515 injured. International outrage over the incident exposed the failures of brands to ensure suppliers were compliant with their codes of conduct and damaged the reputation of many apparel brands with their consumers.

In the aftermath of Rana Plaza, two associations of brands with suppliers in Bangladesh have been formed. The Accord on Factory and Building Safety in Bangladesh is an association of brands primarily based in the EU while the Alliance for Bangladesh Worker Safety is an association of brands primarily based in North America. The efficacy of both associations' efforts to improve fire and building safety in the Bangladeshi apparel industry remains to be seen.

In this chapter, we highlight the equilibrium between apparel brands and their suppliers, the Bangladeshi government, Bangladeshi workers and their allies, as well as apparel consumers that existed prior to the Rana Plaza tragedy. We then trace how various actors have worked to align their interests both within and amongst the clusters of key stakeholders that together create working conditions in the apparel sector to leverage the political opportunity that the Rana Plaza tragedy created. We present the post-Rana Plaza equilibrium along with an analysis of the likely challenges to sustainable change that exist in the new equilibrium. We argue that there has been a change in the beliefs of government officials post-Rana Plaza. Officials have shifted towards the belief that Bangladesh's international reputation as a supplier of consumer goods that meets international labor standards, specifically in the apparel sector, matters for the continued growth of export sector and continued economic development.

The Bangladeshi apparel industry began taking off in the late 1970s, not long after Bangladesh established independence from Pakistan. Apparel exports have grown at an average annual rate of 25 percent in Bangladesh even after the end of the Multi-Fibre Agreement (MFA) in 2005. By 2010, Bangladesh was exporting nearly US$16 billion of apparel and textiles, comprising an overwhelming 82 percent of Bangladesh's total merchandise exports (Bajaj, 2010). The apparel sector generates the largest amount of trade-related foreign exchange of any sector in Bangladesh and employs more than 3 million individuals out of the 70 million working-age population, more than any other manufacturing sector (ibid.).

BUSINESSES

Worker safety standards in all of the major industries in Bangladesh suffer from widespread and well-documented violations of international labor standards (International Labour Organization standards as well as Fair Labor Association or Worker Rights Consortium standards) (Human Rights Watch, 2014a). The most significant industry in Bangladesh is the ready-made garment (RMG) industry. Since the Rana Plaza tragedy involved an apparel factory, we focus in this chapter on the RMG sector although other sectors such as ship breaking, leather production, and textile production have well-documented violations of international worker health and safety standards. We argue that like most businesses, the profit motive is the primary incentive for apparel suppliers in Bangladesh and that beliefs about the sources of competitiveness for apparel suppliers in a global marketplace have shaped the behavior of supplier firms that has led to poor working conditions for apparel workers in Bangladesh. At least until the time of the Rana Plaza tragedy, apparel suppliers seemingly without exception believed that their competitiveness came from offering the lowest-cost apparel production in the world. Whether beliefs about how the reputation of Bangladesh as a source of apparel and the reputations of individual suppliers affect the competitiveness of Bangladeshi apparel suppliers have significantly changed in the aftermath of Rana Plaza is, as yet, an open question.

Much of Bangladesh's comparative advantage in the global apparel market has been based on its low labor costs as well as its guaranteed access to export markets via the quota system of the MFA until 2005 (Rashid, 2006; Rahman et al., 2008; Khan, 2011). Contractors for major apparel firms like Wal-Mart, such as the Li & Fung Group based in Hong Kong, note that their sourcing from Bangladesh increased 20 percent in 2009 while sourcing from China dropped 5 percent (Bajaj, 2010). The change in the sourcing strategies of apparel contractors are in part due to the low wages paid to workers in Bangladesh, about 3000 taka per month (equivalent to about US$37) prior to 2013. By comparison, workers in China's coastal provinces are entitled to a minimum wage between US$117 and US$147 per month. Although Bangladesh's comparative advantage has historically relied on the low cost of labor, Bangladesh Knitwear Manufacturers and Exporters Association (BKMEA) President Fazlul Haq stated in a 2009 interview that he expects that Bangladesh will be able to compete on timely delivery and quality in the future (Saxena and Salze-Lozac'h, 2010). Given the enormous infrastructural challenges that Bangladesh faces in terms of reliable energy delivery as well as road and port infrastructure, the desire for apparel suppliers to compete on dimensions other than cost may be difficult.

The apparel sector is composed of different tiers of contractors. The Export Promotion Bureau of Bangladesh reports that of 2387 firms exporting RMG in 2004, the top 20 percent (500 firms) accounted for 74 percent of total RMG exports.[1] Large firms, such as those in the top 20 percent, have a production capacity of 5000–10 000 dozens of units per month, whereas the smaller firms typically have a capacity of less than 5000 dozen units per month (Rahman et al., 2008).

THE GOVERNMENT

The Bangladeshi state faces enormous challenges both in terms of the natural environment and human development. The per capita GDP in Bangladesh in 2008 was US$520, which places the state firmly in the ranks of low-income developing countries according to the World Bank classification and least developed countries according to the United Nations. The per capita GDP statistic is only one of many statistics that demonstrates 'the accuracy of the general public perception of Bangladesh as a country suffering from immense poverty' (United States Agency for International Development, 2010, p. 5). In this section on the Bangladeshi government, we argue that in Bangladesh's particular political environment and competitive electoral system, the incentive for political parties to win re-election has driven behaviors that align the interests of both major political parties with apparel suppliers and against the interests of workers. We also argue that rent seeking is entrenched within the Bangladeshi bureaucracy and, thus, such behavior is a norm that also drives practices that disadvantage workers and favor apparel suppliers.

Throughout the development of the apparel sector in Bangladesh, the government's policy has been to facilitate the sector's growth via non-interference and a decentralized industrial policy. Indeed, unlike the policies of many East Asian governments, successive Bangladeshi governments have neither picked winners nor exclusively directed state subsidies to the apparel sector. Ahmed et al. (2014, p. 260) argue that a more interventionist industrial policy would 'be untenable in Bangladesh, due to the country's particular political settlement, which has induced rampant government corruption, fierce political competition, inefficient bureaucracies, and weak political leadership'. Oscillating among military regimes and the rule of one of two major political parties, the dynamic of political contestation in Bangladesh is best characterized as a state where 'competitive clientelism' drives politics.

The two rival political parties are the Awami League, led by Sheikh Hasina Wazed, and the Bangladesh Nationalist Party (BNP), led by Begum Khaleda Zia. Although other parties, such as the Jama'at-i Islami have also had an impact on politics, electoral politics remains dominated by the Awami League and the BNP. The Awami League and the BNP espouse competing nationalist narratives and do not compete at the polls on the basis of economic policies. In Bangladesh 'political parties are multi-class organizations that bring together a large number of patron–client networks in a pyramidal structure' (Khan, 2010, p. 11). Moreover,

Bangladesh's level of development and export-led growth strategy has created a situation where 'state-led primitive accumulation has generated intense political competition for control of the state. This in turn has created irresistible short-term incentives for upwardly mobile groups to collectively organize into competing factions' (Khan, 1995, p. 575).

A high level of corruption and frequent regime turnover among the two major political parties and the military generates incentives for the misallocation of public funds yielding poor public goods provision:

> Since political actors compete on the redistribution of formal and informal government rents to win elections, the incentives of politicians are to support policies/programs that ensure a quick payoff. Consequently, there is under-investment in and politicization of long-term public programs, such as government procurement. Poor investment in infrastructure, especially power and roads, is a major obstacle to the continued growth of the apparel sector. (Ahmed et al., 2014, p. 266)

This has emerged as a consequence of the growing politicization of the bureaucracy and the cyclical demotion of senior bureaucrats after every change of the party in power. Consequently, the time horizons of bureaucrats diminish such that they are incentivized to develop party loyalties rather than in their professional capabilities. According to a report prepared for the World Bank (Wescott and Breeding, 2011), 'There has been a decline in the quality of policy engagement between politicians and the public administration'.

The lack of organized labor power has given the state little reason to invest in building the necessary capacity to properly regulate the industry. Bangladesh, like many other apparel-producing countries, suffers from weak regulatory capacity. In the context of labor rights, this problem tends to manifest in the plight of under-funded labor ministries. Nazrul Islam Khan, President of the Jatiyatabadi Sramik Dal (BJSD) workers' federation, laments, 'labor inspectors have power' (in reference to existing legal statutes) but 'our labor inspectors are under staffed, under equipped, and incapable of performing their duties' (Khan [2012] 2014).

Government officials and labor leaders openly acknowledge that the ratio of labor inspectors to workers is hopelessly imbalanced. Moreover, inspectors rarely have the tools they need like cars for travel between factory locations or sufficient salaries to resist bribes. The lack of resources allocated to labor ministries is due to the marginalization of labor from the current political settlement. Although there are technical skills in which labor inspectors may need to be trained, such as how to evaluate efficiencies in different types of production in order to work with suppliers on capturing greater gains, this aspect of labor regulation is far less important than the basic issue of funding.

The allocation of funding for labor regulation can be seen as one way in which pro-labor political parties often support their constituents. However, neither of the dominant political parties in Bangladesh can be described as pro-labor. Scholarly research shows that pro-labor parties spend more on social welfare and adopt more progressive labor laws than other types of political parties (Hibbs, 1977; Huber and Stephens, 2001; Murillo and Schrank, 2005; Iversen and Soskice, 2006). Without such a party in Bangladesh, the outlook for labor is bleak. For example, in the current Bangladeshi Parliament (comprised of 345 members), there are 29 sitting members that are garment manufacturers/owners, compared to only four with a labor union background (Ahmed et al., 2014). Moreover, cross-national work (see Mosley, 2008) shows that trade openness is negatively associated with collective labor rights under centrist or right-wing governments, but positively associated under left-wing governments. As described above, the dominant political parties in Bangladesh can be thought of as sharing an economic ideology based on a liberal, free market approach that emphasizes decentralization and low levels of regulation. This means the Awami League and BNP can both be described as centrist or even right wing and bodes poorly for Bangladeshi workers.

WORKERS

Prior to the Rana Plaza tragedy, the power of apparel workers in relation to the power of the Bangladeshi state and apparel firms was weak. The highly fractionalized nature of the union movement in Bangladesh prevented the formation of an organized labor movement. Moreover, the nature of the political competition between the Awami League and the BNP did not require the two parties to seek the support of organized labor in order to form a winning political coalition. The exclusion of labor from formal political representation has resulted in sporadic, violent worker protests against low wages and poor working conditions. It is only the street-level politics that seem to force political actors to make concessions to labor interests.

Like most countries, Bangladesh has signed a number of conventions on labor rights and passed legislation that formally entitles workers to political and civil rights.[2] Domestic laws as well as international treaties are favorable to workers (International Labour Organization, 2013a). However, most analysis of these conventions and laws suggests serious problems with implementation. For example, the 2010 report on the Convention on Freedom of Association (No. 87) states:

> The Committee recalls that freedom of association and in particular the right to organize under the Convention can only be exercised in a climate that is free from violence, pressure or threats of any kind against the leaders and members of workers' organizations and that detention of trade unionists for reasons connected with their activities in defence of the interests of workers, constitutes a serious interference with civil liberties in general and with trade union rights in particular. In these circumstances, the Committee urges the Government to provide full particulars in respect of all the allegations of killings, physical assaults and detention of trade unionists and trade union leaders. (International Labor Organization, 2010)[3]

The vast majority of apparel workers are women who have migrated from Bangladesh to Dhaka in search of employment opportunities (Afsar, 2001; Mlachila and Yang, 2004; Razzaque, 2005; Kabeer et al., 2011). Jobs for young women in the apparel sector employment have led to an increase in the employment of women in the formal workforce and some report an improvement of their bargaining position within the home as a result of their employment (Kabeer, 2001; Kabeer et al., 2011; Schuler et al., 2013). Jobs in the apparel sector have also enabled some women workers to support their family via increased consumption and increased investments in their family's education, creating positive spillover effects for the overall human development level of the country (Rahman et al., 2008; Heath and Mobarak, 2012; Hossain, 2012). Although jobs in the apparel industry can be transformative for young women in particular, the wages workers earn in the apparel industry are low.

Low wages in the apparel industry are unsurprising given the abundant labor supply in Bangladesh coupled with the relatively low-skill nature of apparel production work. A majority of Bangladeshi workers are not unionized and therefore cannot collectively bargain for higher wages. Although no official statistics are available, most sources (e.g., Bangladesh Institute for Labor Studies, labor leaders) approximate that less than 5 percent of workers in the apparel industry belong to unions. The low unionization rate is unsurprising as interviews with garment workers revealed that joining a union means taking the risk of losing one's job. Moreover, according to Nazrul Islam Khan, President of the BJSD workers' federation, less than 10 percent of all workers in Bangladesh are members of trade unions. According to Khan:

> [T]here are some interesting developments happening regarding the trade unions and labor organizations in the apparel sector. Currently, there are some national-level labor organizations [that] are taking interest in the workers and

do some work but there are very few factory level organizations in the true sense of a trade union operation. (Khan [2012] 2014)

The conflict over the minimum wage demonstrates the way labor is marginalized from the current political settlement and its attempts to exert its potential power. Wages in Bangladesh for apparel manufacturing are amongst the lowest in the world. Bangladesh has a minimum wage significantly below even Cambodia. In fact, the current minimum wage of US$43 per month in Bangladesh was only implemented in November of 2010. Between 1994 and 2006, wages were stagnant at a rate of 930 taka per month (US$14 in 2006) (Hearson, 2006). The fight over the minimum wage increase in 2010 was heated. Bangladeshi labor federations and pro-labor NGOs advocated for an increase of the minimum wage to 5000 taka per month but ultimately lost and had to settle for an increase to 3000 taka per month (International Labor Rights Forum, 2010). During the campaign workers' representatives faced harassment, arrest and torture (Human Rights Watch, 2008; International Trade Union Conference, 2009, 2010). According to a report by International Labor Rights Forum (ILRF), such a wage falls short of constituting a living wage.[4] To put the new minimum wage of 3000 taka per month into perspective, employees of state-owned industries in Bangladesh are entitled to twice that amount.

THE RANA PLAZA TRAGEDY

On 24 April 2013, an eight-story building in the Savar District of Dhaka collapsed killing 1127 people and injuring more than 2500 others. The building housed several apparel factories, employing over 5000 people. The building was originally constructed to house shops rather than factories and the top four floors of the eight-story building had been built without a permit. The day prior to the accident cracks had appeared in the building, compromising the integrity of the structure. The building was evacuated yet workers were ordered to return to work as usual the following day. At least one factory threatened to withhold a month's wages from any worker that didn't comply with the order (Devnath and Srivastava, 2013). As the result of a power outage (a common occurrence in Dhaka), diesel generators were fired up on the top floor of the building around 9:00 am on 23 April and the building collapsed shortly thereafter with over 3100 workers inside at the time. Rescue efforts to pull survivors from the rubble lasted for weeks until the search was finally called to a close on 13 May 2013. The day after the building collapse (25

April 2013), the Dhaka Development Authority filed a case against the owner of the building, Sohel Rana, as well as five of the factory owners who were tenants in the building (Yardley, 2013). Rana was arrested four days after the building collapsed. The case against Rana was pending at the time of writing, when he was released on bail.

Garment workers in Dhaka took to the streets in grief and anger on May Day of 2013 while the search for survivors was still ongoing. Although international media attention sympathized with the conditions faced by Bangladeshi workers at the time, far less coverage of police brutality directed at protesting workers reached an international audience than did coverage of the accident itself. Ongoing intimidation of labor leaders and police brutality against worker-led demonstrations before and after Rana Plaza has been documented by international human rights organizations (Human Rights Watch, 2014a).

As the tragedy unfolded, part of the work of activists and NGOs was to identify the global apparel brands that had placed orders with factories in Rana Plaza and hold them accountable for the working conditions in their supply chains. Brands including Benetton, The Children's Place, Joe Fresh, Mango, Primark, and Wal-Mart, along with 23 others, were identified as having sourced from Rana Plaza. Representatives from only nine of these attended meetings held in November 2013 to discuss a proposal to provide compensation to the victims of the tragedy and their survivors (Ovi, 2013).

The week after Rana Plaza, global apparel brands, NGOs, and labor activists met to discuss how to ensure that garment supply chains were in compliance with international norms of worker safety. Many of the brands that attended the meetings agreed to an Accord on Factory and Building Safety in Bangladesh. The Accord was meant to address the serious health and safety concerns facing workers in the apparel industry. Wal-Mart, along with 14 other North American companies, refused to sign the accord as the 16 May signing deadline passed. In 2011, Wal-Mart had rejected reforms that would have required retailers to pay apparel suppliers in Bangladesh more in order to help factories improve safety standards. In July 2013, a group of 17 major North American retailers, including Wal-Mart, Gap, Target and Macy's, announced an alternative plan (known at the Alliance) to improve factory safety in Bangladesh. Unlike the Accord, the Alliance lacks legally binding commitments to pay for improvements to building safety. Further analysis of both the Accord and the Alliance is detailed below.

POST-RANA PLAZA: A NEW EQUILIBRIUM?

The public nature of the Rana Plaza tragedy, kept in the public eye by the attention of the international media, prompted actions by every cluster of actors involved in the Bangladeshi garment industry. The government responded by passing amendments to its labor laws, which most importantly strengthened workers' right to freedom of association and collective bargaining (International Labor Organization, 2013a). The new amendments (passed in 2013) made it possible for Bangladesh to at last become part of an International Labor Organization-International Finance Corporation (ILO-IFC) Better Work program. Better Work provides in-depth assessment and advice to individual factories to improve working conditions and make compliant supplier factories competitive and profitable.

As discussed in the section above, the business and worker clusters responded to the Rana Plaza tragedy by creating two new major private governance schemes. One is a group of primarily European apparel brands while the other is a group of primarily North American apparel brands. The Accord on Fire and Building Safety is the group of European brands (for a full list of participating brands see the Appendix, Box 8A.1 at the end of the chapter). The Accord is a legally binding agreement signed by over 150 apparel firms, two global trade union federations, Bangladeshi unions, and a number of NGOs with the International Labor Organization serving as its chair. The Accord specifies a process of safety inspections and reporting. The firms also contribute to a fund that is supposed to ensure that signatory factories are able to bring their factories up to code with international safety standards. Inspections by international inspectors began in February 2014.

A number of apparel corporations, primarily those based in North America, resisted post-Rana Plaza pressure to join the legally binding Accord (Greenhouse, 2013). Instead, the corporations created an alternative, the Alliance for Bangladesh Worker Safety (see Appendix Box 8A.2). The Alliance has much weaker legal obligations than the Accord and does not consult local or international unions.

While private politics and governance schemes have emerged from the Rana Plaza tragedy and some consumers have become more aware of working conditions in the apparel industry as a result of the media coverage of the tragedy, very little has changed in practice. As we have detailed above, the balance between the clusters of actors in Bangladesh (government, workers and their allies, and business) is tilted heavily towards favoring an alliance between government and business rather than government and workers. The Rana Plaza tragedy may have constituted a moment where beliefs about the importance of worker health and safety could have changed, shifting the interests of both the government and apparel suppliers toward better working conditions. Old beliefs, that neither global apparel brands nor end consumers would bear an increase in costs in order to fund improved working conditions in supplier factories, could have been replaced with new beliefs that brands and consumers would not only bear a marginal increase in costs but, in fact, would demand such improvements in order to continue purchasing apparel from Bangladesh.

However, new beliefs about the importance of worker health and safety have not been reinforced by sustained consumer attention and pressure or by the behavior of global apparel brands, at least some of whom have resisted taking responsibility for compensating victims of the tragedy (Human Rights Watch, 2014a, 2014b). The vast majority of apparel brands chose to continue sourcing apparel from Bangladesh, which likely signaled to the government that the RMG industry would not suffer as a result of the tragedy. In fact, not only did Bangladesh not suffer a decrease in apparel orders as a result of the Rana Plaza tragedy, clothing exports actually *increased* 16 percent in the 12 months that ended in March 2014 from the period a year earlier (Saha, 2014). Exiting Bangladesh as a source of apparel supply was a strategy that many workers' organizations themselves opposed, since many workers and their representatives in Bangladesh want working conditions to improve and exiting Bangladesh would deprive workers of much-needed jobs and income. However, it is difficult to square what was supposed to be an opportunity for global brands to work in partnership with their suppliers to improve conditions with reports from garment exporters that, 'Global retailers are using the Rana Plaza issue as a bargaining tool to cut prices … the garment sector witnessed price cuts by around 6 percent over the last one year despite a rise in production costs' (ibid.).

In what was an overly optimistic analysis of the government response to Rana Plaza, *The New York Times* in a staff editorial (2014) wrote, 'To its credit, Prime Minister Sheikh Hasina's administration has allowed more workers to unionize, which should empower them to demand better working conditions. The government has registered more than 140 labor unions since the start of 2013'. Yet as we have shown above, the fractionalization of labor unions is one of the major obstacles to worker voice in Bangladeshi politics. While greater freedom of association is indeed important, the blooming number of unions alone will likely have very little impact on the overall working conditions in Bangladesh. Moreover, meaningful freedom of association is still questionable given that labor organizers continue to face violent intimidation. An on-the-ground report published in *Jacobin Magazine* (Long, 2014) raises the same concerns:

> As union officials interested in international worker solidarity, we spent most of our time in Bangladesh with local unionists, workers, and members of left parties. It soon became clear that the incredible fragmentation of Bangladeshi politics and society is replicated on the Bangladeshi left, perhaps in even more extreme form. There are eighty or ninety unions claiming to represent garment workers, ranging from 'yellow' or boss's unions to ones that function like NGO charities and others that attempt to organize workers in their communities since they cannot get into their workplaces.

The hope for the Accord and the Alliance is that inspections beginning in 2014 will mitigate some of the most egregious violations of worker safety, particularly in the areas of fire safety and structural integrity of factory buildings. However, as Long (2014) points out, 'There is a risk that the Accord will alleviate concerns about fire and building safety while doing nothing to prevent the continued exploitation of workers in other ways – over-work, low pay, violence. Concerned citizens in the rich world may consider their work done once the Accord process is under way and most companies have signed up'. Long also points out that the Accord does not have a provision for follow-up inspections to ensure that violations once found have been corrected. As we discussed in Chapter 2, private governance schemes are rarely sufficient to correct working conditions in cases where a second layer of institutions, primarily those of an efficiently functioning government, is not present. As we have demonstrated above, the government in Bangladesh is neither incentivized to correct working conditions nor does it necessarily have the capacity to do so even if the political will were present. This leads us to the rather bleak conclusion that working conditions in Bangladesh are likely to continue to be substandard for the foreseeable future.

CONCLUSION

The Rana Plaza tragedy is an important example of how an exogenous shock, such as a building collapse or a factory fire, can be an important point of leverage for workers and their allies. While such shocks have the potential to shift the existing equilibrium, sustainable change is by no means assured. Even in the case of Bangladesh where significant international media attention was able to, at least temporarily, align end consumers with workers and their allies, the lack of long-term commitment to punishing brands and suppliers who violate workers' rights by end consumers in combination with a domestic political equilibrium that disadvantages workers is likely to result in a missed opportunity to significantly improve working conditions in Bangladesh's RMG industry.

NOTES

1. More recent data with a breakdown of exports by firm size from the Bureau of Export Promotion is not currently available.
2. In fact, Bangladesh ratified many of the fundamental International Labour Organization (ILO) conventions in the early 1970s. Bangladesh has currently ratified seven of the fundamental conventions, including conventions on the Right to Organize and Collective Bargaining (No. 98), the Right to Freedom of Association (No. 87), and the Abolition of Forced Labour (No. 105).
3. The 2010 report to the ILO on the Right to Organize and Collective Bargaining (No. 98) is just as bleak. The report says, 'There is a weak implementation of labour law in general, and more particularly an unwillingness of employers to recognize trade unions and collective bargaining' (International Labour Organization, 2011). The report goes on to note that Bangladeshi law 'provides for the establishment of an EPZ labour tribunal and an EPZ labour appellate' but reports by the International Trade Union Confederation (ITUC) reveals that neither body has been established, leaving garment workers employed in EPZs without access to the judicial system for the resolution of labor grievances. A 2010 survey of 825 factories done by the Bangladesh Factory Inspection Department concluded that 15 percent of factories do not pay their workers on time, 6 percent did not pay overtime, and 1 percent did not even pay workers the minimum wage (International Labor Rights Forum, 2010). The report also notes that during the first six months of 2010 alone, 356 garment workers were killed on the job (ibid.). These deaths are largely due to a series of fires in garment factories, including a fire at a small factory in Dhaka where 22 women workers died from the fire as a result of being locked in to the factory. All exits from the building had been blocked despite the certification of the factory as being 'fully compliant' by a monitoring group (ibid.).
4. According to this report the previous minimum wage of 1662 taka per month is not a living wage; it is, in fact, a malnutrition wage. ILRF calculates that the average garment worker needs 2351 taka per month simply to buy food with enough calories to support a ten-hour workday. According to the report, this wage does not even begin to reflect the other basic needs of workers or the fact that many workers support their families as well as themselves with their wages (International Labor Rights Forum, 2010).

APPENDIX

BOX 8A.1   BRANDS PARTICIPATING IN THE ACCORD ON FIRE AND BUILDING SAFETY IN BANGLADESH

Abercrombie & Fitch	Forever New	Multiline Group
Adidas	Full-Service Handels	N Brown
Åhléns	G-Star	New Look
Aldi North	Gebra Group	Next
Aldi South	Groupe Casino	O'Neill Europe BV
American Eagle Outfitters	H&M	Otto GmbH
Arcadia Group	Helly Hansen	Primark
Auchan	HEMA	Puma SE
Belotex	Hemtex AB	PVH
Benetton	Herding-Heimtextil	PWT Group/Texman
Bestseller	Hess Natur	Rewe Group
Bonmarché	Horizonte	s.Oliver
Brands-Fashion	IC Companys	Sainsbury's
C&A	ICA sverige	Schmidt Group
Camaïeu	Inditex (Zara)	Scoop NYC
Carrefour	JBC	Sean John
Charles Vögele	Jogilo	Shop Direct
Chicca	John Lewis	Specialty Fashion Group
Colombus Textilvertrieb	Jolo Fashion	Stockmann
Comtex	Juritex	Switcher
Coop Denmark	KappAhl	Target Australia
Cotton On	Karstadt	Tchibo
Dansk Supermarked	KiK	Tesco
Datex	Klaus Herding	Topgrade International
Debenhams	Kmart Australia	Uncle Sam GmbH
Distra	LC Waikiki	V&D
DK Company	Lidl	Van der Erve NV
E. Leclerc	Loblaw	Varner Group
El Corte Inglés	LPP	Viania
Ernstings's Family	Mango	Voice Norge AS
Esprit	Marks and Spencer	We Europe
Fashion Linq	Matalan	Woolworths Australia
Fast Retailing	Metro Group	Wunsche Group
Fat Face	Mothercare	Zeeman

BOX 8A.2 BRANDS PARTICIPATING IN THE ALLIANCE FOR BANGLADESH WORKER SAFETY

Ariela and Associates International
Canadian Tire Corporation, Limited
Carter's Inc.
Children's Place Retail Stores Inc.
Costco Wholesale
Corporation
Fruit of the Loom, Inc.
Gap Inc.
Giant Tiger
Hudson's Bay Company
IFG Corp.
Intradeco Apparel
J.C. Penney Company Inc.
The Jones Group Inc.

Jordache Enterprises, Inc.
The Just Group
Kohl's Department Stores
L.L.Bean Inc.
M. Hidary & Company Inc.
Macy's
Nordstrom Inc.
Public Clothing Company
Sears Holdings Corporation
Target Corporation
VF Corporation
Wal-Mart Stores, Inc.
YM Inc.

Note: Supporting associations include: American Apparel & Footwear Association, BRAC, Canadian Apparel Federation, National Retail Federation, Retail Council of Canada, Retail Industry Leaders Association, and United States Association of Importers of Textiles & Apparel. In addition, Li & Fung, a major Hong Kong-based sourcing company, which does business with many members of the Alliance, will serve in an advisory capacity.

9. Labor resistance and local government – supplier collusion in post-1986 China

Since 1979, the Chinese economy has experienced rapid growth, and the quality of life for millions of Chinese citizens has significantly improved. In the 1980s and 1990s, China's economic growth was driven by labor-intensive light manufacturing industries, and businesses moved to China to benefit from the availability of cheap labor, tax breaks, and reduced tariffs offered by local governments. As investment increased in the apparel, footwear, and electronics sectors, migrants from the countryside flocked to coastal China for factory jobs that offered an alternative to backbreaking agricultural work. By 2013, China's annual trade surpassed US$4 trillion, making it the largest trading nation in the world (Monaghan, 2014).

At the same time that China emerged as an engine of the global economy, China also earned the reputation for being the world's sweatshop (Kaufman, 2010). As economic development accelerated in coastal China, labor activists, student groups, NGOs, and the Western media exposed many serious labor rights violations in Chinese factories. Common labor rights violations included forced overtime, often with no overtime pay, corporal punishment and physical abuse, extremely low and below minimum wage hourly wages, wage arrears, no work contracts, no benefits, inadequate fire exits in factories and dormitories, exposure to toxic chemicals, child labor, and in extreme cases, bonded and slave-labor-type conditions (Chan, 1996, 1998; Cushman, 1998; Greenhouse, 1998; Kernaghan, 1998; Doorey, 2011).

While many of these problems are still endemic in China's factories, there have also been some improvements to working conditions in the past 20 years. Remuneration, when actually paid out, has increased over time for the majority of Chinese workers across industries (Bureau of Labor Statistics, 2014; Pi, 2014). By 2010, 71 percent of local residents and 34 percent of migrant workers had labor contracts (Gallagher et al., 2013, p. 12) and were therefore less susceptible to the abuses of informal work. Workers also have more legal rights to good working conditions than ever before. Prior to 1995, when the National People's Congress (NPC) passed the Labor Law of 1995, there was no labor law in China (Chan, 1998). The 2008 Labor Contract Law even entitles workers to social insurance benefits, including medical insurance, unemployment benefits, and pensions (China Labor Watch, 2014c). The legal and regulatory landscape in 2014 for workers is thus significantly different than it was in 1994.

However, implementation has been incremental and slow. Local governments hold responsibility for enforcement of labor standards, resulting in uneven enforcement across time, space, and industry. In many industries, including apparel, footwear, and electronics, there remain serious problems of unpaid wages, basic health and safety standard violations, and excessive overtime.

Chinese workers also continue to lack collective bargaining rights and the freedom to form independent unions. The state-run All China Federation of Trade Unions (ACFTU) remains the only legally permitted union in the country and is under direct supervision of the Chinese Communist Party (CCP) at every level. Workers can only unionize through the ACFTU, and their local branch can only bargain on behalf of workers at firms where it is active.

Chinese workers and their allies have to struggle for their legal rights to be enforced on a day-to-day and factory-by-factory basis. Resistance is episodic, and progress is sporadic, as well as incident, location, and issue specific. The ACFTU is only involved some of the time, and wildcat strikes increased throughout the late 2000s. Victories from these battles very rarely, if ever, transfer to Chinese workers broadly. There can be improvements on a factory floor one week and rollbacks the next.

We argue that violations persist in China because local governments have enormous incentives, due to the cadre evaluation system (CES), to side with suppliers against brands, workers, and sometimes even the central government. Furthermore, collusion between local governments and suppliers has persisted because the Chinese worker cluster remains divided and weak. Under what conditions can local governments be encouraged to uphold labor standards? Can the local government–supplier alignment be broken down?

The remainder of this chapter is divided into five parts. The following section examines the role and incentives of the central government in China. Following that, we focus on the local government, which we argue is the pivotal actor in the Chinese case. We then look at the intra-group conflicts and incentives within the worker cluster. We also provide a discussion of the role and incentives of supplier factories in China. The final section is an in-depth examination of the ongoing labor rights violations at two mega-suppliers to the footwear and electronics industries, Yue Yuen and Foxconn. These cases illustrate the friction that exists between brands and suppliers, collusion between supplier factories and local governments, and the nature of labor resistance in contemporary China.

THE ROLE AND INCENTIVES OF THE CENTRAL GOVERNMENT

Like all politicians and political parties, central government officials and the CCP strive for political survival above all else. Given the failure of the Great Leap Forward and the excesses of the Cultural Revolution following the death of Mao Zedong, the CCP had to significantly reinvent itself. Many China experts assert that the CCP's primary claim to popular legitimacy is its ability to achieve continued economic growth, which keeps the elites happy and the growing middle class content. Furthermore, after the downfall of the majority of the former Communist Bloc by 1989–91, the CCP has increasingly turned towards a form of state-directed capitalism or 'Capitalism with Chinese characteristics' and away from the old socialist anti-capitalist model (Chen, 2004; Huang, 2008).

China's development hinged upon reintegration into the global economy. This required the central government to 'participate in international and transnational institutional environments that embodied global norms' (Foot and Walter, 2010, p. 18). However, the CCP has been very pragmatic about its participation in the international community and has complied with, or at least paid lip service to, global norms when it suits their economic and political goals (Foot and Walter, 2010).

After nearly 20 years of isolation from the West, the Chinese economy was primarily composed of inefficient state-owned enterprises (SOEs) in heavy industry and subsistence agriculture. In 1976, more than 80 percent of the Chinese population was still rural, and the per capita annual income was just US$175 (in 2000 dollars) (World Bank, 2013). None of the Chinese SOEs were major players in world markets, capital was scarce, and so was technology (Chen, 2011). To deal with these problems and encourage development, in December 1978, reformist leaders of the CCP, led by Deng Xiaoping, began the process of Reform and Opening.

Many of these reforms created challenges and opportunities for Chinese workers. In 1980, China created four special economic zones (SEZs) located in the provinces of Guangdong and Fujian: Shenzhen,

Zhuhai, Xiamen, and Shantou. SEZs were intended to serve as laboratories for China's economic reforms. Following the creation of SEZs, millions of peasants left fields for factories and the promise of material gain. The central government issued the Coastal Development Strategy (CDS) in 1988 and claimed that it would 'link the coastal areas with the global marketplace' and 'promote export-oriented economic development through linkages to the inland areas' (Tzeng, 1991, p. 271). The CDS brought all of the open areas together under the same policy.

There were two major consequences of the CDS for working conditions. The first was that local officials were given more autonomy over authorizing and approving foreign investments worth up to US$30 million (Gallagher, 2007). Second, it was the first time that the central government explicitly redirected its focus away from heavy industry and towards labor-intensive light industry.

The central government also created and revised national labor laws. China's current labor law is articulated in the Labor Contract Law, which was passed in late 2007 and enacted in early 2008. The law requires employers to provide a contract for employees who have at least ten years' standing. The push to require contracts is aimed at protecting workers from being dismissed without cause. The law also requires employers to contribute to social security and sets minimum wages for employees on probation and for overtime hours. The formal labor dispute resolution process was established in the 1995 Labor Law, which consists of firm-level mediation, local-level arbitration, and finally civil court litigation. The central government also issues annual directives to local governments instructing them on how to follow national laws.

However, there is skepticism about the legal changes in China. Friedman and Lee (2010, p. 508) view China's legal reforms as 'a strategy of the state to regulate and contain labor resistance'. The CCP has given workers more legal rights on paper, but the government has used the law as a weapon to further divisions between workers and control collective worker mobilization.

There are material rewards to staying in power, and many of the CCP's top officials have benefitted greatly from China's economic successes. The current Premier, Xi Jinping, and his family have amassed fortunes (Forsythe et al., 2012). Past premiers and presidents of China, such as Hu Jintao and Wen Jiabao, and their families are also extremely wealthy and are alleged to have ties to profitable corporations including DreamWorks, Microsoft, Nokia, Merrill Lynch, ICBC, Tsinghua Holdings, and many others (Barboza and Lafraniere, 2012; Rabinovitch, 2012). Top officials of provinces, as well as mayors of Shanghai and other economic hubs, have also greatly profited from their political positions and connections.

However, the structure of China's economy may be changing. The central government realized that economic growth based on low-value-added labor was not sustainable in the long term and in the 2011–2015 Strategic Five Year Plan, announced plans to transition the economy towards high-value-added industries. Central and local governments have started to give tax benefits, as well as other concessions, to these industries. This has already started to shift some of the low-value-added businesses, including apparel, footwear, and low-value-added electronics, to countries such as Vietnam and Indonesia as well as to the interior provinces of China. As the core of China's economy shifts geographically and sectorally in the future, rewards and punishments for upholding labor standards will also change.

THE INCENTIVES OF LOCAL GOVERNMENTS

Ultimately, the central government leaves enforcement of economic policies and labor laws up to local governments. This has meant uneven, and sometimes non-existent, enforcement across industries and places in China. Local governments often collude with business, and supplier factories in particular, against workers because they face a complex set of incentives generated by the CES. Since the late 1970s, the CES has changed from a system that was focused on political attitudes to one that assesses cadres based on work performance and achievements. The exact performance criteria of any evaluation vary and are determined by the immediate superior level of government.

The CES is important because it is linked to material rewards and promotions, as well as punishments and demotions for local officials. The system was reformed in the late 1980s and early 1990s in order to promote competition among local officials at the same level based on 'quantitative measures of performance on the main "social, economic, and cultural" targets' (Whiting, 2004, p. 104). These targets include many items relevant to investment, economic development, and ultimately labor law implementation: increase gross value of industrial output, increase industrial profits, ranking by profit rate on total capital, increase the total value of exports, increase GDP, create new jobs, maintenance of the consumer price index, secure public order, reduce energy consumption, and protect the environment (Whiting, 2004; Wang, 2013). Each criterion is assigned a point value and points are awarded based on how closely local officials come to meeting the target. In theory, local officials who get the best score should be rewarded with promotions or other material benefits, and officials who score poorly are penalized and even demoted.

Due to the rotate and transfer system, most cadres also only have three to five years in any given position or place.

Some tentative predictions are possible about how each CES criterion would lead a local official to favor the interests of suppliers, brands, or workers. The need to increase the gross value of industrial output would lead officials to favor suppliers, as they own the factories that generate industrial output. This may also lead them to be supportive of management styles that increase productivity and output efficiency. The need to increase industrial profits and increase the total value of exports will also lead officials to favor suppliers. Fiscal decentralization in China compounds this effect by making local officials responsible for the majority of their own revenue generation and expenditures.

However, in order to increase industrial profits and any resulting tax revenue, not only will suppliers have to increase productivity, capacity, and output, but they will also have to maintain and increase the number of contracts that they bring in from brands. More contracts may also create more jobs, which means that officials would favor the interests of both brands and suppliers. This is difficult because in order to be competitive and save costs, suppliers may press workers to work harder, faster, and for less.

Wary of their reputation, brands will also be pressuring suppliers to implement their codes of conduct and meet the minimum legal labor standards. Brands may threaten to revoke or move contracts if suppliers fail to do so, as the Yue Yuen case below illustrates. Unless these threats are actually followed through, however, neither local officials nor suppliers are likely to change their behavior.

The situation becomes even more complicated because increased output and pressure on workers may also lead to excessive overtime, high rates of turnover, and ultimately worker unrest. If worker unrest cannot be contained or dealt with by supplier factories and it spills out onto the streets, local officials may be docked, demoted, or even fired for not maintaining public security and social stability in their locality.

On one hand, some officials may have the incentive to work hard to repress or hide worker unrest. This operates in favor of suppliers and, if exposed, against brands and against local officials who are likely to be punished as a result. On the other hand, some officials may realize the value of maintaining contracts with big brands. Under circumstances where media scrutiny domestically and internationally is intense, and labor unrest is disruptive to production, investment and/or daily life for local residents, local officials may order suppliers to respond to the demands of workers. However, this is a rare occurrence because foreign and domestic media and the Internet are strictly monitored and censored by the CCP, making it difficult, though not impossible, for many of these stories to be exposed.

Therefore, local officials have to perform an economic and political balancing act where they must simultaneously achieve economic growth and development, social stability, and environmental protection. This is a difficult task, and, as observed by both Western and Chinese media reports and research, criteria that support economic growth and development have tended to be the focus of many local officials, even while the environment has been ravaged and labor riots and protests exist, to varying extents, all over China.

THE ROLE AND INCENTIVES OF WORKERS

Another factor that contributes to the lack of enforcement is the intense divisions among workers and their allies in China. Chinese workers are divided for many reasons, chief among them being the household registration system (*hukou*), a Mao-era system of labor mobility control. The *hukou* system creates a conflict of interests among workers because it divides workers, legally, into three categories: urban, rural, and migrant. Worker citizenship status confers rewards and punishments in the form of education, healthcare, and social security benefits based on place of registration. Migrant workers in urban areas can only access an extremely limited version of these benefits. For example, a migrant worker with Chengdu *hukou* working in Dongguan cannot access the same benefits, in terms of education, healthcare, and even housing, as a Chinese worker that holds Dongguan *hukou*. This bias applies not only to rural *hukou* holders who come to cities to work from other provinces but to all rural *hukou* holders, including those that work within their home province.

Workers with rural *hukou* are rarely employed as permanent employees and often work without contracts. In the city of Wuxi in 2005, there were 100 000 temporary workers without contracts and 80 000 were rural migrant workers (Zhang et al., 2010, p. 381). Even if workers are not discriminated against based upon the location of their *hukou*, they often face workplace discrimination due to their status as a formal permanent contract worker or a temporary worker (Barrientos, 2001; Zhang, 2010). Local governments have also intentionally changed the incentives of firms to hire temporary workers without contracts by taxing firms based on the number of their formal workers (Zhu et al., 2012).

Furthermore, low-skilled migrant workers, high-skilled workers, and SOE workers all have very different interests and demands that they make on firms and local governments. High-skilled workers and public employees are much more likely to protest or riot about removal of pre-existing or historical privileges, such as pensions and healthcare, whereas migrant workers are more likely to protest or riot regarding wage arrears, health and safety violations, and minimum wage.

Adding to this discord, Chinese workers lack collective bargaining rights and independent unionization is strictly prohibited. The state-backed union, ACFTU, remains subordinate to the CCP, and in most cases, has been in strong alignment with local governments and firm management rather than workers. The majority of Chinese workers therefore believe that the ACFTU is not only unrepresentative, but also completely irrelevant. The lack of free and independent unionization and restrictions on civil society has meant that formal claims-making continues to be individualized, rather than collective in nature.

This is not to say that the ACFTU has never been an important or relevant actor in labor standards outcomes in China. For example, Friedman (2012, p. 461) argues that since the economic downturn in 2008, the 'relationship between the ACFTU and migrant workers is one characterized by divergence and conflict'. As workers radicalized, and strikes, protests, and riots were observed all over coastal China, the union's administrative approach to labor conflict was called into question and resulted in some localized discussion about reform of the union. Many labor advocacy organizations, such as the Fair Labor Association (FLA), China Labour Bulletin (CLB) and China Labor Watch (CLW), have encouraged democratic union elections within factories, but there has been little progress on this issue (Friedman, 2012). Therefore, despite increases in riots and protests in coastal China, a sustained and coordinated countervailing force still does not exist. This equilibrium allows suppliers to continually violate labor rights and Chinese labor laws.

THE ROLE AND INCENTIVES OF SUPPLIERS

As the manufacturing center of the world, China's supplier factories have been the key to the country's economic success and growth since 1978. Like suppliers everywhere, supplier factories in China are profit motivated while also facing upstream business pressures from brands and retailers. Some suppliers in China have adapted to these pressures by creating some of the biggest supply chain cities and industrial clusters in the world. For example, Luen Thai,[1] a Hong Kong-listed firm that specializes in apparel, footwear, and accessories production, has developed its own supply chain city in Dongguan, Shenzhen that is:

a two-million-square-foot-factory, a three-hundred-room hotel, a dormitory for the factory's four thousand workers, and a product-development center. The factory permits apparel manufacturer Liz Claiborne and other Luen Thai customers to work in a single location, their designers meeting directly with technicians from the factory and fabric mills to plan production far more efficiently. The consolidated supply chain is projected to reduce Liz Claiborne and Luen Thai staff by 40 percent, cutting costs and improving turnaround by providing tight coordination over logistics. (Applebaum, 2008, p. 72)

The perceived benefits of supply chain cities are increased efficiency and decreased costs, both of which increase profits. Supply chain cities also serve as counterweights to major apparel and footwear brands in two ways. First, mega-suppliers reduce the number of options for production available to brands. This makes it more difficult for brands to terminate contracts with them. Second, many mega-suppliers are increasingly specialized and are clustered in ways that make it more efficient and cost effective for brands to use mega-suppliers over small and medium-sized enterprises, even if small and medium-sized enterprises have cheaper wages. Supply chain cities also provide economic incentives to brands for investment by cutting costs and turnaround time. They also fit the changing economic goals of the central and local governments towards moving out of labor-intensive light industries by employing not only low-skilled manufacturing workers, but also service workers and high-skilled workers charged with production development and design. Mega-suppliers help keep business, and therefore tax revenue and jobs, in China. China's supply chain cities, which are often funded by foreign direct investment (FDI), have scale-driven specialization that lends the country a competitive advantage over its competitors (Gereffi, 2009).

Although mega-suppliers are helping to keep business in China despite rising wage costs, mega-suppliers still face many of the same incentives as their small and medium-sized counterparts. Chief among these are absorbing material and production cost increases, dealing with quick turnaround demands from buyers, and employee turnover.

Mega-suppliers also share with small and medium-sized enterprises similar beliefs about migrant workers. Namely, they hold a long-term 'belief that rural workers are different from urban workers and should be treated differently' (Zhang et al., 2010, p. 383). In their study of contemporary human resource management (HRM) systems in Mainland China, Zhu et al. (2012) find that both management and the urban workers believe rural workers to be fundamentally different. They quote a human resources manager of an SOE who said that there was no point in paying rural workers the same as urban workers because 'rural migrants usually lack commitment and loyalty to companies. They require strict management ... so we can secure production' (ibid., p. 397). The manager also believed the company offered rural workers a good wage despite their low skill levels.

These beliefs are common throughout SOE factories in China as well as other supplier factories, regardless of size, location, or ownership type. Most managers believe that the primary benefit of employing migrant workers is their low cost, that migrant workers need to be controlled by management, and that migrant workers receive the working conditions and pay that they deserve (and sometimes even better than they deserve) as low-skilled, often transient, workers. We now turn to the cases of Yue Yuen and Foxconn to illustrate mega-supplier behavior and their relationships with workers, brands, and local governments in China.

LABOR RESISTANCE AT NIKE'S BIGGEST SUPPLIER: YUE YUEN

'In the past,' Thomas Shi, a deputy Yue Yuen manager in a Chinese factory told a Financial Times journalist cynically: 'it was all about whether you could hit the workers or slap them. Now we talk about how we should celebrate their birthdays'. (Quoted in Merk, 2008, p. 89)

In 2014, workers went on a two-week strike at Yue Yuen's Dongguan facility. The event illustrates two points important to our argument. First, consumer groups and private politics were of limited influence on the local government. Second, the Dongguan local government was aligned with Yue Yuen, but the alignment had limits. As Yue Yuen began to lose contracts, unemployment increased, and tax revenue decreased. These factors are among the criteria the CES uses to evaluate local officials; so, too, is protracted social unrest. Fear of poor evaluations changed the incentives of local governments, rupturing the alignment with Yue Yuen, at least publicly. Consequently, relevant ministries ordered the company to follow national labor laws and respond to worker demands for the social welfare benefits.

Before going into further detail about the April 2014 strike, a brief description of the Chinese garment industry and Yue Yuen is helpful. In 2012, garments and footwear accounted for less than 10 percent of China's total export revenue, yet the Chinese garment industry remains central to apparel global supply chains (International Trade Centre, 2014). In the same year, China was the world's largest exporter of clothing, exporting over US$153 billion (current dollars) worth of garments (World Trade Organization, 2014). According to the World

Trade Organization there are over 100 000 garment manufacturers, employing more than 10 million workers in China. Seventy percent of the total garment output in China comes from just five coastal provinces: Fujian, Guangdong, Jiangsu, Shandong, and Zhejiang.

One of these garment manufacturers, Yue Yuen Industrial Holdings, was founded in 1988 when Pou Chen, a Taiwan-based firm, decided to move production sites from Taiwan to China to escape labor shortages, rising wages, and currency appreciation. Yue Yuen's rapid expansion and growth in China in the 1980s and 1990s was:

> underpinned by a repressive labor strategy based on preventing workers from organizing and exercising collective bargaining power. Its high productivity rates are the result of long hours and forced overtime, for example, through its use of a piece-rate quota system in which quotas are set very high and are difficult to meet. Further, it enforces a strategy of strict discipline and punishment in a military-style factory regime, sometimes described as 'management by terror and browbeating'. (Merk, 2008, p. 88)

In 1998 Charles Kernaghan presented findings from his book, *Behind the Label: 'Made in China'*, (1998), to the National Labor Committee in the United States. One of the supplier factories that Kernaghan exposed for having poor labor conditions was Yue Yuen. He reported that the company was paying workers very low wages, and that workers were working between 60 and 84 hours per workweek, forced to work overtime, and given no overtime premium. Yue Yuen workers were also exposed to excessive noise pollution and toxic fumes in the factory. Furthermore, although Nike passed its corporate code of conduct in 1992, in 1998 workers at Yue Yuen reported that they had never heard of these codes.

Yue Yuen has maintained dominance in the industry, in part, by creating a supply chain city in Dongguan (Applebaum, 2008). The size of Yue Yuen provides the firm with some bargaining power vis-à-vis brands. According to a competitor, 'If Yuen Yuen said today, "I won't supply anymore to Nike," then Nike would be scared' (Merk, 2008, p. 88). Despite negative press and creation of CSR programs by Nike, Reebok, and Adidas and other major brands, Yue Yuen's factories remain locations of labor violations and worker unrest.

On 14 April 2014, workers at Yue Yuen's Gaobu factory, the very same supplier that Kernaghan criticized Nike for using in 1998, went on strike. Workers walked off the job when the company failed to pay social insurance and housing benefits. According to CLW (China Labor Watch, 2014a), after a week of work stoppage, the factory responded to worker demands by saying that it would increase worker subsidies by 230 RMB per month (less than US$50) and that social insurance would be paid for workers according to the law starting on 1 May 2014. This did not assuage workers, who were already owed millions of dollars in unpaid social insurance, and the strike continued.

Throughout this period, workers and labor NGO groups reported to the media that Yue Yuen and the Dongguan (a district of Shenzhen) government worked together to force workers back into the factory. Workers told the Associated Press that 'the factory has been tricking us for 10 years' and the '[local] government, labor bureau, social security bureau and the company were all tricking us together' (BBC News, 2014). The local government also aided Yue Yuen during the strike by providing coercive force. Two worker representatives, Zhang Zhiru and Lin Dong, from the Shenzhen Chunfeng Labor Dispute Service Center, entered the factory at the beginning of the strike to negotiate with management but were quickly detained by local police. Zhang and Lin reported via social media that they had instructed workers not to use violence or break the law and that most of the strike activities had been non-violent (Chan, 2014; China Labor Watch, 2014a). Police in riot gear took dozens of workers away even though there were no reported clashes between the workers and police (McCombs, 2014).

During the strike, buyers and brands had mixed reactions. A Nike spokesperson was quoted as saying that Nike was in 'close contact with the Yue Yuen management' but stressed that negotiations were between Yue Yuen, its workers, and the government. In subsequent interviews Nike officials told the media that they wanted 'to invest in the partners that are really doing the right thing with the workforce' (Valdmanis, 2014). As the strike entered its second week, Adidas, one of Yue Yuen's biggest customers, transferred some orders out of the factory because they were falling behind production and delivery schedules. However, 'while some orders were shifted to other suppliers at no point did it consider pulling out of the factory' (Borromeo, 2014).

After Adidas moved some contracts (and possibly some specialized footwear machinery), the strike ended when the Dongguan government ordered Yue Yuen to provide back pay to workers for all owed social insurance (Lin et al., 2014). The Dongguan government issued a document that included 'responses to worker demands from the Bureau of Social Insurance, the Bureau of Human Resources, the Housing Fund Management Center, and Yue Yuen factory's management' (China Labor Watch, 2014b), meaning that multiple subnational government bureaus' interests aligned with Yue Yuen, after more than two weeks and high losses in profits and revenue, to respond to the demands of the workers. Government officials and union leaders hailed this as a successful end to the labor dispute, but CLW remained skeptical that Yue Yuen would fully implement the measures. Given the lack of transparency that still exists in China, the exact details regarding the negotiations between the various bureaus, the local government, and Yue Yuen remains unclear.

The 2014 Yue Yuen strike illustrates two points that make it distinct from the United States, Honduras, and Bangladesh cases. First, consumer groups and private politics were of questionable influence on the local government. Adidas reported that it moved contracts because timeliness of orders could not be guaranteed. Nike initially declined to comment about the labor dispute at Yue Yuen but noted its ability for flexible production to *Bloomberg News*. After the strike was over, Nike later claimed that it had worked closely with the Yue Yuen management on the strike issues (McCombs, 2014; Lin et al., 2014). While consumer pressure and negative publicity certainly has affected the behavior of Adidas and Nike in specific cases, in this particular instance it appears to have had limited influence on the outcome.

Second, workers were able to get concessions from Yue Yuen because the strike made non-compliance with Chinese labor law costly for the factory management and the local Dongguan government officials. These changes in incentives also led to a short-term breakdown of alignments between the local government and the firm. The strike lasted more than two weeks, and Yue Yuen began to lose contracts and industrial output. Both of these factors count against government officials when they are being assessed by the CES, as does protracted social unrest. Officials in local government and the relevant ministries responded to these new incentives, and updated their beliefs about the rewards and punishments they might face. This resulted in local government breaking alignment with Yue Yuen, at least publicly, and ordering the company to follow national labor laws regarding social insurance benefits. Yue Yuen's economic calculations about the protest had also changed, as the company estimated a loss of US$27 million in direct costs due to lost profits and additional airfreight costs in just two weeks (Lin et al., 2014). The Foxconn case that follows, though highlighting some differences, similarly illustrates the strong role that the supplier–local-government alignment plays in labor rights outcomes for Chinese workers.

LABOR RESISTANCE AT APPLE'S BIGGEST SUPPLIER: FOXCONN

Hon Hai has a workforce of over one million worldwide and human beings are also animals, to manage one million animals gives me a headache. (Terry Gou, head of Foxconn, quoted in Blodget, 2012)

Foxconn lives the culture of 'random acts of love, people orientation, and green operations'. (Foxconn, 2013, p. 1)

The ongoing labor rights violations at Foxconn demonstrate that even when alignments change between actors in favor of protecting workers, suppliers in China can easily find new local governments to collude with. In the post-suicide period (2011–present), the Dongguan government and Foxconn were forced by an onslaught of negative press and NGO pressure to make visible changes on the factory floors and open factories to FLA audits. At the same time, Foxconn quickly made new alignments with local governments in interior provinces like Henan and Sichuan, and moved a good portion of its production away from the coast. Interior local officials benefitted enormously from the massive investment and employment that Foxconn provided their provinces and districts. However, labor violations have been persistent in the new factories, and in some cases that surfaced in 2012–14 local authorities have not only been complicit but, at times, also directly responsible for the violations.

Of all the businesses manufacturing electronics in Mainland China, few have garnered as much media attention in recent years as Foxconn (Hon Hai Limited). Foxconn is a mega-supplier and the world's largest contract electronic manufacturing firm. In China alone, the Taiwanese business employs over 1 million workers (Foxconn, 2013) and produces electronics for basically all major brands, including Apple, Sony, Dell, IBM, Nokia, Hewlett-Packard, Amazon, Sharp, and Nintendo, to name but a few.

Foxconn and one of its largest buyers, Apple, have suffered the majority of criticisms from media, governments, and labor NGOs, regarding poor working conditions in Foxconn's mega-factories in China since the mid-2000s. As noted in the discussion of Apple in Chapter 2, Foxconn made media headlines in the United States and China in 2006 after the firm sued two Shanghai-based reporters for 30 million yuan, accusing them of negatively affecting its reputation with articles about the firm's labor law violations (*Xinhua*, 2006). In 2010, Foxconn came under fire when 18 Foxconn workers attempted suicide, resulting in 14 deaths and leaving four workers severely injured (Chan, 2013).

The Foxconn suicides shocked consumers, brands, and the media, and left many asking what could possibly be happening in these factories to drive young workers to take their own lives. Lucas et al. (2013, p. 91) argue that Foxconn's 'total institution structure imposed unique indignities on its workers that both raised questions of their self-respect and self-worth, as well as gave rise to multiple episodes of disrespectful communication'. Central to this lack of dignity was overwork and a harsh management style. Workers reported that they were 'made to work like machines' (ibid., p. 97).

The owner and CEO of Foxconn, Terry Gou, has a personal management style laid out in a company document 'Gou's Quotations', that promotes coercion, control, and a culture of absolute obedience (Dean, 2007). In the factories, banners with slogans such as 'A harsh environment is a good thing', 'Hungry people have especially clear minds' and 'Work hard on the job today or work hard to find a job tomorrow' hang around the factory floors (Elmer-DeWitt, 2010). Given that workers were also often isolated from friends or co-workers who spoke their dialect and believed their union representatives to be of little help to their situation, their only recourse to end their suffering and humiliation was death (Lucas et al., 2013).

In response to the suicide crisis, Foxconn strung more than 3 000 000m² of mesh netting around its buildings to catch jumpers and windows were covered with wire and locked. They also set up a 24-hour counseling center, and even forced workers to sign a no-suicide pledge (Chan, 2013). Following intense criticism over the no-suicide pledge, this administrative requirement was eventually dropped.

During this time, the official trade union staff who were supposed to be responsible for managing communication between Foxconn workers and the company were missing in action and had failed to investigate or report the workplace conditions that led up to the 2010 suicides. This is partially due to the fact that:

> from 1988 through 2006, Foxconn, like many other foreign-invested enterprises evaded its basic responsibilities and failed to set up a trade union to strengthen workers' communication and management. When Chinese governments across different levels directly intervened in the mobilization, the Longhua factory was 'unionized' only on the last day of 2006 (IHLO, 2 January 2007). Taking immediate control over the newly formed union, Foxconn CEO Terry Gou appointed his special personal assistant, Chen Peng, as union chairwoman. (ibid., p. 7)

This example illustrates two points about the state-sanctioned union in China. First, many foreign-owned factories, although obligated by national law to have union branches on their factory floors, openly violate Chinese labor law and do not even have the official state-run union available to workers. Second, even when the unions are present they are responsible first to the CCP, then the factory, and last the rank and file workers. In the case of the Foxconn workers pre-2012, the union functioned as a company union and primarily addressed the interests of Foxconn rather than the workers.

In response to international outcry, local officials and Foxconn executives responded in a few ways. First, local government officials publicly criticized Foxconn but also tried to cover up additional negative coverage. They banned negative reporting about Foxconn, and one official was quoted as saying 'all related content before the 12th jump should be locked up … the front pages of news websites and news center pages, blogs, micro-blogs, there should be no news related to "Foxconn" except from official sources' (ibid.).

Second, the suicides, combined with increasing labor shortages and rising pressures for industrial upgrading, also led Foxconn to make the decision to move from its historic location in Shenzhen, Guangdong province to China's interior. While some argue that Foxconn moved inland in order to get cheaper wages, the more compelling argument is that this move was primarily to access the source of Chinese migrant labor in the workers' home provinces such as Sichuan and Henan. An additional benefit to Foxconn of this move was the offer of bargain basement deals on land, taxes, recruitment of workers, and public housing by the local governments in these provinces, eager for both investment and job growth. This again illustrates the intimate relationship between local authorities in China and supplier factories.

In 2011, under the pressure of Apple and continuing popular criticism, Foxconn agreed to let the FLA conduct an audit of its Longhua, Guanlan, and Chengdu factories in 2012. The FLA conducted an audit of the factories, using its Sustainable Compliance Initiative (SCI) methodology, and interviewed more than 35 000 randomly selected Foxconn workers over a month-long investigation (Fair Labor Association, 2012b). The investigation found at least 50 violations of the FLA code of conduct and Chinese labor law in areas of health and safety, worker integration and communication, wages, and working hours (ibid.). After the first inspection, both 'Apple and Foxconn agreed to an action plan of 360 items to be completed by 1 July, 2013. As of January, 98.3 percent of them had been achieved' (Goel, 2013).

While this seems an impressive feat, the media has found continued labor violations at Foxconn's factories, new and old. A Chinese-language report 'Entering the West – An Investigative Report on Foxconn's Move to the Interior' released by Peking University and Tsinghua University, found Foxconn's new internship program with some 200 vocational schools rife with labor abuses, including excessive overtime, low pay, illegal placement and recruitment fees, and a harsh production environment since as early as 2009. The report concluded that in many, if not most cases local authorities were directly involved in the recruitment process and some were given recruitment fees for fulfilling Foxconn's worker quotas. Other officials filed health checks and insurance registrations for employees, a task that is typically the responsibility of the firm (Du, 2011).

From summer 2012 through 2013, media reports corroborated the findings that Foxconn was using unpaid, underage, and sometimes even forced labor in the form of vocational student interns. In Yantai Development Zone, in Northern China's Shandong province, *Xinhua* (2012) reported that the Administration Committee of the Development Zone was responsible for recruiting the interns for Foxconn in order to deal with a severe labor shortage. The interns were later found to be only 14–16 years of age, which violates Chinese labor law. CLW and *The New York Times* alleged that a Foxconn factory in Zhengzhou, Henan province was similarly abusing internship labor (Barboza and Duhigg, 2012; Reuters, 2013). In response, Foxconn released public statements defending its practice by saying that the vocational schools 'recruit the students under the supervision of the local government' (quoted in Barboza and Duhigg, 2012). Apple declined to comment. This, again, illustrates the close relationship between suppliers and local officials in Mainland China, despite brand pressure and strong activist campaigns abroad.

Like most other Fortune 500 companies, Foxconn has a code of conduct and a social and environmental responsibility (SER) committee. The company became a member of the Electronic Industry Citizenship Coalition (EICC) in 2005, created its SER committee in 2005, a Global SER Committee in 2007, and published its first code of conduct in 2008, and an updated version in 2012 (Foxconn, 2013, pp. 6–7). The Global SER Committee is responsible for audits 'to ensure that SER policy is implemented fully and completely at every manufacturing site' using a team of over 1000 professionals, as of 2013, dedicated to carrying out these duties (ibid., p. 6). Following the FLA audits and the update of the code in 2012, Foxconn required that all employees be trained in its terms, which include a focus on 'ethics, employees and human rights, health and safety, environment, management system, and restriction on use of conflict minerals and anti-corruption' (ibid., p. 7).

It is too early to determine the effectiveness of Foxconn's CSR initiatives and the FLA audits. However, it is clear that Foxconn's incentives have changed, as continued violations create tensions with its largest partner, Apple, and draw criticism from the FLA and the media. What remains unclear is whether the upper management at Foxconn has actually changed its beliefs about appropriate labor standards. The move to the interior of China indicates that the company may be trying not only to access China's labor source, but also to escape the attention of the media, who face more restrictions and tighter controls in Western China than coastal China. Additionally, Foxconn's collusion with local authorities on the internship program suggest that both actors are looking for solutions to the labor shortage problem, even if these solutions are at the expense of Chinese workers and violate Chinese labor law.

CONCLUSION

In August 2014, an explosion in Kunshan, Jiangsu province, left at least 75 dead and 186 seriously burned at Zhongrong Metal Factory. Despite having protective laws on the books, worker health and safety in China is still a major problem (Young, 2014). A team of medical doctors who surveyed 7610 female workers in the electronics industry in four provinces in China in 2012 discovered pervasive health and safety problems. The survey found that nearly 52 percent of all workers were exposed to at least one occupational hazard including chemical and ergonomic hazards. Sixty percent of the female workers reported having work-related diseases, such as chronic back pain, hearing and vision loss, and chronic headaches (Yu et al., 2013, p. 193). The medical team concluded that while many see the electronics industry as safe and clean, it poses serious risks to the health of reproductive-age females, and that 'these hazards are often widely disregarded by factory owners, government officials, and health professionals' (ibid.).

As we have argued, these types of violations persist because local governments and suppliers collude against the interests of workers, and often against the interests of multinational brands. Local government officials are willing and eager to work with supplier factories because the CCP has created a political equilibrium through use of the CES and fiscal decentralization, which creates short time horizons and a 'development and investment at all costs' policy outlook. Local officials are motivated to increase export outputs, raise productivity, and attract investment from Fortune 500 companies. Those who perform well are rewarded with promotions and other material benefits. Furthermore, there are intense divisions within the worker cluster stemming from the *hukou* system and strict repression of independent unionization. This has prevented Chinese workers from forming a sustained or coherent countervailing force to business.

These factors all combine to create immense barriers to change, even when opportunities for leverage exist. Transnational campaigns and media attention did, temporarily, change the calculations of Foxconn. Unfortunately, Foxconn still seems to be acting against the interests of its workers, just in different ways and in different locations. Local officials are still complicit. The unusual levels of alignment among workers during the Yue Yuen strike managed to briefly break down the alignment between local governments and suppliers. However, investment and development had to be threatened in order to change the calculations of the firm and the local government. Without a sustained movement, the CLW and other organizations remain skeptical that the firm will even follow through on its promises to pay workers what was owed to them. Long-term beliefs about rewards and punishments for upholding labor standards are incredibly difficult to change. They are even more difficult to change in places where the political system consistently reinforces divisions among workers, prohibits independent unionization, and rewards local officials for economic development and revenue generation above all else.

NOTE

1. In 2004, Luen Thai and Yue Yuen, the Taiwanese mega-supplier of Nike, Adidas, and other famous athletic footwear brands detailed in the case below, created a strategic joint venture called Yuen Thai to leverage their combined sports apparel manufacturing supply chains in the sports apparel market (Yue Yuen Industrial, 2004, pp. 1–2).

10. Conclusion

We began this project aware of the complexities of the supply chain, the difficulties of creating effective alliances for raising labor standards, and the obstacles to sustained improvement. Subsequent thinking and research confirmed our initial assessment but also revealed opportunities for leverage. Our findings are largely consistent with earlier analyses of successful reforms in which protest and organization become political resources (Lipsky, 1968; Lipsky and Levi, 1972). Actors who have little or no government or corporate power can have important and consequential impact on policy; they do so by engaging in actions that capture the attention of the public, particularly those with influence, who then exert their clout to reform practice and policy. Supply chain workers and many of their allies, including the most vocal of student groups, lack direct power over business and government but they have a capacity to tarnish brand and official reputations, mobilize public outrage, and find support within universities, religious organizations, and political parties. When successful, these campaigns lead to brands and governments taking responsibility for enforcing labor standards in factories and among suppliers.

Unfortunately, such campaigns are often most effective in the aftermath of terrible disasters, such as Rana Plaza. Even more unfortunately from our perspective, such protests do not always arise. When they do, they can fail because of opposition, indifference as a result of a failure to provide information or information that moves the public, and divisions among potential allies.

Aligning interests, we find, is not the same as establishing an alliance. Changing incentives and beliefs so that key actors share a common purpose is an important step in the process of crafting a political coalition, but it is only a first step and one very dependent on the quality and credibility of information about public sentiment and the likely behavior of potential allies and opponents. Potential movements and campaigns often struggle with how best to pursue their common goals and disagree forcefully on strategy, sometimes with harmful consequences to their capacity to act collectively and effectively (McAdam, 1982; McAdam et al., 2001; Levi and Murphy, 2006).

In the rest of this conclusion, we consider what we have learned about the opportunities for leverage and the conditions necessary for translating those opportunities for leverage into improved labor standards.

THE ROLE OF INFORMATION

In the United States, the 1911 Triangle Shirtwaist Factory fire played an important role in changing actors' beliefs and incentives around labor standards, by providing new and unavoidable information about the conditions faced by many workers. By taking advantage of an increasing political support within the Democratic Party, workers and their allies were able to use this information as an opportunity for increased leverage to improve labor standards.

The international 'anti-sweatshop' movement initiated in the 1990s also began with revelations of shocking information about working conditions and low pay in factories producing for Nike, Levi Strauss, and other brands. In these cases, however, the source of salient information was not a high-profile disaster but instrumental information gathering and political action by labor and other activist groups. Increasing public awareness of, and shock over working conditions in industries such as footwear and apparel, helped forge opportunities for leverage. The loose alignment of consumer and worker interests generated pressure on global brands by threatening sales and potentially profit margins. The combined pressure of end consumers, alongside workers and their allies, modified the beliefs of global brand executives about acceptable actions and increased their incentives to support workers' rights in at least limited ways. Nike and Levi Strauss, consequently, ramped up their private regulatory programs by creating corporate codes of conduct, conducting audits of some supplier factories, and eventually making their supplier list available to the public.

In the cases presented in the chapter on Honduras, it was local Honduran labor activists themselves who brought information on their illegal treatment under Honduran labor law to the attention of US-based groups, who then used that information to campaign on their behalf.

Our chapter on Bangladesh, on the other hand, most closely resembles the Triangle Shirtwaist Factory fire in that a high-profile incident brought attention to dangerous working conditions that made both the Rana Plaza collapse and its high death toll possible. This case highlighted the interaction of unexpected events and human action. While transnational advocates had been seeking to bring attention to working conditions in the country's ready-made garment sector for years, it was this incident that thrust those conditions (and advocates' interpretations of them) into the global media spotlight in a way that realigned many actors' interests and beliefs, creating a momentary opportunity for leverage.

Finally, in our chapter on China, Yue Yuen workers exposed their grievances by staging one of the largest strikes in recent history for two weeks. Additional information was brought to light by watchdog organizations based in Hong Kong and the United States. Information about working conditions in Foxconn factories spread both because of a high-profile series of worker suicides and because of increased attention from Western media like *The New York Times*. This attention was heightened because of the connection to Apple, one of the world's most well-known brands.

These cases illustrate that workers or their allies often generate information that can be used to change incentives and, ultimately, alignments between the actor clusters. Even when new information is the result of a high-profile incident like the Rana Plaza factory collapse, workers and their allies still play a role in disseminating and framing that information. The role of information highlights how the media itself plays an important role. Freedoms of speech, media, and information are important in enabling workers and their allies to gather and spread information. Firms and governments themselves also engage in strategic information politics, attempting to frame situations in their preferred ways to prevent or mitigate reputational damage. While information is critical for the rest of the process to occur, it is ultimately how the actor clusters respond to this new information that leads to changes in labor standards.

CONFIGURATIONS OF ALIGNMENT

Our framework highlights how different configurations of interest and conflict across the clusters of actors can create new opportunities for leverage. Actors in a given cluster will have more opportunities to advance their interests when they have greater alignment of interests within their own cluster, when they have greater alignments of interest, or outright coalitions, with actors in other clusters, and when there are conflicts among the actors in the cluster they seek to influence.

Increased alignment among members of a cluster can facilitate their ability to exert influence on actors in other clusters; intra-cluster divisions can be a hindrance to such influence. In the Russell and Nike cases in Honduras, Honduran workers and their allies locally and in the United States were able to work closely together to pursue a cohesive strategy, facilitating their ability to influence institutional consumers, and ultimately brands. On the other hand, the loss of confidence in unions by their historical allies contributed to the decline of labor standards in the United States.

Alignments of interest across clusters also create opportunities for leverage. Importantly, these alignments can be formalized in alliances or can occur with little or no coordination. The chapter on China is illustrative of this point. The local governments' interests in both the Yue Yuen and Foxconn cases became aligned with the interests of workers, not because of communication or incorporation of workers into the local government, but because of intense media scrutiny, international criticism, consumer pressure, and brand pressure that threatened local stability and economic growth. There was no formal coalition of workers and the local governments, nor is there evidence of coordination between the rank-and-file workers and the local officials during the negotiations. In the Yue Yuen case, some union and labor representatives did negotiate with the factory management directly and may have even met with local officials, but by and large the alignment was informal and short-lived.

On the other hand, alignments across clusters were more formalized in the Honduras case. The local union, CGT Honduras, has formal links with both the Worker Rights Consortium, the AFL-CIO, and with unions in other Central American countries. A great deal of communication and coordination took place between these groups and United Students Against Sweatshops chapters on US university campuses. Through effective organization on the part of NGOs and worker allies, unions in Honduras were in direct and sustained communication with representatives within the university trademarks and licensing offices of influential institutional purchasers. As pressure began to build, workers were also eventually granted access to Nike and Russell representatives.

The cross-cluster alignment of interests that emerged between institutional purchasers and factory workers was what led to the ultimate concessions by brands. The alignment of interests between consumers and workers could be leveraged in ways that directly threatened the sales of global brands, causing the interests of the brands in question to shift. In order to ensure that profits were not threatened and business was not lost, brands gave way to worker and consumer demands, allowing for some tangible improvements to labor standards in the factories in question. In some cases, management norms changed, modifying their beliefs about the appropriate course of action. More likely is that the campaigns altered management beliefs about when and how they were likely to face exposure and punitive action for tolerating labor violations.

Finally, divisions among the actors in a cluster can serve not just as a barrier but also sometimes as an opportunity to actors seeking to influence them. One of the most notable ways in which this can occur is when workers and their allies are able to take advantage of conflicts between suppliers and brands. When workers and their allies are able to bring the interests of brands into alignment with their own, through alliances with ethical consumers or institutional purchasers, by creating meaningful risks to the brand's reputation, or through effective persuasion, those brands must then try to put pressure on suppliers to improve labor standards. Although the divisions between brands and suppliers mean that suppliers are likely to resist these efforts, they also mean that pressure to improve standards can become part of brands' overall strategies of dealing with suppliers in ways that seek to improve quality and efficiency and reduce costs. When confronted with uncooperative suppliers, brands may also take more substantial action on their own, as Nike was ultimately pressured to do after its suppliers in Honduras shut down without compensating workers.

However, it is important to note that divisions among worker and government clusters can also create greater opportunities for business actors to exert their own leverage. As documented here, conflicting interests among workers has facilitated business influence in the United States and in China. Further, the many misalignments of interest between local officials and the central government in China have created opportunities for businesses to capture local government.

SUSTAINABILITY OF IMPROVEMENTS

Our analysis of brand and country cases illustrates that wins for supply chain workers and improvements in labor standards are often temporary and issue-specific, and can easily be reneged. We argue that in order for labor standards to be upheld in a sustainable and long-term fashion there must be government institutionalization of labor rights through regulation and effective enforcement. Additionally, workers and their allies have to keep constant pressure on brands and governments to follow through and implement laws and contracts. As the work of Locke and co-authors (2007b, 2013) shows, private codes of conduct and regulation are markedly limited. The results of our quantitative chapter provide additional nuances to the conditions for raising labor standards. The findings reveal the importance of democratic governments, left-wing political parties in power, and state capacity in ensuring improvements, especially in terms of enforcement in practice.

Finally, neither do our case study chapters provide a basis for optimism in their long-term outlook. The victory for workers in Nike factories in Honduras was explicitly one time only and not applicable to workers anywhere else in Nike's supply chain. The changes presented in the China chapter were largely one-off improvements that are already being undermined by shifting more production into the country's interior. In Bangladesh, it may be too soon to draw conclusions on long-term sustainability, but already there are indications that the response by global brands has been weak, non-committal, and impeded by division into two competing initiatives. While the US chapter shows a case where labor standards improvements were written into law, enforced, and effective over many decades, the recent trends indicated declining labor standards in a context of weakening labor unions and an increasingly unfriendly political environment. In none of our cases can we be sanguine over a long-term horizon.

A POLITICAL PROCESS

This book underlines the fact that doing business and upholding labor rights are fundamentally political processes. Brands must develop new market strategies to remain competitive in global supply chains, but also political strategies to deal with workers, local governments, and their supplier factories. Governments and brands have to find a modus operandi for establishing regulations that level the playing field for businesses, ensuring that they can maintain competitiveness while also creating, enforcing, and applying labor standards universally. Finding a basis for coordination between business and government is particularly difficult where corruption is rife or where the interests of local and central governments diverge.

Supply chain workers and their allies also have to recognize the politics of these complicated and interdependent relationships. While workers in labor-repressive contexts are often limited in power and influence, their allies frequently miss opportunities for leverage that would enable them to target the interests and beliefs of those holding political or economic power. Moreover, advocates of improved labor standards may share a common purpose and, in that sense, a common interest, but the distinctive interests of the members of the potential coalition may cause them to founder on the shoals of the collective action problem. Strategic differences may be an additional source of rifts. Overcoming these internal obstacles requires political entrepreneurship and the establishment, itself a political act, of common beliefs about the best way to act in the given situation. Promoters of change must turn protest into a political resource. When they do, improved labor standards can result.

References

Aaronson, S.A. and J.M. Zimmerman (2007), *Trade Imbalance: The Struggle to Weigh Human Rights Concerns in Trade Policymaking*, New York: Cambridge University Press.

Aeppel, T. (2008), 'U.S. shoe factory finds supplies are Achilles' heel', *The Wall Street Journal*, 3 March, accessed 12 January 2015 at http://online.wsj.com/news/articles/SB120450124543206313.

AFL-CIO (2014a), 'The Union Shop', *AFL-CIO*, accessed 16 January 2015 at http://www.aflcio.org/Get-Involved/The-Union-Shop.

AFL-CIO (2014b), 'Honduras', *AFL-CIO – Solidarity Center*, accessed 16 January 2015 at http://www.solidaritycenter.org/where-we-work/americas/629-2/.

Afsar, R. (2001), 'Sociological implications of female labour migration in Bangladesh', in R. Sobhan and N. Khundker (eds), *Globalization and Gender: Changing Patterns of Women's Employment in Bangladesh*, Dhaka: Centre for Policy Dialogue and University Press Limited.

Ahlquist, J.S. (2012), 'Public sector unions need the private sector (or why the Wisconsin protests were not labor's Lazarus moment)', *The Forum*, **10**(1), accessed 16 January 2015 at http://www.degruyter.com/view/j/for.2012.10.issue-1/1540-8884.1499/1540-8884.1499.xml.

Ahlquist, J.S. and M. Levi (2013), *The Interest of Others: Organizations and Social Activism*, 1st edition, Princeton, NJ: Princeton University Press.

Ahlquist, J.S., A.B. Clayton and M. Levi (2014), 'Provoking preferences: unionization, trade policy, and the ILWU puzzle', *International Organization*, **68**(01), 33–75.

Ahmed, F.Z., A. Greenleaf and A. Sacks (2014), 'The paradox of export growth in areas of weak governance: the case of the ready made garment sector in Bangladesh', *World Development*, **56**(1), 258–71.

Amengual, M. (2010), 'Complementary labor regulation: the uncoordinated combination of state and private regulators in the Dominican Republic', *World Development*, **38**(3), 405–14.

Amengual, M. (2014), 'Pathways to enforcement: labor inspectors leveraging linkages with society in Argentina', *Industrial and Labor Relations Review*, **67**(1), 3–33.

Anner, M.S. (2011), *Solidarity Transformed: Labor Responses to Globalization and Crisis in Latin America*, Ithaca, NY: ILR Press.

Anner, M. (2012), 'Corporate social responsibility and freedom of association rights: the precarious quest for legitimacy and control in global supply chains', *Politics & Society*, **40**(4), 609–44.

Anner, M. and T. Caraway (2010), 'International institutions and workers' rights: between labor standards and market flexibility', *Studies in Comparative International Development*, **45**(2), 151–69.

Apple (2013), *Apple Supplier Responsibility: 2013 Progress Report*, accessed 13 January 2015 at https://www.apple.com/supplier-responsibility/pdf/Apple_SR_2013_Progress_Report.pdf.

Apple (2014), *Apple Supplier Responsibility: 2014 Progress Report*, accessed 13 January 2015 at https://www.apple.com/supplier-responsibility/pdf/Apple_SR_2014_Progress_Report.pdf.

Applebaum, R.P. (2008), 'Giant transnational contractors in East Asia: emergent trends in global supply chains', *Competition & Change*, **12**(1), 69–87.

Applebaum, R.P. and G. Gereffi (1994), 'Power and profits in the apparel commodity chain', in G. Gereffi and M. Korzeniewicz (eds), *Commodity Chains and Global Capitalism*, Westport, CT: Praeger, pp. 95–122.

Areddy, J.T. (2010), 'Levi's faced earlier challenge in China', *The Wall Street Journal*, 14 January, accessed 12 January 2015 at http://online.wsj.com/news/articles/SB100014240527487046751045750008315813155788.

Arkans, N. (2010), Interview with Norm Arkans, Brand Responsibility Project, Seattle, WA: University of Washington [audio], accessed 16 January 2015 at http://depts.washington.edu/brandrp/transcripts/audio_video/NormArkans.mp3.

Bajaj, V. (2010),'Bangladesh, with low pay, moves in on China', *The New York Times*, 16 July, accessed 16 January 2015 at http://www.nytimes.com/2010/07/17/business/global/17textile.html.

Barboza, D. and C. Duhigg (2012), 'China contractor again faces labor issue on iPhones', *The New York Times*, 10 September, accessed 17 January 2015 at http://www.nytimes.com/2012/09/11/technology/foxconn-said-to-use-forced-student-labor-to-make-iphones.html.

Barboza, D. and S. Lafraniere (2012), '"Princelings" in China use family ties to gain riches', *The New York Times*, 17 May, accessed 17 January 2015 at http://www.nytimes.com/2012/05/18/world/asia/china-princelings-using-family-ties-to-gain-riches.html.

Barrientos, S. (2001), 'Gender, flexibility and global value chains', *IDS Bulletin*, **32**(3), 83–93.

Barrientos, S. and S. Smith (2007), 'Do workers benefit from ethical trade? Assessing codes of labour practice in global production systems', *Third World Quarterly*, **28**(4), 713–29.

BBC News (2014), 'China's Yue Yuen shoe factory workers in large strike', *BBC News*, 15 April, accessed 17 January 2015 at http://www.bbc.com/news/world-asia-china-27033186.

Berliner, D. and A. Prakash (2012), 'From norms to programs: the United Nations Global Compact and global governance', *Regulation & Governance*, **6**(2), 149–66.

Berliner, D. and A. Prakash (2014), 'The United Nations Global Compact: an institutionalist perspective', *Journal of Business Ethics*, **122**(2), 217–23.

Berliner, D. and A. Prakash (2015), '"Bluewashing" the firm?: voluntary regulations, program design and member compliance with the United Nations Global Compact', *Policy Studies Journal*, **43**(1), 115–38.

Blanc, P.D. (2009), *How Everyday Products Make People Sick: Toxins at Home and in the Workplace*, Berkeley, CA: University of California Press.

Blodget, H. (2012), 'CEO OF APPLE PARTNER FOXCONN: 'Managing one million animals gives me a headache', *Business Insider*, 19 January, accessed 28 September 2012 at http://www.businessinsider.com/foxconn-animals-2012-1.

Blyth, M. (2013), *Austerity: The History of a Dangerous Idea*, Oxford/New York: Oxford University Press.

Bores, A. (2011), Interview with Alex Bores, Brand Responsibility Project, Seattle, WA: University of Washington, accessed 16 January 2015 at http://depts.washington.edu/brandrp/transcripts/AlexBores_Final.pdf.

Borromeo, L. (2014), 'How Adidas supported worker rights in China factory strike', *The Guardian*, 12 June, accessed 17 January 2015 at http://www.theguardian.com/sustainable-business/sustainable-fashion-blog/adidas-worker-rights-china-factory-strike.

Browning, E.S., S. Russolillo and J.E. Vascellaro (2012), 'Apple now biggest-ever U.S. company', *The Wall Street Journal*, 21 August, accessed 12 January 2015 at http://online.wsj.com/news/articles/SB10000872396390443855804577601773524745182.

Bueno de Mesquita, B., R.M. Siverson, J.D. Morrow and A. Smith (2003), *The Logic of Political Survival*, Cambridge, MA: MIT Press.

Bureau of Labor Statistics (2014), 'Manufacturing in China', *Bureau of Labor Statistics*, accessed 17 January 2015 at http://www.bls.gov/fls/china.htm.

Burkhalter, H. (2012), 'Fair Food Program helps end the use of slavery in the tomato fields', *The Washington Post*, 2 September, accessed 13 January 2015 at http://www.washingtonpost.com/opinions/fair-food-program-helps-end-the-use-of-slavery-in-the-tomato-fields/2012/09/02/788f1a1a-f39c-11e1-892d-bc92fee603a7_story.html.

Bussolo, M., R. de Hoyos and O. Nunez (2008), 'Can Maquila booms reduce poverty? Evidence from Honduras', *The World Bank*, accessed 16 January 2015 at http://documents.worldbank.org/curated/en/2008/12/10064148/can-maquila-booms-reduce-poverty-evidence-honduras-can-maquila-booms-reduce-poverty-evidence-honduras.

Buy American (2014), 'Buy American', accessed 16 January 2015 at http://buyamerican.com/.

California (2010), *California Transparency in Supply Chains Act of 2010*, accessed 16 January 2015 at http://www.state.gov/documents/organization/164934.pdf.

Caraway, T. (2010), 'Labor standards and labor market flexibility in East Asia', *Studies in Comparative International Development*, **45**(2), 225–49.

Central American Free Trade Agreement (2004), 'CAFTA-DR (Dominican Republic-Central America FTA)', *Office of the United States Trade Representative*, accessed 16 January 2015 at http://www.ustr.gov/trade-agreements/free-trade-agreements/cafta-dr-dominican-republic-central-america-fta.

Chan, A. (1996), 'Boot camp at the shoe factory', *The Washington Post*, 17 November, accessed 17 January 2015 at http://www.oocities.org/wilfratzburg/bootcamp.html.

Chan, A. (1998), 'Labor standards and human rights: the case of Chinese workers under market socialism', *Human Rights Quarterly*, **20**(4), 886–904.

Chan, J. (2013), 'A suicide survivor: the life of a Chinese migrant worker at Foxconn', *The Asia-Pacific Journal*, **11**(31), accessed 17 January 2015 at http://www.japanfocus.org/-Jenny-Chan/3977.

Chan, J., N. Pun and M. Selden (2013), 'The politics of global production: Apple, Foxconn and China's new working class', *New Technology, Work and Employment*, **28**(2), 100–115.

Chan, W. (2014), 'Adidas shifts orders after massive strike at Chinese shoe factory', *CNN*, 25 April, accessed 17 January 2015 at http://www.cnn.com/2014/04/25/world/asia/adidas-chinese-factory-strike/index.html.

Chen, C. (2011), *Foreign Direct Investment in China: Location Determinants, Investor Behaviour and Economic Impact*, Cheltenham, UK and Northampton, MA, USA: Edward Elgar Publishing.

Chen, J. (2004), *Popular Political Support in Urban China*, Washington, DC: Woodrow Wilson Center Press.

Cheng, R. (2013), 'A US-made Mac Pro is a token gesture', *CNET*, accessed 13 January 2015 at http://www.cnet.com/news/a-us-made-mac-pro-is-a-token-gesture/.

China Labor Watch (2014a), 'Yue Yuen worker strike enters its second week, Adidas pulls out of factory', *China Labor Watch*, 22 April, accessed 17 January 2015 at http://www.chinalaborwatch.org/newscast/234.

China Labor Watch (2014b), 'Dongguan union releases response to Yue Yuen workers' demands', *China Labor Watch*, 27 June, accessed 17 January 2015 at http://www.chinalaborwatch.org/report/62.

China Labor Watch (2014c), *Beyond Foxconn: Deplorable Working Conditions Characterize Apple's Entire Supply Chain*, accessed 16 January 2015 at http://www.chinalaborwatch.org/report/62.

Clark, A.M. and K. Sikkink (2013), 'Information effects and human rights data: is the good news about increased human rights information bad news for human rights measures?' *Human Rights Quarterly*, **35**(3), 539–68.

Cohen, Wilbur, J. and J. Barr (1944), 'The 1944 International Labor Conference', Social Security Bulletin, accessed at http://www.ssa.gov/policy/docs/ssb/v7n6/v7n6p11.pdf.

Compa, L. (2004), 'Trade unions, NGOs, and corporate codes of conduct', *Development in Practice*, **14**(1), 210–15.

Compa, L. and T. Hinchliffe-Darricarrere (1995), 'Enforcing international labor rights through corporate codes of conduct', *Columbia Journal of Transnational Law*, **33**(3), 663–89.

Cook, T. (2013), 'Tim Cook receiving the IQLA Lifetime Achievement Award', Auburn University, 14 December, *YouTube*, accessed 13 January 2015 at http://www.youtube.com/watch?v=dNEafGCf-kw&feature=youtube_gdata_player.

Cooke, W.N., A.K. Mishra, G.M. Spreitzer and M. Tschirhart (1995), 'The determinants of NLRB decision-making revisited', *Industrial and Labor Relations Review*, **48**(2), 237–57.

Cornell University (2014), 'Remembering the 1911 Triangle Factory fire', School of Industrial and Labor Relations Online Exhibit, accessed 12 January 2015 at http://www.ilr.cornell.edu/trianglefire/story/introduction.html.

Cosgrove-Mather, B. (2003), 'Levi Strauss shuts all U.S. plants', *Associated Press*, 25 September, accessed 12 January 2015 at http://www.cbsnews.com/news/levi-strauss-shuts-all-us-plants/.

Cushman, J.H. (1998), 'Nike pledges to end child labor and apply U.S. rules abroad', *The New York Times*, accessed 12 January 2015 at http://www.nytimes.com/1998/05/13/business/international-business-nike-pledges-to-end-child-labor-and-apply-us-rules-abroad.html.

Dark, T.E. (2000), 'Labor and the Democratic Party: a report on the 1998 elections', *Journal of Labor Research*, **21**(4), 627–40.

Dark, T.E. (2001), *The Unions and the Democrats: An Enduring Alliance*, Ithaca, NY: Cornell University Press.

Dean, J. (2007), 'The forbidden city of Terry Gou', *The Wall Street Journal*, 12 August, accessed 17 January 2015 at http://online.wsj.com/news/articles/SB118677584137994489.

Devnath, A. and M. Srivastava (2013), '"Suddenly the floor wasn't there" factory survivor says', *Bloomberg*, 25 April 2015, accessed 16 January 2015 at http://www.bloomberg.com/news/2013-04-25/-suddenly-the-floor-wasn-t-there-factory-survivor-says.html.

Doorey, D.J. (2011), 'The transparent supply chain: from resistance to implementation at Nike and Levi-Strauss', *Journal of Business Ethics*, **103**(4), 587–603.

Du, Ke (2011), 'Report finds Foxconn internship program rife with abuse', *Caixin Online*, 24 June, accessed 17 January 2015 at http://english.caixin.com/2011-05-24/100262522.html.

Duhigg, C. and K. Bradsher (2012), 'How the U.S. lost out on iPhone work', *The New York Times*, accessed 12 January 2014 at http://www.nytimes.com/2012/01/22/business/apple-america-and-a-squeezed-middle-class.html.

Eidelson, J. (2013), 'Alt-Labor', *The American Prospect*, 29 January, accessed 16 January 2015 at http://prospect.org/article/alt-labor.

Elmer-DeWitt, P. (2010), 'This man makes 137,000 iPhones a day – Fortune', *Fortune*, 10 January 2015 at http://fortune.com/2010/09/10/this-man-makes-137000-iphones-a-day/.

Emmert, M. (2010), Personal interview with former University of Washington President, Brand Responsibility Project, Seattle, WA: University of Washington, accessed 16 January 2015 at http://depts.washington.edu/brandrp/transcripts/MarkEmmert_Final.pdf.

Esbenshade, J.L. (2004), *Monitoring Sweatshops: Workers, Consumers, and the Global Apparel Industry*, Philadelphia, PA: Temple University Press.

European Court of Human Rights (2008), '*Demir and Baykara* v. *Turkey*', Strasbourg: European Court of Human Rights.

Ewing, K.D. and J. Hendy (2010), 'The dramatic implications of Demir and Baykara', *Industrial Law Journal*, **39**(1), 2–51.

Fair Labor Association (2012a), 'Apple joins FLA', *Fair Labor.org*, 13 January, accessed 17 January 2015 at http://www.fairlabor.org/blog/entry/apple-joins-fla.

Fair Labor Association (2012b), *Independent Investigation of Apple Supplier, Foxconn*, accessed 13 January 2015 at http://www.fairlabor.org/sites/default/files/documents/reports/foxconn_investigation_report.pdf.

Farber, H.S. (2007), 'Job loss and the decline in job security in the United States', Working Paper No. 520, Princeton University Industrial Relations Section, revised 2009, accessed 16 January 2015 at http://harris.princeton.edu/pubs/pdfs/520revision2.pdf.

Fariss, C.J. (2014), 'Respect for human rights has improved over time: modeling the changing standard of accountability', *American Political Science Review*, **108**(2), 297–318.

Featherstone, L. (2000), 'The new student movement', *The Nation*, 27 April, accessed 16 January 2015 at http://www.thenation.com/article/new-student-movement.

Fine, J. (2006), *Worker Centers: Organizing Communities at the Edge of the Dream*, Ithaca, NY: Cornell University Press.

Finnemore, M. and K. Sikkink (1998), 'International norm dynamics and political change', *International Organization*, **52**(4), 887–917.

Foot, R. and A. Walter (2010), *China, the United States, and Global Order*, Cambridge, UK/New York: Cambridge University Press.

Forbes (2014), 'The world's biggest public companies list', *Forbes.com*, accessed 12 January 2015 http://www.forbes.com/global2000/list/.

Forney, M. (2004), 'How Nike figured out China', *Time*, 17 October, accessed 12 January 2015 at http://content.time.com/time/magazine/article/0,9171,725113,00.html.

Forsythe, M., S. Oster, N. Khan and D. Lawrence (2012), 'Xi Jinping millionaire relations reveal fortunes of elite', *Bloomberg*, 20 June, accessed 17 January 2015 at http://www.bloomberg.com/news/2012-06-29/xi-jinping-millionaire-relations-reveal-fortunes-of-elite.html.

Foxconn (2013), *2013 CSER Annual Report*, accessed 17 January 2015 at http://ser.foxconn.com/SelectLanguageAction.do?language=1&jump=/cser/Annual_Report.jsp.

Francia, P.L. (2006), *The Future of Organized Labor in American Politics*, New York: Columbia University Press.

Frank, D. (2000), *Buy American: The Untold Story of Economic Nationalism*, Boston, MA: Beacon Press.

Freeman, R.B. (2007), *America Works: The Exceptional U.S. Labor Market*, New York: Russell Sage Foundation.

Friedman, E. (2012), 'Getting through the hard times together? Chinese workers and unions respond to the economic crisis', *Journal of Industrial Relations*, **54**(4), 459–75.

Friedman, E. and C.K. Lee (2010), 'Remaking the world of Chinese labour: a 30-year retrospective', *British Journal of Industrial Relations*, **48**(3), 507–33.

Gallagher, M.E. (2007), *Contagious Capitalism: Globalization and the Politics of Labor in China*, Princeton, NJ: Princeton University Press.

Gallagher, M.E., J. Giles, A. Park and M. Wang (2013), 'China's 2008 Labor Contract Law: implementation and implications for China's workers', Policy Research Working Paper No. WPS6542, Washington, DC: World Bank, accessed 17 January 2015 at http://elibrary. worldbank.org/doi/pdf/10.1596/1813-9450-6542.

Gereffi, G. (1994), 'The organization of buyer-driven global commodity chains: how U.S. retailers shape overseas production networks', in G. Gereffi and M. Korneniewicz (eds), *Commodity Chains and Global Capitalism*, Westport, CT: Praeger.

Gereffi, G. (2009), 'Development models and industrial upgrading in China and Mexico', *European Sociological Review*, **25**(1), 37–51.

Gereffi, G. (2013), 'Response: host countries can act', *Boston Review*, accessed 12 January 2015 at http://new.bostonreview.net/BR38.3/ndf_gary_gereffi_global_brands_labor_justice.php.

Gereffi, G., J. Humphrey and T. Sturgeon (2005), 'The governance of global value chains', *Review of International Political Economy*, **12**(1), 78–104.

Glass, I. (Producer) (2012), 'Mr. Daisey and the Apple Factory', *This American Life*, audio retracted, accessed 16 January 2015 at http://www.thisamericanlife.org/radio-archives/episode/454/mr-daisey-and-the-apple-factory.

Godoy, A. (2010), Interview with Angelina Godoy, Brand Responsibility Project, Seattle, WA: University of Washington, accessed 16 January 2015 at http://depts.washington.edu/brandrp/transcripts/Angelina Godoy_Final.pdf.

Goel, V. (2013), 'Foxconn audit reveals workweek still too long', *The New York Times*, 16 May, accessed 17 January 2015 at http://www.nytimes.com/2013/05/17/business/foxconn-audit-reveals-workweek-still-too-long.html.

Goldfield, M. and A. Bromsen (2013), 'The changing landscape of US unions in historical and theoretical perspective', *Annual Review of Political Science*, **16**(1), 231–57.

Goldman, D. (2012a), 'Why Apple will never bring manufacturing jobs back to U.S.', *CNN Money*, 17 October, accessed 16 January 2015 at http://money.cnn.com/2012/10/17/technology/apple-china-jobs/index.html.

Goldman, D. (2012b), 'Throwing cold water on Apple's made-in-the-U.S.A. Mac', *CNN Money*, accessed 16 January 2015 at http://money.cnn.com/2012/12/06/technology/apple-mac-made-in-usa/index.html.

Gould, W.B. (2001), *Labored Relations: Law, Politics, and the NLRB – A Memoir*, Cambridge, MA: MIT Press.

Government of Honduras (1959), *Código Del Trabajo Y Sus Reformas. Decreto 189-59 Publicado El 15 de Julio de 1959, Gaceta No. 16,82 7*, accessed 16 January 2015 at http://www.trabajo.gob.hn/biblioteca-y-documentos/leyes/codigo%20de%20trabajo%20y%20sus%20reformas.pdf.

Government of India (2014), 'Child Labour Acts, Rules and Schedules', *Ministry of Labour and Employment*, accessed 13 January 2015 at http://labour.gov.in/content/division/acts-and-rules.php.

Greenhill, B., L. Mosley and A. Prakash (2009), 'Trade-based diffusion of labor rights: a panel study, 1986–2002', *American Political Science Review*, **103**(4), 669–90.

Greenhouse, S. (1998), 'Anti-sweatshop coalition finds itself at odds on garment factory code', *The New York Times*, 3 July, accessed 15 January 2015 at http://www.nytimes.com/1998/07/03/us/anti-sweatshop-coalition-finds-itself-at-odds-on-garment-factory-code.html.

Greenhouse, S. (2008), *The Big Squeeze: Tough Times for the American Worker*, New York: Alfred A. Knopf.

Greenhouse, S. (2013), 'US retailers see big risk in safety plan for factories in Bangladesh', *The New York Times*, 22 May, accessed 16 January 2015 at http://lateralpraxis.com/download/Supply%20chain%20and%20Ethics.pdf.

Greenhouse, S. (2014), 'Report cites forced labor in Malaysia's electronics industry', *The New York Times*, 17 September, accessed 13 January 2015 at http://www.nytimes.com/2014/09/17/business/international/report-cites-forced-labor-in-malaysia.html.

Greenstone, D.J. (1977), *Labor in American Politics*, Chicago, IL: University of Chicago Press.

Greyser, S.A. (2009), 'Corporate brand reputation and brand crisis management', *Management Decision*, **47**(4), 590–602.

Gross, D. (2012), 'Tim Cook: Apple will make computers in the U.S. next year', *CNN Tech*, accessed 13 January 2015 at http://www.cnn.com/2012/12/06/tech/innovation/apple-made-in-us-cook/.

Guglielmo, C. (2013), 'Apple's supplier labor practices in China scrutinized after Foxconn, Pegatron reviewed', *Forbes*, 12 December, accessed 26 August 2014 at http://www.forbes.com/sites/connieguglielmo/2013/12/12/apples-labor-practices-in-china-scrutinized-after-foxconn-pegatron-reviewed/.

Gutiérrez Rivera, L. (2010), *Territories of Violence: State, Marginal Youth, and Public Security in Honduras*, New York: Palgrave Macmillan.

Hagel, J. and J.S. Brown (2005), *The Only Sustainable Edge: Why Business Strategy Depends on Productive Friction and Dynamic Specialization*, Boston, MA: Harvard Business School Press.

Hainmueller, J., M.J. Hiscox and S. Sequeira (2014), 'Consumer demand for the fair trade label: evidence from a multi-store field experiment', SSRN Scholarly Paper, Rochester, NY, accessed 13 January 2015 at http://papers.ssrn.com/abstract=1801942.

Harrison, A. and J. Scorse (2010), 'Multinationals and anti-sweatshop activism', *American Economic Review*, **100**(1), 247–73.

Hassel, A. (2008), 'The evolution of a global labor governance regime', *Governance*, **21**(2), 231–51.

Hathaway, O.A. (2002), 'Do human rights treaties make a difference?' *The Yale Law Journal*, **111**(8), 1935–2042.

Hayter, S. and V. Stoevska (2011), *Social Dialogue Indicators: International Statistical Inquiry 2008–2009*, International Labour Office, accessed 13 January 2015 at http://laborsta.ilo.org/applv8/data/TUM/TUD%20and%20CBC%20Technical%20Brief.pdf.

Hearson, M. (2006), 'Let's clean up fashion', *Cleanclothes.org*, accessed 16 January 2015 at http://www.cleanclothes.org/resources/national-cccs/06-09-cleanupfashion.pdf.

Heath, R. and M. Mobarak (2012), 'Supply and demand constraints on educational investment: evidence from garment sector jobs and the female stipend program in Bangladesh', Working Paper, Yale School of Management, accessed 16 January 2015 at http://www.econ.yale.edu/conference/neudc11/papers/paper_363.pdf.

Heymann, J. and A. Earle (2010), *Raising the Global Floor: Dismantling the Myth That We Can't Afford Good Working Conditions for Everyone*, Stanford, CA: Stanford University Press.

Hibbs, D. (1977), 'Political parties and macroeconomic policy', *American Politic Science Review*, **71**(1), 467–87.

Hill, D.W., W.H. Moore and B. Mukherjee (2013), 'Information politics versus organizational incentives: when are Amnesty International's "naming and shaming" reports biased?' *International Studies Quarterly*, **57**(2), 219–32.

Hiscox, M. (2001), 'Class versus industry cleavages: inter-industry factor mobility and the politics of trade', *International Organization*, **55**(1), 1–46.

Hiscox, M. (2002), *International Trade and Political Conflict: Commerce, Coalitions, and Mobility*, Princeton, NJ: Princeton University Press.

Hoggan, K. (2010), Interview with Kathy Hoggan, Brand Responsibility Project, Seattle, WA: University of Washington, accessed 16 January 2015 at http://depts.washington.edu/brandrp/transcripts/KathyHoggan_Final.pdf.

Hollie, P.G. (1985a), 'Shoe industry's struggle', *The New York Times*, 28 May, accessed 12 January 2015 at http://www.nytimes.com/1985/05/28/business/shoe-industry-s-struggle.html.

Hollie, P.G. (1985b), 'Footwear response prepared', *The New York Times*, 27 August, accessed 12 January 2015 at http://www.nytimes.com/1985/08/27/business/footwear-response-prepared.html.

Hopkins, T.K. and I. Wallerstein (1986), 'Commodity chains in the world economy prior to 1800', *Review (Fernand Braudel Center)*, **10**(1), 157–70.

Hossain, N. (2012), 'Exports, equity and empowerment: the effects of readymade garments manufacturing employment on gender equality in Bangladesh', Background Paper for the World Bank *World Development Report 2012*, accessed 16 January 2015 at http://siteresources. worldbank.org/INTWDR2012/Resources/7778105-1299699968583/77 86210-1322671773271/Hossain-Export-Equity-employment.pdf.

Huang, Y. (2008), *Capitalism with Chinese Characteristics: Entrepreneurship and the State*, Cambridge, UK/New York: Cambridge University Press.

Huber, E. and J.D. Stephens (2001), *Development and Crisis of the Welfare State: Parties and Policies in Global Markets*, Chicago, IL: University of Chicago Press.

Human Rights Watch (2008), 'Bangladesh: labor activists in export sector harassed', *Human Rights Watch*, accessed 16 January 2015 at http://www.hrw.org/news/2008/01/30/bangladesh-labor-activists-export-sector-harassed.

Human Rights Watch (2014a), 'Bangladesh: Rana Plaza victims urgently need assistance', *Human Rights Watch*, 21 April, accessed 16 January 2015 at http://www.hrw.org/news/2014/04/23/bangladesh-rana-plaza-victims-urgently-need-assistance.

Human Rights Watch (2014b), 'Bangladesh: protect garment workers' rights', 6 February, accessed 17 January 2015 at http://www.hrw.org/news/2014/02/06/bangladesh-protect-garment-workers-rights.

Inter-American Court of Human Rights (2009), *'Escher et al. v. Brazil'*, San José: Inter-American Court of Human Rights.

International Labour Organization (1958), *ILO Convention No. 111 on Discrimination in Employment and Occupation*, accessed 13 January 2015 at http://www.ilo.org/dyn/normlex/en/f?p=NORMLEXPUB:1210 0:0::NO::P12100_ILO_CODE:C111.

International Labour Organization (1999), *Recommendation 190 Concerning the Prohibition and Immediate Action for the Elimination of the Worst Forms of Child Labour*, accessed 13 January 2015 at http://www.ilo.org/public/english/standards/relm/ilc/ilc87/com-chir.htm.

International Labour Organization (2010), *Observation on Freedom of Association and Protection of the Right to Organise Convention, 1948 (No. 87)*, *International Labour Organization*, accessed 16 January 2015 at http://www.ilo.org/dyn/normlex/en/f?p=NORMLEXPUB:131 00:0::NO::P13100_COMMENT_ID:2333760.

International Labour Organization (2011), *Observation on the Right to Organise and Collective Bargaining Convention, 1949 (No. 98)*, accessed 16 January 2015 at http://www.ilo.org/dyn/normlex/en/f?p=1000:13100:0::NO:13100:P13100_COMMENT_ID:2333772.

International Labour Organization (2013a), 'ILO statement on reform of Bangladesh labour law', accessed 16 January 2015 at http://www.ilo.org/global/about-the-ilo/media-centre/statements-and-speeches/WCMS_218067/lang–en/index.htm.

International Labour Organization (2013b), *International Labour Organization Social Protection Program: Honduras*, accessed 20 January 2015 at http://www.social-protection.org/gimi/gess/ShowProjectSpe Wiki.do?wid=860.

International Labour Organization (2014a), 'International Labour Conference', accessed 13 January 2015 at http://www.ilo.org/global/about-the-ilo/how-the-ilo-works/international-labour-conference/lang–en/index.htm.

International Labour Organization (2014b), 'Applying and promoting International Labour Standards', accessed 13 January 2015 at http://www.ilo.org/global/standards/applying-and-promoting-international-labour-standards/lang–en/index.htm.

International Labour Organization (2014c), 'Representations', accessed 13 January 2015 at http://ilo.org/global/standards/applying-and-promoting-international-labour-standards/representations/lang–en/index.htm.

International Labour Organization (2014d), 'Complaints', accessed 13 January 2015 at http://www.ilo.org/global/standards/applying-and-promoting-international-labour-standards/complaints/lang–en/index.htm.

International Labour Organization (2014e), 'Committee on Freedom of Association', accessed 13 January 2015 at http://ilo.org/global/standards/applying-and-promoting-international-labour-standards/committee-on-freedom-of-association/lang–en/index.htm.

International Labour Organization (2014f), 'Better Work', *International Labour Organization*, accessed 13 January 2015 at http://www.ilo.org/washington/areas/better-work/lang–en/index.htm.

International Labor Rights Forum (2010), *Enemies of the Nation or Human Rights Defenders? Fighting Poverty Wages in Bangladesh*, accessed 20 January 2015 at http://www.laborrights.org/sites/default/files/publications-and-resources/enemiesofthenation.pdf.

International Trade Centre (2014), 'Trade performance HS: exports of China (2009, in USD thousands)', *Trade Competitiveness Map*, accessed 17 January 2015 at http://legacy.intracen.org/appli1/TradeCom/TP_EP_CI.aspx?RP=156&YR=2009.

International Trade Union Conference (2009), 'Bangladesh: three workers killed during a peaceful protest', *ITUC*, accessed 16 January 2015 at http://www.ituc-csi.org/bangladesh-three-workers-killed.

International Trade Union Conference (2010), 'Bangladesh: government must support decent minimum wage, and cease harassment of union rights supporters', *ITUC*, accessed 16 January 2015 at http://www.ituc-csi.org/bangladesh-government-must-support.

Iversen, T. and D. Soskice (2006), 'Electoral institutions and the politics of coalitions: why some democracies redistribute more than others', *American Political Science Review*, **100**(02), 165–81.

Jepperson, R.L., A. Wendt and P.J. Katzenstein (1996), 'Norms, identity, and culture in national security', in P.J. Katzenstein (ed.), *The Culture of National Security: Norms and Identity in World Politics*, New York: Columbia University Press, pp. 33–78.

Jones, T.Y. (2012), 'What Apple can learn from how Nike dealt with its Chinese labor scandal', *Businessinsider.com*, 6 March, accessed 12 January 2015 at http://www.businessinsider.com/what-apple-can-learn-from-how-nike-dealt-with-its-chinese-labor-scandal-2012-3.

Kabeer, N. (2001), *The Power to Choose: Bangladeshi Women Workers and Labour Market Decisions*, Dhaka: University Press.

Kabeer, N., S. Mahmud and S. Tasneem (2011), 'Does paid work provide a pathway to women's empowerment? Empirical findings from Bangladesh', accessed 16 January 2015 at http://dspace.bracu.ac.bd:8080/handle/10361/2598.

Kang, S.L. (2012), *Human Rights and Labor Solidarity: Trade Unions in the Global Economy*, Philadelphia, PA: University of Pennsylvania Press.

Katznelson, I. (2013), *Fear Itself: The New Deal and the Origins of Our Time*, 1st edition, New York: Liveright.

Kaufman, L. (1999), 'Levi is closing 11 factories; 5,900 jobs cut', *The New York Times*, 23 February, accessed 15 January 2015 at http://www.nytimes.com/1999/02/23/business/levi-is-closing-11-factories-5900-jobs-cut.html.

Kaufman, W. (2010), 'China aims to move past "sweatshop" rep.' *NPR.org*, accessed 17 January 2015 at http://www.npr.org/2010/12/20/132205458/china-aims-to-move-past-worlds-sweatshop-rep.

Kell, G. and J.G. Ruggie (1999), 'Global markets and social legitimacy: the case of the global compact', *Transnational Corporations*, **8**(3), 101–20.

Kernaghan, C. (1998), *Behind the Label: 'Made in China'*, Collingdale, PA: Diane Publishing.

Khan, M. (1995), 'Class, clientelism and communal politics in contemporary Bangladesh', in K.N. Panikkar, T.J. Byres and U. Patnaik (eds), *The Making of History: Essays Presented to Irfan Habib*, London: Anthem Press, pp. 572–606.

Khan, M. (2010), 'Bangladesh: partitions, nationalisms and legacies for state-building', unpublished paper, accessed 16 January 2015 at http://eprints.soas.ac.uk/11685/.

Khan, M. (2011), 'The political settlement and its evolution in Bangladesh', accessed 16 January 2015 at http://eprints.soas.ac.uk/12845/1/The_Political_Settlement_and_its_Evolution_in_Bangladesh.pdf.

Khan, N.I. ([2012] 2014), Interview at the Bangladesh Institute of Labour conducted by Faisal Ahmed, quoted in F.Z. Ahmed, A. Greenleaf and A. Sacks (2014), 'The paradox of export growth in areas of weak governance: the case of the ready made garment sector in Bangladesh', *World Development*, **56**(1), 258–71.

Kollman, K. (2008),'The regulatory power of business norms: a call for a new research agenda', *International Studies Review*, **10**(3), 397–419.

Korpi, W. (1978), *The Working Class in Welfare Capitalism: Work, Unions, and Politics in Sweden*, Boston, MA: Routledge & Kegan Paul.

Korpi, W., J.S. O'Connor and G.M. Olsen (1998), *Power Resources Theory and the Welfare State: A Critical Approach: Essays Collected in Honour of Walter Korpi*, Toronto: University of Toronto Press.

Kreps, D.M. (1990), 'Corporate culture and economic theory', in J.E. Alt and K.A. Shepsle (eds), *Perspectives on Positive Political Economy*, Cambridge, UK/New York: Cambridge University Press.

Lafer, G. (2011), 'Defining and defending workers' rights in international trade treaties', paper presented at the American Political Science Association Annual Meeting, Seattle, WA.

Landler, M. (1998), 'International business: reversing course, Levi Strauss will expand its output in China', *The New York Times*, 9 April, accessed 12 January 2015 at http://www.nytimes.com/1998/04/09/business/international-business-reversing-course-levi-strauss-will-expand-its-output.html.

Lee, E. (2006), 'Chinese journalists in trouble for iPod story', *SFGate*, accessed 12 January 2015 at http://blog.sfgate.com/techchron/2006/08/29/chinese-journalists-in-trouble-for-ipod-story/.

Levi, M. (2003), 'Organizing power: the prospects for an American labor movement', *Perspectives on Politics*, **1**(01), 45–68.

Levi, M. and A. Linton (2003), 'Fair trade: a cup at a time?' *Politics & Society*, **31**(3), 407–32.

Levi, M. and G.H. Murphy (2006), 'Coalitions of contention: the case of the WTO protests in Seattle', *Political Studies*, **54**(4), 651–70.

Levi, M. and D. Olson (2000), 'The battles in Seattle', *Politics & Society*, **28**(3), 309–29.

Levi, M., A. Greenleaf and M. Lake (2011), 'Ensuring brand responsibility: firm behaviour and institutional purchasing power in the apparel industry', Brand Responsibility Archive Project, Seattle, WA: University of Washington.

Levi, M., M. Moe and T. Buckley (2009), 'Institutionalizing trustworthiness through the NLRB?' in R. Hardin (ed.), *Distrust*, New York: Russell Sage Foundation.

Levi, M., M. Myrdal and G. Robertson (2007), 'Remodeling the house of labor', *New Political Science*, **29**(4), 521–8.

Levi, M., T. Melo, B. Weingast and F. Zlotnick (2014), 'Opening access by ending the violence trap', in N.R. Lamoreaux and J.J. Wallis (eds), *Organizations, Civil Society, and the Roots of Development*, Chicago, IL: Chicago University Press.

Levi Strauss & Co. (2013), *Sustainability Guidebook*, accessed 12 January 2015 at http://lsco.s3.amazonaws.com/wp-content/uploads/2014/01/LSCO-Sustainability-Guidebook-2013-_-December.pdf.

Levi Strauss & Co. (2014a), 'Heritage timeline', *Levi Strauss.com*, accessed 12 January 2015 at http://www.levistrauss.com/our-story/heritage-timeline/.

Levi Strauss & Co. (2014b), 'Investor FAQs', *Levi Strauss.com*, accessed 12 January 2015 at http://www.levistrauss.com/investors/investor-faqs/.

Levi Strauss & Co. (2014c), 'Suppliers & operations', *Levi Strauss.com*, accessed 12 January 2015 at http://www.levistrauss.com/sustainability/innovative-practices/suppliers-operations/.

Lichtenstein, N. (2006), *Wal-Mart: The Face of Twenty-First-Century Capitalism*, 1st edition, New York: New Press.

Lichtenstein, N. (2010), *The Retail Revolution: How Wal-Mart Created a Brave New World of Business*, 1st edition, New York: Picador.

Lichtenstein, N. (2013), *State of the Union: A Century of American Labor (Revised and Expanded)*, Princeton, NJ: Princeton University Press.

Lin, L., D. Roberts and J. Fellman (2014), 'Yue Yuen says 80% of workers return after plant strike', *Bloomberg*, 25 April, accessed 17 January 2015 at http://www.bloomberg.com/news/2014-04-25/china-tells-nike-shoemaker-to-rectify-striker-benefits-by-today.html.

Linton, A. (2012), *Fair Trade from the Ground Up: New Markets for Social Justice*, Seattle, WA: University of Washington Press.

Lipsky, M. (1968), 'Protest as a political resource', *American Political Science Review*, **62**(4), 1144–58.

Lipsky, M. and M. Levi (1972), 'Community organization as a political resource', in H. Hahn (ed.), *People and Politics in Urban Society*, Beverly Hills, CA: Sage Publications.

Locke, R.M. (2013), *The Promise and Limits of Private Power: Promoting Labor Standards in a Global Economy*, Cambridge, UK/New York: Cambridge University Press.

Locke, R.M., M. Amengual and A. Mangla (2009), 'Virtue out of necessity? Compliance, commitment, and the improvement of labor conditions in global supply chains', *Politics & Society*, **37**(3), 319–51.

Locke, R.M., F. Qin and A. Brause (2007a), 'Does monitoring improve labor standards? Lessons from Nike', *Industrial and Labor Relations Review*, **61**(1), 3–31.

Locke, R.M., T. Kochan, M. Romis and F. Qin (2007b), 'Beyond corporate codes of conduct: work organization and labour standards at Nike's suppliers', *International Labour Review*, **146**(1–2), 21–40.

Long, C. (2014), 'After Rana Plaza', *Jacobin Magazine*, accessed 20 January 2015 at https://www.jacobinmag.com/2014/06/after-rana-plaza/.

Lucas, K., D. Kang and Z. Li. (2013), 'Workplace dignity in a total institution: examining the experiences of Foxconn's migrant workforce', *Journal of Business Ethics*, **114**(1), 91–106.

Mares, I. and M.E. Carnes (2009), 'Social policy in developing countries', *Annual Review of Political Science*, **12**, 93–114.

Marx, K. and F. Engels ([1848] 1952), *Capital by Marx: Manifesto of the Communist Party*, Chicago, IL: Encyclopaedia Britannica.

McAdam, D. (1982), *Political Process and the Development of Black Insurgency, 1930–1970*, Chicago, IL: University of Chicago Press.

McAdam, D., S.G. Tarrow and C. Tilly (2001), *Dynamics of Contention*, New York: Cambridge University Press.

McCombs, D. (2014), 'Adidas deals with striking China factory by moving orders', *Bloomberg*, 24 April, accessed 17 January 2015 at http://www.bloomberg.com/news/2014-04-24/adidas-to-move-some-out put-from-strike-disrupted-factory.html.

Mendeloff, J.M. (1979), *Regulating Safety: An Economic and Political Analysis of Occupational Safety and Health Policy*, Cambridge, MA: MIT Press.

Merk, J. (2008), 'Restructuring and conflict in the global athletic footwear industry: Nike, Yue Yuen and labour codes of conduct', in M.

Taylor (ed.), *Global Economy Contested: Power and Conflict Across the International Division of Labor*, London: Routledge, pp. 79–139.

Miller, G.J. (1992), *Managerial Dilemmas: The Political Economy of Hierarchy*, Cambridge, UK/New York: Cambridge University Press.

Mlachila, M. and Y. Yang (2004), 'The end of textiles quotas: a case study of the impact on Bangladesh', IMF Working Paper, accessed 16 January 2015 at http://books.google.com/books?hl=en&lr=&id=eKnxEOhCGv8C&oi=fnd&pg=PA4&dq=Mlachila,+M.+and+Yang,+Y.+2004.+&ots=gkOK73U_Cu&sig=4bgf0l6FMr3qXhE5uBgFt_J1ZbE.

Monaghan, A. (2014), 'China surpasses US as world's largest trading nation', *The Guardian*, 10 January, accessed 17 January 2015 at http://www.theguardian.com/business/2014/jan/10/china-surpasses-us-world-largest-trading-nation.

Morley, S., E. Nakasone and V. Pineiro (2008), *The Impact of CAFTA on Employment, Production, and Poverty in Honduras*, accessed 16 January 2015 at http://www.ifpri.org/publication/impact-cafta-employment-production-and-poverty-honduras.

Mosley, L. (2008), 'Workers' rights in open economies global production and domestic institutions in the developing world', *Comparative Political Studies*, **41**(4–5), 674–714.

Mosley, L. (2010), *Labor Rights and Multinational Production*, Cambridge, UK/New York: Cambridge University Press.

Mosley, L. and S. Uno (2007), 'Racing to the bottom or climbing to the top? Economic globalization and collective labor rights', *Comparative Political Studies*, **40**(8), 923–48.

Murillo, M.V. (2001), *Partisan Coalitions and Labor Competition in Latin America: Trade Unions and Market Reforms*, New York: Cambridge University Press.

Murillo, M.V. and A. Schrank (2005), 'With a little help from my friends. Partisan politics, transnational alliances, and labor rights in Latin America', *Comparative Political Studies*, **38**(8), 971–99.

National Oceanic and Atmospheric Association (NOAA) (2011), 'Mitch: the deadliest Atlantic hurricane since 1780', *NOAA National Climatic Data Research Center*, accessed 16 January 2015 at http://www.ncdc.noaa.gov/oa/reports/mitch/mitch.html.

Neumayer, E. and I. de Soysa (2006), 'Globalization and the right to free association and collective bargaining: an empirical analysis', *World Development*, **34**(1), 31–49.

New York Times, The (2014), 'One year after Rana Plaza', *The New York Times*, 27 April, accessed 16 January 2015 at http://www.nytimes.com/2014/04/28/opinion/one-year-after-rana-plaza.html.

Nielsen, M.E. (2005), 'The politics of corporate responsibility and child labour in the Bangladeshi garment industry', *International Affairs*, **81**(3), 559–80.

Nike, Inc. (2014), 'Manufacturing map', *Nikeinc.com*, accessed 12 January 2015 at http://manufacturingmap.nikeinc.com/#.

Nova, S. (2011), Interview with Scott Nova, Worker Rights Consortium, Brand Responsibility Project, Seattle, WA: University of Washington, accessed 16 January 2015 at https://depts.washington.edu/brandrp/transcripts/ScottNova_Final.pdf.

O'Rourke, D. (2001), 'To fix sweatshop conditions in factories, we must listen to workers', *The Boston Globe*, 27 February, accessed 13 January 2015 at http://nature.berkeley.edu/orourke/media/globe-op-ed.html.

O'Rourke, D. (2003), 'Outsourcing regulation: analyzing nongovernmental systems of labor standards and monitoring', *Policy Studies Journal*, **31**(1), 1–29.

Ovi, I.H. (2013), 'Buyers' compensation for Rana Plaza victims far from reality', *Dhaka Tribune*, accessed 16 January 2015 at http://www.dhakatribune.com/business/2013/nov/17/buyers%E2%80%99-compensation-rana-plaza-victims-far-reality.

Padilla, R. (2012), 'Labor law in Honduras', *Central Law: Medina, Rosenthal & Associates*, accessed 16 January 2015 at http://abogados.hn/publicaciones_detalle.asp?id=215.

Pi, X. (2014), 'China wages seen jumping in 2014 amid shift to services', *Bloomberg*, 6 January, accessed 17 January 2015 at http://www.bloomberg.com/news/2014-01-06/china-wages-seen-jumping-in-2014-amid-shift-to-services-.html.

Polaski, S. (2006), 'Combining global and local forces: the case of labor rights in Cambodia', *World Development*, **34**(5), 919–32.

Pollack, A. (1989), 'Jeans fade but Levi Strauss glows', *The New York Times*, 26 June, accessed 12 January 2015 at http://www.nytimes.com/1989/06/26/business/jeans-fade-but-levi-strauss-glows.html.

Powers, M. (2011), Interview with Mike Powers, Brand Responsibility Project, Seattle, WA: University of Washington, accessed 16 January 2015 at http://depts.washington.edu/brandrp/transcripts/MikePowers_Final.pdf.

Prince, M. and W. Plank (2012), 'A short history of Apple's manufacturing in the U.S.', *WSJ – Digits*, accessed 12 January 2015 at http://blogs.wsj.com/digits/2012/12/06/a-short-history-of-apples-manufacturing-in-the-u-s/.

Prior, A. (2014), 'Levi Strauss to eliminate 800 jobs to cut costs', *The Wall Street Journal*, 26 March, accessed 12 January 2015 at http://

online.wsj.com/news/articles/SB10001424052702303779504579463320030695530.

Rabellotti, R., A. Morrison and C. Pietrobelli (2008), 'Global value chains and technological capabilities: a framework to study learning and innovation in developing countries', *Oxford Development Studies*, **36**(1), 39–58.

Rabinovitch, S. (2012), 'Wen family disputes $2.7bn wealth claims', *Financial Times*, 28 October, accessed 17 January 2015 at http://www.ft.com/cms/s/0/5a6b767a-20bd-11e2-babb-00144feabdc0.html#axzz3P4zu6nbN.

Rahman, M., D. Bhattacharya and K.G. Moazzem (2008), *Bangladesh Apparel Sector in Post MFA Era: A Study on the Ongoing Restructuring Process*, Dhaka: Centre for Policy Dialogue.

Rashid, M.A. (2006), 'Rise of readymade garments industry in Bangladesh: entrepreneurial ingenuity or public policy', paper presented at the Workshop on Governance and Development, Dhaka, 11–12 November, accessed 16 January 2015 at http://www.scribd.com/doc/81099280/READYMADE-GARMENTS-INDUSTRY#scribd.

Raynolds, L., D. Murray and J. Wilkinson (2007), *Fair Trade: The Challenges of Transforming Globalization*, 1st edition, London/New York: Routledge.

Razzaque, A. (2005), *Sustaining RMG Export Growth after MFA Phase-out: An Analysis of Relevant Issues with Reference to Trade and Human Development*, Final Report of a Preparatory Assistance Project of Ministry of Commerce and United Nations Development Programme, Dhaka, Bangladesh.

Reich, R.B. (2008), *Supercapitalism: The Transformation of Business, Democracy, and Everyday Life*, reprint, New York: Vintage.

Reuters (2013), 'Students by millions fill labor gap in China', *The New York Times*, 7 January, accessed 17 January 2015 at http://www.nytimes.com/2013/01/08/business/global/students-by-millions-fill-labor-gap-in-china.html.

Risse-Kappen, T., S.C. Ropp and K. Sikkink (1999), *The Power of Human Rights: International Norms and Domestic Change*, New York: Cambridge University Press.

Rivoli, P. (2005), *The Travels of a T-Shirt in the Global Economy: An Economist Examines the Markets, Power and Politics of World Trade*, Hoboken, NJ: John Wiley & Sons.

Rodgers, G., E. Lee, L. Swepston and J. Van Daele (2009), *The International Labour Organization and the Quest for Social Justice, 1919–2009*, New York: Cornell University Press.

Rodríguez-Garavito, C.A. (2005), 'Global governance and labor rights: codes of conduct and anti-sweatshop struggles in global apparel factories in Mexico and Guatemala', *Politics & Society*, **33**(2), 203–333.

Rodríguez-Garavito, C.A. and B. de Sousa Santos (2005), *Law and Globalization from Below: Towards a Cosmopolitan Legality*, Cambridge, UK/New York: Cambridge University Press.

Rodrik, D. (1995), 'Getting interventions right: how South Korea and Taiwan grew rich', *Economic Policy*, **20**(2), 53–97.

Ron, J., H. Ramos and K. Rodgers (2005), 'Transnational information politics: NGO human rights reporting, 1986–2000', *International Studies Quarterly*, **49**(3), 557–88.

Rosner, D. and G.E. Markowitz (eds) (1994), *Deadly Dust: Silicosis and the Politics of Occupational Disease in Twentieth-Century America*, Princeton, NJ: Princeton University Press.

Rudra, N. (2008), *Globalization and the Race to the Bottom in Developing Countries: Who Really Gets Hurt?*, Cambridge, UK/New York: Cambridge University Press.

Ruggie, J.G. (2002), 'The theory and practice of learning networks', *Journal of Corporate Citizenship*, **2002**(5), 27–36.

Ruggie, J.G. (2007), 'Business and human rights: the evolving international agenda', *American Journal of International Law*, **101**(4), 819–40.

Ruwanpura, K.N. and P. Rai (2004), *Forced Labour: Definition, Indicators and Measurement*, InFocus Programme on Promoting the Declaration on Fundamental Principles and Rights at Work, International Labour Office, accessed 13 January 2015 at http://digitalcommons.ilr.cornell.edu/cgi/viewcontent.cgi?article=1000&context=forcedlabor.

Saha, S. (2014), 'Garment exports show resilience', *The Daily Star*, 23 April, accessed 16 January 2015 at http://www.thedailystar.net/garment-exports-show-resilience-21162.

Saxena, S.B. and V. Salze-Lozac'h (2010), 'Competitiveness in the garment and textiles industry: creating a supportive environment', Occasional Paper No. 1, The Asia Foundation, accessed 16 January at http://asiafoundation.org/resources/pdfs/1OccasionalPaperNo.1BGGARMENTwithCover.pdf.

Schalch, K. (2005), 'Hondurans brace for pros, cons of CAFTA', *NPR.org*, accessed 16 January 2015 at http://www.npr.org/templates/story/story.php?storyId=4657525.

Schoenberger, K. (2000), 'Tough jeans, a soft heart and frayed earnings', *The New York Times*, 25 June, accessed 12 January 2015 at http://www.nytimes.com/2000/06/25/business/tough-jeans-a-soft-heart-and-frayed-earnings.html.

Schrank, A. (2011), 'Co-producing workplace transformation: the Dominican Republic in comparative perspective', *Socio-Economic Review*, **9**(3), 419–45.

Schuler, S.R., R. Lenzi, S. Nazneen and L.M. Bates (2013), 'Perceived decline in intimate partner violence against women in Bangladesh: qualitative evidence', *Studies in Family Planning*, **44**(3), 243–57.

Schwartz, A. (2010), Interview with Andrew Schwartz, Brand Responsibility Project, Seattle, WA: University of Washington, accessed 16 January 2015 at http://depts.washington.edu/brandrp/transcripts/Andrew Schwartz_Final.pdf.

Seidman, G.W. (2007), *Beyond the Boycott: Labor Rights, Human Rights, and Transnational Activism*, New York: Russell Sage Foundation.

Sethi, S.P. and D.H. Schepers (2014), 'United Nations Global Compact: the promise–performance cap', *Journal of Business Ethics*, **122**(2), 193–208.

Shamir, R. (2010), 'Capitalism, governance, and authority: the case of corporate social responsibility', *Annual Review of Law and Social Science*, **6**(1), 531–53.

Silver, B.J. (2003), *Forces of Labor: Workers' Movements and Globalization since 1870*, Cambridge, UK/New York: Cambridge University Press.

Simmons, B.A. (2009), *Mobilizing for Human Rights: International Law in Domestic Politics*, Cambridge, UK/New York: Cambridge University Press.

SITRAJERZEESH (2011), Interview with SITRAJERZEESH members, Brand Responsibility Project, University of Washington, in San Pedro Sula, Honduras, accessed 16 January 2015 at http://depts. washington.edu/brandrp/transcripts/SITRAJERZEESH_Notes.pdf.

Smith, J. (2001), 'Globalizing resistance: the Battle of Seattle and the future of social movements', *Mobilization: An International Journal*, **6**(1), 1–20.

Sullivan, M.P. (2006), *Honduras: Political and Economic Situation and U.S. Relations*, CRS Report for Congress Order Code RS21103, Washington, DC: The Library of Congress, accessed 16 January 2015 at http://fas.org/sgp/crs/row/RS21103.pdf.

Tarrow, S. (2000), 'Mad cows and activists: contentious politics in the trilateral democracies', in R.D. Putnam (eds), *Disaffected Democracies: What's Troubling the Trilateral Countries?*, Princeton, NJ: Princeton University Press.

Tarrow, S. (2005), *The New Transnational Activism*, New York: Cambridge University Press.

Taylor-Robinson, M.M. and J. Ura (2010), 'From strengthening institutions to a coup: Explaining the ouster of President Zelaya as an outcome of a game of institutional emergence', Paper presented at the Coloquio Centroamericano, San José, Costa Rica, June 3–4, sponsored by Tulane University and CIAPA, accessed 29 March 2015 at http://stonecenter.tulane.edu/uploads/Taylor-Robinson_and_Ura_paper.pdf.

Tharp, M. (1981), 'South Korea's shoe industry seeking a comeback; other nations cut into sales', *The New York Times*, 2 April, accessed 12 January 2015 at http://www.nytimes.com/1981/04/02/business/south-korea-s-shoe-industry-seeking-a-comeback-other-nations-cut-into-sales.html.

Tzeng, F.-W. (1991), 'The political economy of China's coastal development strategy: a preliminary analysis', *Asian Survey*, **31**(3), 270–84.

United Nations Global Compact (2014), 'The ten principles', *UN Global Compact*, accessed 13 January at https://www.unglobalcompact.org/AboutTheGC/TheTenPrinciples/index.html.

United Nations Office of Drugs and Crime (2014), 'Statistics', *United Nations Office of Drugs and Crime (UNODC) Database*, accessed 16 January 2015 at http://www.unodc.org/unodc/en/data-and-analysis/statistics/index.html.

United States Agency for International Development (2010), *Bangladesh: Economic Performance Assessment*, accessed 16 January 2015 at http://egateg.usaid.gov/sites/default/files/Bangladesh_Economic_Performance_Assessment.pdf.

United States Department of State (2013), *Honduras 2013 Human Rights Report*, US State Department Country Human Rights Reports, accessed 16 January 2015 at http://www.state.gov/documents/organization/220663.pdf.

United Students Against Sweatshops (2012), '3 years after signing historic agreement, Honduran workers and Fruit of the Loom lead the way', *USAS.org*, accessed 16 January 2015 at http://usas.org/2012/10/10/3-years-after-signing-of-historic-agreement-honduran-workers-and-fruit-of-the-loom-lead-the-way/.

Valdmanis, R. (2014), 'Nike CEO says could shift China production over labor strife', *Reuters*, 1 May, accessed 17 January 2015 at http://www.reuters.com/article/2014/05/01/nike-labor-china-idUSL6N0NN3DO20140501.

Vogel, D. (1995), *Trading Up: Consumer and Environmental Regulation in a Global Economy*, Cambridge, MA: Harvard University Press.

Vogel, D. (2012), *The Politics of Precaution: Regulating Health, Safety, and Environmental Risks in Europe and the United States*, Princeton, NJ: Princeton University Press.

Wang, Z. (2013), 'Who gets promoted and why? Understanding power and persuasion in China's cadre evaluation system', SSRN Scholarly Paper ID No. 2299491, Rochester, NY: Social Science Research Network.

Warren, D. (2005), 'Wal-Mart surrounded: community alliances and labor politics in Chicago', *New Labor Forum*, **14**(3), 17–23.

Warren, D.T. (2010), 'Labor in American politics: continuities, changes, and challenges for the twenty-first-century labor movement', *Polity*, **42**(3), 286–92.

Weil, D. (2014), *The Fissured Workplace: Why Work Became So Bad for So Many and What Can Be Done to Improve It*, Cambridge, MA: Harvard University Press.

Wescott, C. and M. Breeding (2011), 'Bangladesh: World Bank engagement on governance and Anticorruption', IEG Working Paper No. 2011/7, accessed 16 January 2015 at http://lnweb90.worldbank.org/oed/oeddoclib.nsf/b57456d58aba40e585256ad400736404/1f49a3bdfafe2d9a85257984006ea323/$FILE/GACBangladeshWPFinal.pdf.

Whiting, S. (2004), 'The cadre evaluation system at the grassroots: the paradox of party rule', in B. Naughton and D. Yang (eds), *Holding China Together: Diversity and National Integration in the Post-Deng Era*, New York: Cambridge University Press, pp. 101–20.

Whoriskey, P. (2011), 'New Balance struggles as last major athletic shoe brand manufacturing in U.S.', *The Washington Post*, accessed 12 January 2015 at http://www.washingtonpost.com/business/economy/new-balance-struggles-as-sole-remaining-major-us-athletic-shoe-manufacturer/2011/07/22/gIQAZsq9eI_story.html.

Wikileaks (2014a), 'Honduran coup: the 'White Team', accessed 16 January 2015 at http://wikileaks.org/cable/2009/07/09TEGUCIGALPA568.html.

Wikileaks (2014b), 'Negotiations begin on minimum wage', accessed 16 January 2015 at https://wikileaks.org/cable/2010/01/10TEGUCIGALPA13.html.

Williamson, O.E. (1975), *Markets and Hierarchies: Analysis and Antitrust Implications: A Study in the Economics of Internal Organization*, New York: The Free Press.

Williamson, O.E. (1985), *The Economic Institutions of Capitalism: Firms, Markets, Relational Contracting*, New York/London: Free Press/Collier Macmillan.

Worker Rights Consortium (2008), *Worker Rights Consortium Assessment: Jerzees de Honduras (Russell Corporation), Findings and Recommendations*, 7 November, accessed 16 January 2015 at http://www.workersrights.org/freports/Jerzees%20de%20Honduras%2011-07-08.pdf.

Worker Rights Consortium (2009), *Worker Rights Consortium Assessment Re Hugger de Honduras and Vision Tex Honduras, Findings, Recommendations and Status Report*, accessed 16 January 2015 at http://archive.jconline.com/assets/PDF/BY146086115.PDF.

Worker Rights Consortium (2010), *Worker Rights Consortium Progress Report: Implementation of Russell Athletic/Fruit of the Loom Remediation Agreements for Operations in Honduras*, accessed 16 January 2015 at http://depts.washington.edu/brandrp/cases/Jerzees/WRC_implementation_Jerzees-Russell_2-17-10.pdf.

Worker Rights Consortium (2011), *Second Progress Report: Implementation of Russell Athletic/Fruit of the Loom Remediation Agreements for Operations in Honduras, Findings and Status Report*, accessed 16 January 2015 at http://depts.washington.edu/brandrp/cases/Jerzees/WRC_update_on_Jerzees-Russell_8-16-11.pdf.

World Bank (2013), *World Development Indicators 2013*, accessed 16 January 2015 at http://databank.worldbank.org/data/download/WDI-2013-ebook.pdf.

World Bank (2014), 'Unemployment, youth male (% of male labor force ages 15–24)', accessed 18 January 2014 at http://data.worldbank.org/indicator/SL.UEM.1524.MA.ZS.

World Governance Indicators (2014), 'The Worldwide Governance Indicators (WGI) project', accessed 14 January 2015 at http://info.worldbank.org/governance/wgi/index.aspx#home.

World Justice Project (2012), *The Rule of Law Index 2012–2013 Report*, accessed 14 January 2015 at http://worldjusticeproject.org/publication/rule-law-index-reports/rule-law-index-2012-2013-report.

World Trade Organization (2014), *Statistics Database*, accessed 17 January 2015 at stat.wto.org/Home/WSDBHome.aspx.

Xinhua (2006), 'Journalists sued over iPod story', *Shanghai Daily*, 29 August, accessed 12 January 2014 at http://news.xinhuanet.com/english/2006-08/29/content_5019710.htm.

Xinhua (2012), 'China voice: Foxconn labor scandal embarrassment to gov't service', *Global Times*, 18 October, accessed 17 January 2015 at http://www.globaltimes.cn/content/739196.shtml.

Yanz, L. (2011), Interview with the Director of the Maquila Solidarity Network, Brand Responsibility Project, Seattle, WA: University of Washington, accessed 16 January 2015 at http://depts.washington.edu/brandrp/transcripts/LyndaYanz_Final.pdf.

Yardley, J. (2013), 'Report on deadly factory collapse in Bangladesh finds widespread blame', *The New York Times*, 22 May, accessed 16 January 2015 at http://www.nytimes.com/2013/05/23/world/asia/report-on-bangladesh-building-collapse-finds-widespread-blame.html?_r=0.

Young, A. (2014), 'Zhongrong metal parts factory explosion: how does it affect General Motors in China?', *International Business Times*, 4 August, accessed 17 January 2015 at http://www.ibtimes.com/zhongrong-metal-parts-factory-explosion-how-does-it-affect-general-motors-china-1648224.

Yu, W. et al. (2013), 'A survey of occupational health hazards among 7,610 female workers in China's electronics industry', *Archives of Environmental & Occupational Health*, **68**(4), 190–95.

Yue Yuen Industrial (2004), 'Yue Yuen and Luen Thai form strategic alliance to develop sports and active wear supply chain business', *YueYuen.com*, 20 June, accessed 17 January at http://www.yueyuen.com/attachments/article/76/040620.pdf.

Zhang, H. (2010), 'The hukou system's constraints on migrant workers' job mobility in Chinese cities', *China Economic Review*, **21**(1), 51–64.

Zhang, M., C. Nyland and C.J. Zhu (2010), 'Hukou-based HRM in contemporary China: the case of Jiangsu and Shanghai', *Asia Pacific Business Review*, **16**(3), 377–93.

Zhu, C.J., M. Zhang and J. Shen (2012), 'Paternalistic and transactional HRM: the nature and transformation of HRM in contemporary China', *The International Journal of Human Resource Management*, **23**(19), 3964–82.

Zlotnick, F. (2014), 'Demography is destiny: demographic change and political leverage in organized labor', Working Paper, Stanford University.

Index

Accord on Factory and Building Safety
    in Bangladesh 131–2, 139, 140,
    142, 144
ACFTU *see* All China Federation of
    Trade Unions
activists 29, 31, 112, 139
Advisory Committee on Trademarks
    and Licensing (ACTL) 123
Adidas 157, 158
AFL-CIO *see* American Federation of
    Labor-Congress of Industrial
    Organizations
aircraft industry 102
alignment 29–30, 34–5, 36–7, 38–9, 40,
    167–9
All China Federation of Trade Unions
    (ACFTU) 147, 153
Alliance for Bangladesh Worker Safety
    132, 139, 140, 142, 145
Alta Gracia 21–2
American Federation of
    Labor-Congress of Industrial
    Organizations (AFL-CIO) 16,
    103, 121, 168
'anti-sweatshop' movement 166
Apparel Industry Partnership (AIP) 109
apparel production 10, 24, 114–45,
    155–8
Apple 11, 18–21, 110, 111, 159, 161,
    167
Argueta, Evangelina 124
Arkans, Norm 127–8
autocracy 65, 69, 71
auto manufacturers 102, 111
Awami League 134, 136

Ballinger, Jeff 16
Bangladesh 9, 10, 24, 52, 75, 131–45,
    166–7, 170

    government 3, 76
Bangladesh Jatiyatabadi Sramik Dal
    (BJSD) workers' federation 137
Bangladesh Knitwear Manufacturers
    and Exporters Association
    (BKMEA) 133
Bangladesh Nationalist Party (BNP)
    134, 136
Battle of Seattle 106–7
beliefs 30–32, 40, 141, 165, 166, 168
Better Work 13, 54–5, 140
BJSD *see* Bangladesh Jatiyatabadi
    Sramik Dal
BNP *see* Bangladesh Nationalist Party
Boeing 102
Bores, Alex 122
boycotts 39
Bozich, Joe 21, 22
brands 7, 11–22, 29, 37, 38, 98, 103, 108
    and Accord on Fire and Building
        Safety 131–2, 144
    affect of campaigns 111
    and Alliance for Bangladesh Worker
        Safety 132, 145
    in China 151, 156, 157
    contracting out 105
    in Honduras 115
    and incentives 130
    influencing 166, 168
    and locational decisions 7–9
    and mega-suppliers 154
    and political strategies 170
    and reputation 39, 112, 169
    and suppliers 141
    and tax 110
    using Rana Plaza 139
Brown University 126
bureaucracy 100, 112, 131, 134, 135